WHITE RAT

A Life in Baseball

Whitey Herzog

AND

KEVIN HORRIGAN

1817

HARPER & ROW, PUBLISHERS • New York
Cambridge, Philadelphia, San Francisco, Washington
London, Mexico City, São Paulo, Singapore, Sydney

FIRST EDITION

Designer: Helene Berinsky

Copy editor: Rick Rennert

Library of Congress Cataloging-in-Publication Data

Herzog, Whitey
  White rat.

  1. Herzog, Whitey. 2. Baseball—United States—
Coaches—Biography. 3. Baseball—United States—
Managers—Biography. I. Horrigan, Kevin. II. Title.
GV865.H47A3   1987   796.357'092'4 [B]   86-45660
ISBN 0-06-015694-5

87 88 89 90 91 HC 10 9 8 7 6 5 4 3 2 1

Contents

◇   ◇   ◇

A section of photographs follows page 118.

The Manager—One Game

Shea Stadium, New York, April 14, 1986. Another opening, another show. And a Monday, no less.

Some genius in the league scheduling office has decided that the New York Mets' home opener should be against me and my St. Louis Cardinals. We beat out the Mets in our division last year—although many of their fans still don't believe it—and they're favored to finish first, ahead of us, this year. From a public relations standpoint, this game ought to be a beauty. From a baseball standpoint, it may be a disaster. Hell of a place to start a book, too.

I get up at 6 A.M., as usual, eat breakfast, and read the papers, which are full of "early season showdown" stuff. If I was at home, I'd probably go fishing for a couple of hours—get away from the phones and the bullshit for a while, and try to catch some bass. Instead, I take the subway from Grand Central Station to Shea and get there a little after nine—four and a half hours before game time. You've heard of chronically late people? I'm chronically early.

Shea is not my favorite place to watch a baseball game, but what the hell. After thirty-seven years in professional baseball, I figure that one place is just about as good as another. I've played in, or coached in, or managed in baseball games in three countries in

North America, in more leagues than I care to count—from Nava-joa, Mexico, to Montreal, Quebec—and two things are for sure: if your team is playing well, you can win in a cow pasture; if it's not, you can be playing outside the pearly gates and you're still going to get hammered. The Cardinals are 4–1 right now, but we're not hitting worth a damn, and today the Mets are pitching Mr. Dwight Gooden. I'm fifty-four and he's twenty-one, but I always call him "Mr. Gooden" because he's the damnedest pitcher I've ever seen.

We won our home opener a week ago—and three out of the next four games at home—so we're sitting on top of the Eastern Division in the middle of April, with only 157 games to play. We're the defending National League champions, but that was last year. There isn't anything in baseball that means less than last year. We're 4–1, but the club isn't hitting and Mr. Dwight Gooden is pitching. So I'd better manage great today. What I'll do is I'll get my pitcher, Rick Horton, to throw a no-hitter, and I'll tell the guys in the lineup to get about fifteen runs. And then I'll let people tell me again what a genius I am.

◇   ◇   ◇

Here's what I know about managing a baseball team: if you get good players and they play well, you're a genius. Sometimes a bad manager will have good players who play well, so for a year or two he'll be a genius. Sometimes a genius manager will have bad players who play poorly, which will make people wonder how come a genius got so dumb so fast. The only thing a manager can do is try to see to it that his club gets good players (which is a tricky thing to do) and then see to it that the players play hard and hustle (which is also a tricky thing to do).

Once a manager gets good players, about 75 percent of his job is handling the pitching. The rest of it is to keep the players happy, keep the writers happy, and try to see that he's got the right players in the right situations during the game. Then he makes damned sure that the players hustle and play smart baseball, which makes the fans happy and keeps them coming back to the park, which makes the owner of the club happy. If everything goes right, his club will contend every year and win a pennant every four or five years, so he'll keep his job, which any manager will tell you is a lot more important than being a genius.

When was the last time everything went right for a manager? Casey Stengel, the greatest manager I've ever known, told me that unless a manager owns the club or dies on the job, he's going to get fired. It happened to Casey; it's happened to me *twice;* and for all I know, it could happen again. So why worry about it?

A lot of nice things have been said about me over the past dozen years. Newspapers have polled big-league players about which manager they'd like to play for most, and my name came out on top. My name was also mentioned by other managers and general managers when they were asked who they'd hire to run their clubs if they couldn't. I've been called "the best manager in baseball," which is a nice compliment, but it doesn't mean a thing. Those polls are always taken after the season, and if your club has won the pennant, you're bound to get some votes.

The only way to prove who is the best manager would be to make all of us play the same hand—the way it's done in duplicate bridge. (I happen to be a very good bridge player, by the way. One year, when I was playing with the Kansas City A's, an outfielder named Bill Tuttle and I walked into the team hotel in spring training and found that there was a duplicate bridge tournament going on. The hotel was full of little old ladies playing cards, but they were one team short, so they invited us to play . . . I guess they thought we were cute. Well, Tuttle and I had never played duplicate before, but baseball is good training for bridge. We finished second in that tournament and really pissed off those ladies.) In a lot of ways, playing bridge is the same as managing a baseball team. You've got strategy and bluffing and finesse, but in the end you'd better hope that you've got more trump cards than the other guy, and you'd better hope that you continue to get dealt good cards. If someone could figure out a way to make all managers play with the same hand—the same players, the same stadium, the same schedule, the same injuries—then we could decide who is the best manager. I'd take my chances in that competition.

On a day-to-day basis, the art of managing a baseball team just isn't as mysterious as it's cracked up to be. A good manager, with a good club, might steal a half-dozen games a year—at the most. A lot of the really hard part of the job takes place away from the field—working with the organization to get the right kind of players, handling the press, and handling the players.

As far as handling the players goes, they're men, and so I treat them like men. But I'm the boss, and they'd better realize it.

◇　◇　◇

The first thing I do when I get to Shea this morning is to go over the charts I keep. It's the first thing I do before every ball game. There are two different sets of charts: my hitters against the other teams' pitchers, and my pitchers against the other hitters. My public relations department keeps my hitting charts, but I do the pitching charts myself.

Every manager has his own system for keeping track of things like this. Davey Johnson, the Mets' manager, uses a computer. Earl Weaver, the manager at Baltimore, keeps his charts on file cards which he sticks in his pocket. I've got a file on every hitter I've ever managed against, on every ball he has hit against every pitcher of mine he's ever faced. I've got a set of colored pens, and I use a different color ink for every pitcher. I trace each ball hit —a broken line for a ground ball, a solid line for a ball hit in the air. Over the years, I've found that by keeping the charts myself, I get a mental picture of where each hitter is likely to hit each pitcher. Before the first series of the year against each team, I hold a meeting and go over the right places for every defensive player to be in. Some of my players, particularly Tom Herr, my second baseman, and Ozzie Smith, my shortstop, study these charts as much as I do, which is why you never see them out of position.

I also use the charts when making out my lineups. Baseball is a game of percentages, and I believe in giving myself every percentage advantage. The most important percentage is the lefty-righty one: because of the way breaking pitches break, left-handed hitters don't hit left-handed pitchers as well as they do right-handed ones, and right-handed hitters don't hit right-handers as well as they do left-handers. A hundred years of baseball experience has proven this to be true, and everything on my charts also shows that it's true.

There are exceptions, of course, and that's why I pay as much attention to my charts as I do. I was a left-handed hitter when I played, and I kept my own charts. I was a platoon player used mostly against right-handed pitching, especially late in my career. The funny thing was that the one pitcher in the league that I owned was a left-hander, Don Mossi, who pitched for Cleveland and Detroit. I used to tear him up. But there was a right-hander on that same Cleveland club named Ray Narleski, and he used to tear me up. I took my charts to my managers and told them, "Look, I know what the percentages are, but I'm telling you—I can hit Mossi and I can't hit Narleski."

The managers would just give me a funny look and strap me out there against Narleski anyway. That's why I believe so much in my own charts—they prove to me when the percentages aren't working. Some hitters just can't hit some pitchers, and it wouldn't make any difference if the pitcher walked off the mound and put the ball on a tee for the guy. Jack Clark, my first baseman, can't hit Rick Reuschel of Pittsburgh. Jack Clark is one of the best hitters in baseball—against right-handers as well as left-handers—but he can't hit Rick Reuschel. So when we play Pittsburgh and they start Reuschel, Clark gets the day off. You cut yourself every advantage you can.

On the other hand, when Mr. Gooden is pitching, it doesn't take very long to go over the charts—nobody on my club hits him very well. So I take out a lineup card, write down the names, and hope for the best.

◇　◇　◇

There's no mystery to making out the lineup card. The first thing you decide, of course, is who's pitching—but you've already decided that days in advance. You've got to look at the schedule weeks ahead of time to make sure you have the pitchers you want ready to face any particular club when you play them. Coming out of spring training this year, I had my pitching rotation set for a month ahead of time. It'll work out just fine if we don't get rained out and I don't have to get into my bullpen too early, too often. I knew coming out of Florida that I wanted my two left-handed starters, John Tudor and Rick Horton, to work against the Mets. The Mets are a little tougher against right-handers than left-handers, so left-handed starting pitching may give us a slight advantage.

Horton will pitch today, we'll have a day off tomorrow, and Tudor (who started and won the first and fourth games of the season for us) will be ready to pitch later in the week. I didn't think I'd have to pitch Horton against Mr. Gooden since he was scheduled to pitch two days ago. But the Mets were rained out, and so they decided to save him for the home opener. Thank you very much, Dave Johnson. Horton vs. Gooden looks like a mismatch, but you never know.

The rest of the lineup card is easy, mostly because I've got a lot of switch-hitters. I've got Vince Coleman, the best base stealer in the history of baseball, leading off. I've got Willie McGee, who hit .353 for me last year and who may have more pure speed than Coleman, hitting second. Behind them is Tom Herr, a very disciplined hitter who can take a pitch to let the speed guys steal a base. Tommy is also a situation hitter; he can make contact when he wants to, hit the ball to right or left when he wants to, get the ball in the air when he has to. He can also run pretty well, so that makes him a perfect No. 3 hitter. All three of these guys—Coleman, McGee, and Herr—are switch-hitters. So if they hit like they're supposed to, it doesn't make any difference who is pitching for the other team.

I write down Jack Clark's name in the fourth position—cleanup. He hits right-handed, but he can handle right-handed pitching, too. He's the greatest fastball hitter I've ever managed, and he's very good with runners on base. Our whole offensive game is geared to getting guys on base ahead of Clark, and everyone in the league knows it.

That's why I always hit my right-field platoon player behind Clark—either Andy Van Slyke, a left-handed hitter, or Tito Landrum, a right-handed hitter. We just have to protect Jack, especially late in the game with runners on base. We don't want the other manager going to the bullpen when Clark is at bat. He won't do that if Van Slyke, a left-handed hitter, is behind Clark, because if he does, I'll pinch-hit for Van Slyke with Landrum. Ideally, you'd have a switch-hitter behind Clark to protect him from any kind of relief pitcher, but you can't have everything you want.

The sixth and seventh hitters in the lineup is where I have to pay attention to who's pitching. If it's a left-hander, I'll put in a right-handed hitter there, and turn it around with a right-handed pitcher. My third baseman, Terry Pendleton, is a switch-hitter, but he's not hitting left-handers well, so that's another factor. With Mr. Gooden pitching, I'll stick Terry in the No. 6 hole and use Mike Heath, a right-handed hitting catcher we got in a trade over the winter, in the No. 7 slot. I don't know if Heath's going to hit right-handers or not, particularly Mr. Gooden. But he's a very good defensive catcher, so he goes into the lineup anyway.

In the National League—the only league in baseball where the pitchers still bat—the No. 8 hitter is probably more important to the lineup than the sixth- and seventh-place hitters. He has to have a good on-base percentage; and he has to be able to run well enough to get to second on a bad bunt, or steal the base if the pitcher doesn't get the bunt down, which often happens. Why pitchers can't learn to bunt is a mystery to me, but that's where the National League gets screwed by the designated hitter rule. These guys never have a bat in their hands until they get to the big leagues, and by then it's damned near impossible to teach them anything.

The No. 8 hitter has to have a little pop in his bat so he can drive in a run in the late innings. A lot of times the other team will pitch to him with runners on base in the late innings because they know you're going to pinch-hit for the pitcher coming up behind him. I use Ozzie Smith, my shortstop, in the eighth position, and he's perfect for it. Because he's such an outstanding defensive player, a lot of people overlook how good an offensive player he's become in the last few years. He's a switch-hitter, he gets on base a lot with walks, he can steal a base, and he'll drive in forty or fifty runs a year.

So there's my lineup—Coleman, McGee, Herr, Clark, Van Slyke, Pendleton, Heath, Smith, and Horton. Heath is new, but the rest of this lineup worked like a charm last year, when Herr drove in 110 runs. But last year is over. Tommy's not hitting right now, and I don't know what I'm going to do about the No. 5 hitter. If a club's not hitting, it doesn't make any difference what the lineup is—you can draw the names out of a hat.

I send a clubhouse boy over to Davey Johnson's office with a copy of the lineup card and post another copy on the clubhouse wall. Players like to see the lineup as soon as they get to the ballpark because it helps them prepare for what they have to do that day. So I get out the lineup early, and then I put on my uniform.

◇　◇　◇

Lord only knows how many baseball uniforms I've put on in my life. The first one belonged to the junior town team in New Athens, Illinois (my hometown), and the latest belongs to the St. Louis National Baseball Club, Inc., a subsidiary of Anheuser-Busch Companies, Inc., the fifty-ninth-largest industrial corporation in America. In between, there were other town teams and high-school teams and eight or nine minor-league clubs and Army clubs and Mexican League clubs. I wore five major-league uniforms in eight seasons as a player, counting the New York Yankee pin-stripes I wore only in spring training. I was a coach for three teams: the Kansas City A's, the New York Mets, and the California Angels. I've managed three clubs: the Texas Rangers, the Kansas City Royals, and the Cardinals. I've kept a cap from each big-league club I've worked for, and now I've got them lined up behind the bar in the basement of my home in Independence, Missouri. They're quite a testimonial to my travels, if nothing else.

I've also had jobs in baseball where I didn't wear a uniform. I was a territorial scout for the A's, special assignment scout and director of player development for the Mets, and general manager of the Cardinals. I don't know that there's anyone else in baseball today who has worked at every level of a big-league club—as a player, coach, scout, front office man, manager, and general manager. It doesn't necessarily make you any smarter, but it sure gives you a good idea of what's going on where.

The one thing I've decided after looking at baseball from top to bottom is that unless the whole organization is working together for one common purpose and under one common philosophy, the club isn't going to win and it isn't going to make money and you're not going to keep your job. The scouts have to find good players; the coaches have to teach; the minor-league staff has to keep the pipeline full of young players; the manager and the general manager and the front office have to keep the players happy and the budget in line; and the owner has to find good people and let them do their jobs. It sounds easy, but it's not.

Baseball is a unique business because it's a sport and it's entertainment—as well as the national pastime—with all sorts of people wanting to tell you what you're doing wrong. But it's also a hard-nosed business in which you've got to make some money. I probably worry about the budget as much as any manager in baseball since Connie Mack—and he owned the club. But to be successful in baseball today, that's the way you've got to operate. Your manager and the other baseball people have got to think business, and your business people have got to think baseball. I think the Cardinals do it as well as anybody, certainly as well as any club I've ever been associated with, and that's a bunch.

I grew up in Cardinals' territory, across the Mississippi River southeast of St. Louis, during the 1940s—a decade in which the Cardinals won four pennants, three World Championships, finished second five times and third once. Most of my buddies were big Cardinals fans, but I was always trying to be a little different.

My favorite team was the Yankees—the only club more successful than the Cardinals.

Even so, I would listen to the Cardinals' broadcasts every night on the big old radio in our house in New Athens. The thing that stuck in my mind was the gung-ho way they played—full speed, fundamentally sound, taking the extra base, running hard all of the time. I grew up thinking that was the way baseball ought to be played. I still do.

Later on, when I was playing minor-league ball in the Midwest, I was still in the middle of Cardinals territory. Back then, before the Dodgers and Giants moved to the West Coast and before expansion came along, the Cardinals were the westernmost and southernmost team in the big leagues, making them the home team for two-thirds of the country. Even later, in the mid-1960s, when I was scouting the Midwest for the Kansas City A's, the team that most people cared about was the Cardinals. You'd be at a game in some small town somewhere in Iowa, and there might be a dozen scouts there, but the one that the local people wanted to hear about was the guy from the Cardinals.

The Cardinals always did a hell of a selling job. The broadcaster back then was Harry Caray, who now does the Cubs' games, and Harry really sold those Cardinals in the Midwest. People were just nuts about them and wild about Harry, and a lot of them still are. It amazes me that no matter where our club goes, there'll be dozens of Cardinals fans hanging around our hotel and draped over the dugout at the ballpark. It doesn't make any difference where we are—Cincinnati or Montreal, Houston or San Francisco—there'll be a bunch of Cardinals fans. Old guys and middle-aged guys, women and kids, all wearing Cardinals caps. I think the Cardinals were America's Team long before the Dallas Cowboys were born and a hell of a long time before Ted Turner put the Atlanta Braves on cable television. You wouldn't believe the mail I get from all over the world.

The thing about Cardinals fans is that they're not front-runners. They're with you, win or lose. They'd rather the Cardinals win than lose, of course, but they don't expect them to win every year, and they don't desert the club when it's losing. They're smart baseball fans; Busch Stadium is one of the few places where you'll hear the crowd applaud a player for hitting a ground ball to the right side to move a runner from second to third.

There's just a great, great baseball tradition in St. Louis. The town has a football team and a hockey team, and it's had a couple of pro basketball teams, but baseball is really the only sport in town for most people. People grew up with good baseball, good heads-up, hard-charging baseball played by guys like Stan Musial, Red Schoendienst, Bob Gibson, and Lou Brock, and they love it. They love the players—sometimes they love them too much, as I discovered when I started shipping some of their heroes out—but mostly they just want the team to hustle and play hard. And that's not too much to ask.

There are a lot of people responsible for the great Cardinals tradition. Branch Rickey got the Cardinals started with the farm system before anybody else. Billy Southworth managed some great teams in the 1940s, and Red Schoendienst managed some great clubs that Bing Devine put together for him in the 1960s. Stan Musial was not only one of the greatest left-handed hitters ever, but also a hell of a gentleman whom the whole town is proud of. Newspaper guys like Bob Burnes and Bob Broeg—guys whose stories I read when I was growing up and delivering newspapers in New Athens—are still writing about the team, and broadcasters like Harry Caray and Jack Buck educated the fans.

But I think that if there's one man more responsible than any other for the Cardinals' success today, it's August A. Busch, Jr., my boss. I haven't always thought very highly of the people I've worked for—hell, a lot of the time I've thought they were dumb asses—but Gussie Busch is one of the finest men I've ever met.

I've worked for a lot of owners and a lot of good people, but I don't think anyone ever appreciated me or my talents until I met Gussie Busch. The very first time I met him, on a Sunday morning in the middle of June in 1980, he cut through a lot of bullshit, gave me a three-year contract to manage his team, and told me he didn't care what it took, just bring him a winner. He was eighty-one years old at the time, but I could see how he got to where he was. The smartest people are those who hire good people and then just get the hell out of the way.

For forty years, from the end of Prohibition in 1933 until he retired in 1973, Gussie Busch ran Anheuser-Busch the same way I try to run the Cardinals. He hustled, he played smart, and he was two or three steps ahead of the competition. They tell me he was absolutely furious in the late 1940s, when Anheuser-Busch fell to the No. 2 spot. He set about getting his brewery so far ahead that nobody would ever catch up. He spent money to make money. He hired good people and pushed them to be better. If a guy didn't do the job, Gussie got someone who could. He played some hardball, man. He got himself connected in Washington and in the state capital and in city hall, and I guess he is probably the most powerful man St. Louis has ever known.

In 1953, there were rumors that the Cardinals were going to be moved out of St. Louis. The owner, a guy named Fred Saigh, was running a shoestring operation, and the shoestrings were getting a little frayed. Gussie pushed the Anheuser-Busch brewery into buying the team, although there were a lot of people at the time who couldn't see what possible use a brewery could have with a sports team. Once again, Gussie was miles ahead of everybody else.

Hell, yes, he did it because he liked St. Louis and didn't want the town to lose the team. But years before anyone else, Gussie also saw the marketing potential. Although he had to back off from his plan to change the name of Sportsman's Park to Budweiser Stadium, that was all he backed off from. He earned tons of good will, made Anheuser-Busch synonymous with baseball, and ran the Cardinals the same way he ran everything else—first class.

In the early 1960s, it was Gussie who pushed the brewery into putting up seed money to tear down the slums on the south side of downtown St. Louis and build hotels and office buildings around a brand new stadium. Yes, he got a new stadium out of it, but he knew that what was good for St. Louis was good for his brewery and his baseball team. There's not a thing in the world wrong with enlightened self-interest.

Like any hard-headed German, Gussie's made some mistakes. He got rid of Steve Carlton in 1972 because Carlton wanted a $30,000 raise. If he'd kept Carlton, he might have won two or three more pennants. But overall, I'd say that Gussie Busch is one of the smartest owners baseball has ever had. He's surely the best one I've ever worked for. I wish I'd met him earlier; he and I might have won three or four more pennants, with or without Steve Carlton. Every time I put on my uniform, with its embroidered red birds on a yellow bat, I think about what a great guy Gussie Busch is.

◇   ◇   ◇

In 1985, the Cardinals and the Mets battled it out until the last week of the season for the championship in the National League's Eastern Division. We've got quite a little rivalry going. So on Opening Day in New York, there are even more newspaper and broadcast guys than usual hanging around before the game. They all want to talk about the rivalry, so I oblige them, even though the Cardinals' big rivalry is with the Chicago Cubs back in the Midwest.

Casey Stengel was the guy who taught me how important the press is to a manager. You've got to bullshit with them, Casey would say, you've got to talk baseball, you've got to give them a story. If you don't give them one, he'd say, they'll get one someplace else, and you might as well have them writing your story as someone else's.

Handling the press is one of the most important things a manager has to do—and one of the hardest. A lot of managers get themselves in trouble by starting feuds with writers, or by not answering their questions. It's not easy to sit there, night after night, and answer questions about what you did wrong. It's not easy to go out there, night after night, and talk to television reporters and answer the same questions over and over again. A manager has got to be a pretty good public relations man.

I've made it a policy not to lie to the writers, nor to mislead them. If I don't want to answer a question, I won't answer it. I don't ever say something negative about a player to a writer before I've said it to the player to his face. Some managers try to use the newspapers to do the hard part of their jobs. I think I've got a pretty good rapport with Rick Hummel and Rob Rains—the baseball writers who cover my club for the St. Louis papers—and with most of the other veteran writers around the big leagues. I have to respect them because they've got a job to do, and when your club is going bad, it makes their jobs that much tougher. It's not easy, night after night, for them to come into a clubhouse full of unhappy players and try to get a story. I don't blame them when they write tough things—as long as they're fair—and most of the writers are.

I have a tougher time dealing with the television and radio reporters. The writers who are around me all the time know when I'm saying something confidentially or off the record. These other guys, with their cameras and tape recorders, come in after the game and stick their microphones in my face while I'm trying to eat, or turn the tape recorder on when I'm trying to give some background to a writer. I'll do an interview with ESPN in August or September, then I'll turn on a TV in Colorado when I'm skiing in January, and there I'll be, saying something that I really said five months earlier. TV and radio people can be a real plague, but I'll put up with almost anything.

The one thing I can't stand is when a writer writes something he knows isn't true. It happened to me one time when I was managing the Kansas City Royals. Amos Otis, my center fielder, came to me and asked to sit down against certain hard-throwing right-handed pitchers. Since he couldn't hit them anyway, I thought that it was a pretty good idea. Well, one of the writers for the Kansas City papers went to Otis and asked him why he didn't play one day against Nolan Ryan. Otis said he didn't know, it was all my fault, and the writer put that in a story even though he knew as well as I did what the situation was since I had already told him.

Any writer or broadcaster who pulls something like that on me is through; I won't talk to him anymore. In the spring of 1985, I invited my old friend Bill Virdon to spring training to help coach my young outfielders. Bill is a former big-league manager and one of my best friends in the game. One of the St. Louis television sportscasters decided that Virdon had been brought into camp to get to know the club because the Cardinals were going to hire him if the club went to hell and I got fired. I explained to the sportscaster what the deal was, and so did Virdon, but he went on the air with his story anyway. I haven't talked with him or anybody else from his station since.

I won't put up with a writer who plays the game of getting me to say something about a player, and then telling the player what I said, and then bringing the player's comments back to me. The guy is just trying to stir up some trouble. So I tell him that if I have anything to say to a player, I don't need a messenger to deliver it. I'll bring the player in privately, sit him down and get it out. It seems to me that's the right way to do things, and I know my players appreciate it.

Managers all have different styles. Some are rah-rah types, some are hard-ass disciplinarians, some are buddy-buddy with the players. I don't know exactly how to describe my style. I'm not a cheerleader; if we're horseshit, I'll say so. I'm not a real strict disciplinarian with a lot of rules; the fewer rules you've got, the better the chances are they'll be obeyed. I'm not buddy-buddy with the players; if they need a buddy, let them buy a dog. I'm the manager, and I've got a job to do.

I just try to treat the players like professional athletes. To me, this means treating them with respect, having enough courtesy to tell them face-to-face when they screw up and patting them on the back when they make a good play. I leave the teaching to my coaches—if a man coaches for me, I expect him to be a teacher, not a bobo who's only job is to pick up baseballs—but if I see something that a player is doing wrong, I'll try to help him. When I was a coach, I always figured my job was to teach. I wasn't afraid to come out to the park early to work with players, and I did a pretty good job. Luckily, I was a lot better as a teacher than I was as a player. When I hire coaches, I look for guys who are the same way, and I tell them, "You see something that needs doing, do it. That's what you're being paid for."

I don't have any patience with players who won't work hard. When I put a club together, I look for guys who aren't afraid to work, who don't bitch and moan and blame their troubles on somebody else—guys who can get along with each other and make the clubhouse a decent place. The writers call this "chemistry," but to me, it's just common sense. I really only have two iron-clad rules: Be on time, and hustle. I want my players to run out every ball, to go full tilt on every play. If they do that, they don't have trouble with me.

The little rules—dress codes and stuff like that—I leave up to the players. I just tell them I expect them to act like gentlemen and let it go at that. I don't want to be some kangaroo-court judge who's always laying petty fines on them. I don't need their money, and I don't want it. The players have a clubhouse meeting every spring and draw up rules, and then I expect them to enforce their own code. They like doing it. They take five or ten bucks from each other, throw it into a kitty, and then have a hell of a party at the end of the year.

When I have a clubhouse meeting (and I don't have many of them), I don't rant and rave. I try to explain, as clearly as I know how, what we're doing wrong and how to do it right. I know what it takes to be a big-leaguer, and I figure my players do, too. If they don't, I'll remind them, but it doesn't happen very often. There have been a couple of times in my managing career when players got the idea that they were beyond the rules, and even one time when one of my coaches did. I got rid of them, even though they were all big stars—even the coach.

I'm flattered that players say they like to play for me. Luckily, everywhere I've been we've managed to win—and winning does more than anything else to keep the players happy.

I meet with the players briefly this morning to go over the defenses for the Mets. We talk about who hits the ball where in what situations, who's running well and who we can throw out, how we want to play certain situations with certain guys at the plate, which of their pitchers have good moves to first base and which of them we can run on. I do that before the first series of the year with each of the teams, which is one reason why my 1985 Cardinals were the best defensive team in baseball. The other reason is we had guys who could flat catch the baseball when it was hit to them. I think our 1986 team has a chance to be one of the best defensive clubs in the history of the game, but we shall see.

Still, it doesn't make any difference how good your defense is when you can't score runs. Facing Dwight Gooden, you have to hope to scratch a run or two early, stay ahead, and then try to put away the Mets if Davey Johnson pinch-hits for Gooden late in the game. That isn't much of a game plan, but that's all I have.

◊　　◊　　◊

Since this is the Mets' home opener, we have time for batting practice but don't get to take infield because they have a bunch of ceremonies scheduled before the game. I usually try to watch our team hit in BP, particularly the pitchers and the guys who have not been hitting well. Watching our pitchers try to hit drives me crazy, but I keep thinking I might see something that would help. Sometimes pitchers in the National League get to the majors without having hit since Little League. A lot of them are pathetic, absolutely defenseless up there. It's one reason I wouldn't mind seeing the designated hitter rule used in both leagues; watching pitchers hit is just not a pleasant experience.

I talk a lot of baseball during batting practice. The writers want to talk; there's always a coach or manager on the other team who's an old buddy; the TV guys want to drag you off and hook a microphone to you. On the road, you only get to use the batting cage for forty minutes or so, so you make sure your regulars get most of the work. At home, you can get your pitchers and extra men out early and give them all the work they need. Which is a lot.

We finish BP, duck back inside to change into our game uniforms, and then go out for another Opening Day ceremony. One year we not only had our home opener, but we were the visiting team for three other home openers. That's a lot of parades, ceremonies, marching bands, and speeches to sit through. I want my club to take infield, not stand on the foul line and tip their caps.

We finally get the game started at about 1:45. Mr. Gooden is just like he has always been. Ninety-plus-mile-an-hour fastball, nasty curveball, all the poise in the world. The good thing is that on this day, anyway, Mr. Horton is just as good. He has his good stuff along with good control, and while he can't throw as hard as Mr. Gooden can, he's a smart son of a gun. I tell our pitchers that in the big National League parks, with the greatest defense in baseball behind them, all they need to do is to move the ball around, throw strikes, and let McGee, Coleman, and Van Slyke run down their mistakes.

Horton does that, except in the third inning. He loses track of the plate, walks three guys, and the Mets get a run out of it on a sacrifice fly. The worst part of it is that two of the guys he walks are the seventh- and eighth-place hitters, which lets Gooden come to the plate in a sacrifice situation. You just can't let the pitcher get into the offense of the game, especially with the Mets, who have too many other guys who can hurt you.

That run in the third inning is the only one Horton allows, which is an excellent job of pitching. I always watch a game from the corner of the dugout with Mike Roarke, my pitching coach. One of the few things a manager can do during a game is to watch his pitcher and be ready to take him out if things start to go wrong. Roarke is very good at picking up little mechanical flaws in a guy's delivery—flaws which tell Roarke when the pitcher is beginning to lose his stuff or get tired. Roarke and I use the next day's starting pitcher to chart our pitcher: count his pitches, their type and location. We knew we didn't want Horton going much beyond ninety pitches or so. All we wanted was six or seven good innings out of him, and we got them.

We get the Mets' run back in the sixth when Coleman triples and McGee singles him home. Horton gets us through the Mets' sixth and seventh, so we're in pretty good shape: tied against Gooden, with two to play, and a chance to get into their bullpen if they pinch-hit for him. In most games, you only get one shot at the other guys, and I prefer to take my shot late.

When you get into the late innings, you have to go for it if you get the chance. Managers try to get their bullpen and bench stacked and ready for the lefty-righty matchups that they want. Some managers will take their shots at you early, sending up pinch-hitters in the fourth and fifth innings. If you know the other guy's tendencies, sometimes you can get him to commit his bench early. If I have to relieve a left-hander early, I do it with a right-hander, and vice versa, so I can force the other guy to decide if he wants to play his hand. If he does, then I go right back the other way. When I managed in the American League, I could always count on Gene Mauch to start running his bench out as soon as I changed pitchers the first time. But you can get away with that more in the American League because of the designated hitter rule.

Me, I just hope our starter can give us six innings, and then I start making my moves. We're lucky in that we have five switch-hitters in our regular starting lineup, so it takes away some of the moves the other manager can make. If I were managing against my club, I'd use left-handed relievers in the late innings and make our switch-hitters hit from the right side. The first baseman could then afford to hold the runners closer, and the hitters would have two steps further to run when trying to beat out a double-play ground ball.

We get our shot at Gooden in the eighth inning. Ozzie leads off with a single, and I send Clint Hurdle, a left-handed hitter, up to hit for Horton. Rick has given us seven great innings, and while he might be able to bunt Ozzie over and give us another inning on the mound, I know I have two other left-handers in the bullpen. It's time to take my shot. I've told Ozzie before he goes up that if he gets on, I'm not going to bunt him over. I've told him to steal the base if he thinks he can make it, but if he does go, to be alive for the hit-and-run. The hit-and-run is a great play if you've got a fast man on first base and a guy at the plate who can hit the ball through the right hole when the runner moves.

When the count goes to 2-1 on Hurdle, I flash the hit-and-run sign to Nick Leyva, my third base coach, who relays it to Ozzie and Clint. I know that if Gooden throws a breaking ball on 2-1, Ozzie will probably make the steal anyway, because a breaking ball is harder than a fastball for the catcher to handle. If Gooden throws a fastball, I figure Clint can handle it. Gooden comes in with a fastball, Hurdle hits it through the left side, and Ozzie moves to third.

Now we've got runners on first and third and nobody out, and the top of the order is coming up. Almost anything gets us a run. Coleman pops to short left, but McGee hits a line drive out to George Foster in medium-deep left field. Foster couldn't have thrown me out on that play, much less Ozzie Smith. He tags and scores, and we have a one-run lead with two innings to play.

In 1985, my bullpen was almost perfect in that kind of situation. We didn't blow a ninth-inning lead until the sixth game of the World Series, and we had some help there. We blew an eighth-inning lead only once or twice. Since I have the same guys in the bullpen this year, I figure our chances are pretty good.

I bring in Ken Dayley, a left-hander, and he gets us through the eighth without any damage. But he walks the leadoff hitter, Tim Teufel, in the ninth, which is a cardinal sin. The next guy up is Keith Hernandez, one of the best clutch hitters in baseball, especially against us. Keith hits a shot up the middle, which is a base hit against any club in baseball that doesn't have Ozzie Smith playing shortstop. Ozzie dives, gloves it on one bounce, and we damned near get a double play out of it. But he has some trouble getting the ball out of his glove, so although we get the force out at second, his toss to Herr covering second is a little late, and Tommy's timing is thrown off just a bit. After pivoting, his throw to Clark at first goes skipping by.

We're still OK, with one man out and Hernandez on first. Davey Johnson sends Wally Backman in to run for Keith, hoping he can steal a base. I bring in Todd Worrell, a right-hander, to pitch to Gary Carter, their right-handed-hitting cleanup hitter. I want Todd to get Carter out, so even if Backman steals the base, I've got first base open so I can intentionally walk Darryl Strawberry, the left-handed hitter who bats behind Carter. Then I'd have two men out, runners on first and second, and Worrell pitching to George Foster, another right-handed hitter. Worrell throws very hard, and I don't think Foster can handle him.

All this great strategy shows how unimportant a manager can be to a game if his players don't get the job done. Backman steals second as Mike Heath, my catcher, hesitates in throwing. So now it comes down to Worrell getting Carter out. Which he doesn't. He walks him, and Strawberry singles Backman home to tie the game. However, Worrell handles Foster and Howard Johnson, so we go into extra innings.

From this point on, it becomes the Battle of the Bullpens. Horton has given me seven innings, and Mr. Gooden has given Davey Johnson eight, so it comes down to the most important question in any manager's career: Can my bullpen outpitch the other guy's? Roger McDowell gives Davey two scoreless innings, and Jesse Orosco gives him two more. After the ninth, Worrell pitches scoreless ball in the tenth and eleventh, and then I bring in left-hander Pat Perry, and he shuts them down in the twelfth.

By now we are more than four hours into the game, and most of our bench is shot. It is beyond anything a manager can do.

The whole game turns on my having one more dependable reliever than Davey does—and on Howard Johnson not making a play he should have. But there's nothing a manager can do about that.

Speed also has something to do with the outcome. For me, speed is the most important factor in putting together a club. Speed never slumps, and a ballplayer who is fast is never too small. When you've got a player who is fast and who can swing the bat, too, you've got someone special. On my club, that guy is Willie McGee.

Willie not only closes out a Mets' threat in the twelfth by running down a line drive by Len Dykstra in center field, he opens the thirteenth by beating out an infield hit. I put down the bunt sign for Herr, who is normally a very good bunter, but he puts a little too much on it, and Randy Niemann, who has come on to pitch in the thirteenth, pounces on it. Niemann thinks he has a shot at Willie at second, but McGee is too fast and he beats the throw. Davey brings in Bruce Berenyi, a right-hander, to pitch to Clark. This is the right move, but Berenyi screws it up for Davey the same way Worrell screwed it up for me in the ninth: he walks Clark.

So here we are, with the bases loaded. Tito Landrum, a right-handed hitter who replaced Van Slyke when the Mets brought in their first left-hander, hits a hard ground ball right at Johnson at third. It was a tailor-made, third-to-home-to-first double-play ball. But it went right through Johnson's legs for a two-run error. Ozzie doubles in two more runs, and Perry shuts them down in the bottom of the thirteenth, and that is the ball game. Cardinals 6, Mets 2.

I go back to my office, shaking my head. I made my move with the hit-and-run with Smith and Hurdle in the eighth, and it worked. I made my move with Worrell pitching to Carter in the ninth, and it didn't work. After that it was up to the relief pitchers, and they did the job.

There isn't much to say to the writers after the game. I sure managed great to get that ground ball through Johnson's legs.

The writers all want to know if I think this is a "crucial" win in a "crucial" series. I have to laugh. It's the second week of the season, and already we've got a crucial series—we've got more damned crucial series these days. If we're one game up on the Mets on the last day of the season, then this will have been a crucial victory. These games count just as much as those in the last days of the season, but asking me to decide in April how much it all means is a little crazy.

We've got a hell of a long way to go. But then, I've already come a hell of a long way.

New Athens

When I took over the Cardinals in 1980, a lot of people made a big deal out of my "coming home." I didn't think of it that way. For twenty-two years, my home has been 220 miles west of St. Louis, in Independence, Missouri. Just exactly where I call home became one of the subplots of the 1985 World Series, when the Cardinals played the Kansas City Royals and I stayed in my own home when my team was on the road.

What they meant about "coming home" in 1980 is that I was born and raised about forty miles from St. Louis, in a little farming and coal-mining town on the Kaskaskia River called New Athens, Illinois. It's not exactly noted for its culture, like the original Athens. In fact, they don't even pronounce it like the Greeks. It's pronounced "New Ay-thens," with a long *A*. New Athens is just a country town, full of decent, hard-working people. The population is about 1,400 and hasn't changed much since I left there in 1949.

New Athens is strictly a German town. The Herzogs are two generations removed from the Hamburg area of northern Germany. They came from a farming and coal-mining area of Germany and moved into a farming and coal-mining part of Illinois. My mother's maiden name was Fanke, and her mother's maiden name was Maul, and my grandmother on my dad's side was named Kaiser. They all emigrated from Hamburg, and most of them kept the classic German personality traits: solid, meticulous, and slow to change. For some reason, people around St. Louis refer to people of German heritage as "Dutchmen," and New Athens is full of hard-headed Dutchmen. People do the same things at the same time every day, every week, every year.

I'll give you an example. When I was in the Army in 1953, they assigned me to manage the baseball team at Fort Leonard Wood in southern Missouri. We scheduled a game at Southern Illinois University in Carbondale, and to get there we had to take a bus south on Illinois Route 13, right down what was then the main drag in New Athens. I told the guys on the bus what guys would be sitting where on the street, what guys would be sitting on which stools in which bars. We rolled in at about 11 A.M. and stopped for lunch, and I told the guys who'd be in the cafe, who'd be at the barber shop playing checkers, who'd be at the hardware store. I walked them around town, and sure enough, everyone was just exactly where I said he'd be. And unless they're dead, that's where they are right now.

If Thursday is their day to mow the lawn, that's the day they mow the lawn, come hell or high water. One of my brothers still lives there, in the house where we were raised, and he's that way, too. If we have a ball game on a Thursday night, he won't come unless he gets the lawn mowed first. The women are the same way. They do the laundry on Monday and iron on Tuesday. That's the way it's always been, and by God, that's the way they want it always to be.

There's a lot of my upbringing left in me. My mother was a very strict housekeeper. We'd get our tails whipped if we ever tracked mud in the house. I think that's why we played outside all the time —so we wouldn't have to hear her gripe about the mud in the house. Now I find I'm like that. Every clubhouse man in the league tells me how clean and tidy my team is. I tell the players, "Hang up your uniforms. Don't throw stuff all over the place. Don't make people clean up behind you." It's the New Athens in me. I still make my bed first thing every morning when I'm home.

Another New Athens thing about me is that I'm never late. I sometimes think I overdo it on punctuality. I get to the ballpark at least four hours before game time (and usually closer to five). I only have about an hour's work to do, going over my charts and filling out the lineup cards, so then I've got three or four hours to kill. I do it because I think a player ought to know as soon as he gets to the park whether he's playing or not.

And I do it because that's just the way I am. My buddies know that if I tell them I'll be by their house to pick them up to go fishing at 5:30 A.M., I'm usually there at 5:20. My wife, Mary Lou, is the same way. We've tried to teach our kids how important it is to be punctual. Most of our friends are like that, too; we just don't bother with people who are chronically late. Our eldest son, David, is a little different. He and his wife are usually an hour late. It's gotten so that if we've asked them over for dinner at six, we tell them dinner is at five so they'll be on time.

My dad, Edgar Herzog, was the same way. He worked for the Mound City Brewing Company in New Athens and later for the Illinois Highway Department, and I don't think he ever missed a day or showed up late. My mother, Lietta Herzog, worked in a shoe factory, and she was the same way. They both quit school when they were sixteen and went to work, which was what people did in those days. We never had a whole lot of money, so my two brothers and I always had jobs. My dad told me something that I told my kids when they started to work: be there early and give them a day's work, so when it comes time to lay someone off, it'll be the other guy who gets fired.

I was lucky in the way I grew up because I learned the value of a dollar. I've made more money in baseball than I ever thought I'd see in my life, but I don't go pouring it away. I'm not tight, mind you, and I'm not afraid to spend my money. But I don't want to waste it or gamble it away. That's a little bit of New Athens, I guess; I get ticked off when I lose ten bucks playing cards or blow a hundred dollars on a horse. I don't mind as much losing at cards because I'm a good enough card player that I win more often than I lose. But you'll hardly ever see me at the track.

It's all the New Athens influence. I'm careful, I'm punctual, I'm organized, and I like to work hard.

◇ ◇ ◇

I did a little bit of everything when I was growing up. I delivered newspapers mornings and evenings. I'd get up early, pick up and fold my papers—although when I got to the last one, I'd open it up and read the box scores and the baseball stories.

Later on I worked for a funeral home. I'd dig the graves first, then I'd go home and wash up, change into a suit and tie, and drive the hearse. I worked at the Mound City Brewery as the cleanup man in the brewhouse—about the only time I ever hit cleanup. I'd start at the top floor and work my way down, and one of the benefits was that I could lower a pail from a rope and one of the guys at the bottom would fill it up with beer. I'd drink beer all day long, and then when I got off work in the afternoon, I'd stop at the tavern and have two or three more cold drafts.

Maybe that's why Gussie Busch and I have gotten along so well. In a German family, kids grow up drinking beer. You have a glass or two at meals, and then when you grow up, you drink beer all day long and don't think anything about it. When I was in high school it was nothing to go into a tavern, plunk down a nickel, and get a beer. Hell, we were Germans, or at least not very far removed. Beer was part of our food.

I was seventeen years old when I signed my first pro baseball contract and wound up playing in McAlester, Oklahoma, for a manager named Vern Hoscheit, who's now the bullpen coach with the Mets. One day Vern took me to Sunday dinner before a game, and I ordered a beer.

"What the hell do you think you're doing?" Vern asked.

"What do you mean?" I said. "I'm ordering a beer to drink with dinner."

"You can't do that. You're seventeen years old, and you've got a game to play."

"But I always drink beer with meals."

"Not anymore you don't," Vern said.

I think that's when I first realized I was out of New Athens. Back there, they're still stopping by their favorite tavern—and they always go to the same one, of course—and having a beer after work. They watch television in the evenings now, but when I was growing up, the men would all go back to the tavern after having supper. We'd go to the Dugout Tavern after a ball game, sit in there with our uniforms on, drink beer, and think we were the hottest things around.

You never saw a woman in a tavern. The women wouldn't think of going in there, and the men wouldn't have known what to do if they had. They'd drink beer all evening, play rummy at a penny or two cents a point, and then go home and do it all over again the next day.

Lord, the work they did was hard. There was a big industry, the Auto Stove Works, and a lot of little industries that did pretty well until they unionized, and then the owners moved them to the South. New Athens had two lumber yards, a foundry, a brewery, a shoe factory, and thirteen grocery stores. And sixteen taverns to make it all bearable.

There's a lot of strip coal-mining in New Athens now, but when I was a kid, a lot of the men worked in shaft mines. My granddad worked the Golden Rule Mine down in Lenzburg, Illinois. They'd go underground with a pick and shovel and work their asses off. Peabody Coal Company came in with the first strip mine in 1948, and a lot of my high-school classmates went to work for them. They worked the vein until it played out, and then the pits flooded, and now that's where I do most of my fishing. My buddy, Herb Fox, was a foreman superintendent for Peabody, and he's got a place on a strip pit in Freeburg. When the Cardinals are at home, I start most every day out on Herb's lake, fishing for bass. It's peaceful out there, and there aren't any phones, and that's where I recharge my batteries.

I don't get back to New Athens much any more, not since my mother died in December of 1981. She was seventy years old and was getting the vacuum cleaner out one day—she used to vacuum two or three times a day in between watching soap operas—when she suffered a massive heart attack. My dad died in 1955 at the age of forty-eight. He drank a lot, never went to the doctor, and never took care of himself.

Both of my parents had pretty good lives. They lived the way they wanted to and were happy with what they were doing. They raised three sons and let us play all the sports we wanted to. And I like to think we made them happy.

◇   ◇   ◇

The only thing I've never been able to figure out is why my parents named us what they did. Their firstborn was named Therron Herman, but we called him Ronnie until he started idolizing Billy Herman, the Dodgers' second baseman, so then we called him Herman, which just happened to be his middle name. We went to a Dodgers-Cardinals game one time in St. Louis when we were kids and snuck down on the field when it was over. My brother Herman went out toward second base, reached down, and scooped up a bunch of the dirt that Billy Herman had walked on. He filled his pockets with the dirt and took it home.

I was born on November 9, 1931, a year after Herman, and my brother Butzie came two years after me and was named Codell. I was named Dorrel Norman Elvert Herzog. I've always wondered if my mother was trying for "Darrell" and screwed it up on the birth certificate. Nobody ever gets Dorrel right; even the Cardinals' press guide spelled it "Dorrell" for years.

My family and everyone else in New Athens always called me "Relly"—my New Athens friends still do. When I got to McAlester, a sportscaster named Bill Speith started calling me Whitey because my hair was even lighter than it is now. And that's what I was called until I got to Denver with the Yankees' chain in 1955. Johnny Pesky, who'd just finished his playing career with the Red Sox, signed on as coach, and he thought I looked like a guy named Bob Kuzava, a left-handed pitcher whom the Yankees had had for a while. Kuzava's nickname was the "White Rat," so that's what

Pesky started calling me. Today I sign checks "Dorrel N." but answer to Relly, Whitey, or Rat. Anything is better than Dorrel, I suppose.

Growing up with two brothers as close in age as we are helped me make it to the big leagues. When one of the kids in town was trying to get a game up—basketball, baseball, whatever—the first place they stopped was at our house because there were three of us there. And someone was always trying to get a game up. Usually me.

There wasn't much of anything to do in New Athens except play ball. Play ball, work, and go to school—that's all we did, and I was a lot better at playing and working than I was at studying. I wasn't a bad student. I could do about as well as I wanted to, and all I wanted was to do well enough to stay eligible for the sports teams. If there hadn't been a couple of smart girls around, including a girl named Mary Lou Sinn who later became my wife, I never would have made it.

My best friend was a guy named Edgar "Buddy" Wirth, Jr., whose dad managed us in the summer baseball leagues and always scrounged up uniforms for us. If it hadn't been for the Wirths, I would probably have grown up to be the business agent for the laborer's union in New Athens. Buddy was one of the guys I went to school with, hung around with, played fifty innings of baseball a day with. I was lucky in that from about the sixth grade on through high school I had the same bunch of sports-crazy friends. Ardell Schoep. Marvin Huth. Jim Schmulbach. Butch Leinecke. Harold Wilderman. The Klingenfus brothers. There was always somebody to play ball with. I'd have never made the big leagues, never become a big-league manager, never made the kind of money I've made, if I hadn't been a small-town kid with nothing to do but play ball.

Kids today don't realize the way it was back then. It was nothing for us to play five or six nine-inning games every day. We'd play uptown against downtown, choose up sides with a bat. Every day. We'd get more at-bats in one day than kids today get in a whole season of Little League. They get bats and balls and uniforms and concession stands, and mom and dad drive them to practice a couple of times, and they think they're learning baseball. They play on Little League fields that look a lot better than some of the fields I played on in professional ball. My first field was a little different.

Behind our house, beyond the alley, was a plowed field. Just a regular farm field, with nothing growing on it. I looked at it one day and said to myself, "Hot damn. That's a baseball field." I asked around and found out that a man named Louis Berthold owned it, so I went down and asked him whether he'd mind if we used it for a baseball field. He said go ahead, so my brothers and my buddies and I laid out a field, built a mound, and we had a baseball field.

We played out there every day, all day, right along Route 13. If it rained, we moved down to the schoolyard and played there until the sun dried the mud out. If we didn't have enough guys for a whole game, we'd play Indian Ball or Workup . . . any damned thing. That's all we did. There wasn't any television back then, or any video games, or anyplace to hang out; and our parents were working too hard to entertain us. So we did it ourselves. Maybe the real reason we did it is because it was the only way to show off for the girls. They didn't have anything to do, either, but ride their bicycles over to watch us play.

That field is gone now; houses were built on it. The kids in New Athens who bother to play ball do it at a new park they built when the Corps of Engineers rechanneled the Kaskaskia River. And I'm proud to say that the high-school field has been named after me: Whitey Herzog Field. I tell people it's got a capacity of 20,000—if they don't mind standing in the cornfield beyond the outfield. When I played on it, the field was laid out in the direction opposite of the way it's laid out now, with the town cemetery out beyond the right-field fence. I used to hit an awful lot of balls in there, rattle them around the tombstones and wake the dead.

I really think we had it better then. For kids today, everything is organized. Everybody tells them where to be, what to do. You don't see them playing mumblety-peg; you don't see them playing shinny with a couple of sticks and a tin can out in the street getting up a hockey game. Nobody plays hopscotch anymore. We used to make the hopscotch squares so big that you really had to be able to jump.

We had something going all the time. Marbles—we had marbles coming out of our ears, and the guy with the biggest bag was always the best player. We used to shoot them so hard we'd break them, really pop them. Mumblety-peg. You'd stick a matchstick in the ground and get five cracks at it with your jackknife, and the loser would have to chew the stick out of the ground. "Chew the Root," we called it. You'd come home with your mouth all full of mud and catch hell from your mother, but those were the rules.

Today you don't see any of that. I've never seen any of my children get a game up on their own. They'd say, "Basketball season opens November 2," like all of a sudden they're going to be basketball players. Or, "Baseball season opens April 2," and they're going to be baseball players. But as far as playing basketball or baseball before they were told to, they'd never do it.

I'd tell them, "If you want to be a baseball player, for Chrissakes, go out and play. If you want to be a basketball player, go nail a hoop up. Go shoot. But no, everything had to be structured. Practice would start and they'd run out there, thinking they were Elgin Baylor or Willie Mays. I didn't shoot a basketball in a gym until I was in the seventh grade, but by God, I had a pretty good idea of what to do when I got there. Today I don't see kids having much fun.

We always had something to do. We didn't just sit in the house like kids today. I don't care what the weather was like, we were always outside doing something. Maybe you can't do it if you grow up in a city, but where I grew up, we could always ride our bicycles four miles down the road to another town to stir something up. Now you can't even get kids to ride their bikes to school.

One time we built an airplane on the roof of the shed behind my cousin's house. We modeled it after one of those balsawood jobs with the rubberband motor, only we used an inner tube from a truck tire as a motor. We wound that sucker up, and I jumped in and hollered to let it go. Went right off the shed and landed on my head. I was lucky I didn't break every bone in my body.

Halloween was our favorite day of the year. Very few people had indoor plumbing at the time, so we'd go down the alleys and dump the outhouses. A lot of times those old Dutchmen would be sitting on their back porches with shotguns, and they'd let go and scare us half to death, but we'd still get fifteen to twenty outhouses on a good Halloween. The other thing we'd do would be to go by the firehouse, which was next to the grammar school at the time, and grab the old horse-drawn firewagon and run it up the school flagpole. We'd come to school the next day, pleased with ourselves, but then the principal would ask around and find out who'd done it and dock us a week's worth of recess. That just about killed us, losing recess.

◇   ◇   ◇

When I got older and was in high school, I'd hitchhike over to Belleville, the biggest town around us. Every truck driver on Route 13 knew me by name. I'd get to Belleville and catch the bus over to St. Louis. Cost a dime to get to downtown St. Louis. There I'd pay another dime to get the Washington-Page streetcar out to Grand Avenue and grab a transfer north on Grand to Sportsman's Park, where the Cardinals and the Browns played. I'd buy a grandstand ticket for $1.25. So, for $1.45, I was in the ballpark.

If it was a day game, I'd skip school, especially if the Yankees, my favorite team, were in town to play the Browns. I'd sneak up into the upper deck, which they usually had chained off. I'd sneak in during batting practice and fill up my pockets with baseballs that were fouled off. Five or six balls. One day Freddie Hoffman, a coach for the Browns, spotted me and yelled at me to throw them back. I threw back two or three and kept the rest.

I'd take the balls back downstairs when the game started and sell four of them for a buck apiece, and still go home with a couple. That would make my trip. I'd have enough profits for a couple of hotdogs and Coke, and I'd go home with two brand new American League baseballs. I'd have a hell of day.

The only thing was that I'd get caught once in a while. I'd skip school, and the principal didn't know where I was, and my mom didn't know where I was, and I'd get in trouble. After a while, though, the principal, a fine man named John Vogler, figured out that I had a better chance of being a ballplayer than a Rhodes scholar, so he kind of protected me a little bit.

I'd see him in the hall and say, "Well, sir. Newhouser is pitching tomorrow so I won't be at school."

He'd say, "Hal Newhouser, huh? You're going to see the Tigers and the Browns, is that it?"

"Yes sir."

"Well, have a good time."

I never missed Opening Day, no matter who was playing. I'd skip school, hitchhike over there. The first major-league game I ever saw, Mickey Owen and Walker Cooper got into a fight. I went over to see the first game that Jackie Robinson played in St. Louis. Thirty thousand people were in the ballpark, but it was rained out. I remember during the war, when Branch Rickey put the Dodgers into satin uniforms—light blue satin for night games. I remember Howie "Steeple" Schultz looked particularly fine.

As my taste for culture developed, I'd hitchhike over to the burlesque shows, or go to the Grand Theater at Eighth and Market, just a block from where Busch Stadium is now. I'd go out and see the old St. Louis Bombers play basketball. They played a lot of Sunday afternoon games in those days, so after the game, I'd stop at the Grand Theater and see Billy "Zoot" Reed, the burlesque comedian, who became a good friend of mine.

I was always on the go. I didn't have a car until I left New Athens to play pro ball, so I'd either hitchhike or ride with a friend. Anything to get out and see the world.

If I wasn't over in St. Louis at the ball game or the burlesque house, I'd be back home, playing ball myself, or talking about baseball or basketball or thinking about it. It was all I ever wanted to do. This was in the 1940s, remember, before television came in and ballplayers were the only kind of heroes we had. There were fifty-three minor leagues after the war, and minor-league ballplayers were really looked up to. It was considered a privilege to be a ballplayer, a real status thing. A ballplayer could always come home and find a job in the off-season, even if times were hard.

About the biggest hero New Athens had when I was growing up was a guy named Mickey Haefner, a left-handed pitcher who eventually won 78 big-league games for the Senators and the White Sox. Mickey was my hero. In the off-season, I'd wait on his front porch for him to come home from work. Every night I'd be out there, waiting to see if he'd play catch with me and talk about baseball. Later on, after I was playing minor-league ball, I'd come home and I'd be the hero. There was a kid named Richie Hacker who used to wait on my porch like I'd waited on Mickey Haefner's. Richie only played about seven games in the big leagues, but he became a fine minor-league coach and instructor, and in 1986, I made him my first-base coach with the Cardinals.

◇   ◇   ◇

Lord, did I ever want to be a ballplayer. I was a skinny little kid —5′ 10″, 150 pounds as a senior in high school—and today a big-league scout wouldn't give me a second look. Maybe not even a first look. The reason I made it is because of the kids I grew up with, because we played ball all of the time. They made me into a ballplayer. We all played together in sandlot ball; and from seventh grade on, in school ball.

I guess there were only ninety-five to one hundred kids in our high school—maybe forty-seven or forty-eight boys—but because we played together for so long, we had some hellacious sports teams. In Illinois in those days, there were no big-school, small-school classifications at playoff times. We had to beat the big guys to get into the state tournament, and we did it.

If it hadn't been for me, we might have won the state baseball tournament in 1948. We were leading Granite City, 1–0, late in the game, when I lost a fly ball in the lights at the old Caterpillar Field in Peoria. Hell, it was the first time I'd ever played under the lights. The batter hit a fly ball beyond the light standard, I lost it and turned it into a triple. The next guy up singled and we were down,

3–1. I came up in the ninth with two runners on and a chance to redeem myself. Instead, I lined into a double play and we lost.

That may be one reason why people in New Athens remember me best as a basketball player. I'd go back to New Athens when I was playing in the major leagues, and people would say to me, "Your brother Herman was a better player than you. Why aren't you playing basketball?"

I'd say, "I don't know. Why don't you ask him? He's carrying mail right here in town."

Actually, Herman was a better ballplayer than I was. He signed a pro contract and made it to Class C minor-league ball before he got tired of fighting it. And I was a good enough basketball player to be offered seven college scholarships—your basic small, scrappy guard. Our basketball team finished 35–2 in my senior year. We lost in the sectionals of the state tournament when we had to play our first game in a gym with glass backboards. I remember shooting 6 for 12 from the field and going 0 for 6 from the foul line. Our team lost by one point, 36–35.

But when it came time to choose between a college basketball scholarship and playing professional basketball, my mind was already made up. I knew I wasn't any student, and playing ball was all I ever wanted to do. I played on the town team during the summer, against some pretty good competition all over southern Illinois, and I started getting some attention from the scouts. I could run and I could throw, and I could hit most anything but an off-speed breaking pitch.

I started thinking hard about it when I was a junior in high school. Our team was getting pretty good, and I got pretty good playing center field and pitching. The St. Louis Browns were the first club I heard from. They wanted me as a pitcher. I knew I wasn't a pitcher, but my mother and I went over to the Browns' offices at Sportsman's Park to listen to their offer. Their farm director, Jack Fournier, wanted to sign me as a pitcher for their Marshall, Texas, farm club for $200 a month. No bonus, no nothing. I remember being insulted, and the last thing I said when I left their offices was, "Now I know why you guys are in last place all the time, if you wanted to sign a wild-ass left-hander like me."

Then the Chicago Cubs started coming around, and Joe Kernan, one of their scouts, told me not to sign with anyone until he got back to me because they'd better anybody else's offer. I thought that was great, but I knew it was baloney. In those days, anyone getting over a certain amount of money in a signing bonus had to be kept on the big-league roster, and I knew I wasn't that good.

One of the finest compliments I've ever been paid came from Hank Peters, the general manager of the Baltimore Orioles and a man I worked for with the Kansas City A's. Hank said that someday I'd be inducted into the Hall of Fame, and they'd say that I was the greatest judge of baseball talent in the history of the game. Maybe I've always had that talent because back in New Athens I knew that Relly Herzog wasn't good enough to make a big-league roster at the age of eighteen.

The day after I got out of high school, Buddy Wirth and I were invited down to Branson, Missouri, to a tryout camp that the New York Yankees were holding. The Yankees had always been my team, even though I was living across the Mississippi River from the two St. Louis teams. I guess I was a front-runner at heart. I'd always go over to see the Yankees against the Browns. The Yankees were the only American League team I ever really liked. They had a first baseman named Nick Etten during the war years—a left-hander like me—and he was my idol. Of course, I liked Joe DiMaggio and Charlie Keller, too, but Etten for some reason was my hero.

The Yankees played me just right. After the tryout camp, they sent scouts around who told me that DiMaggio was getting old and they'd be needing a replacement for him in center field. This was before I knew they'd also told the same thing to a kid down in Springfield, Missouri, named Bill Virdon, and another kid down in Commerce, Oklahoma, named Mickey Mantle. I signed with them for a $1,500 bonus and $150 a month, which was more than Virdon or Mantle got. This goes to show you that some scouts are better than others.

I was assigned to the Yankees' Class D farm team in McAlester,

Oklahoma—the farthest I'd ever been away from home in my life. The day after I signed, I packed my bag and headed to the bus depot in New Athens to go to St. Louis and pick up the old M-K-T Rocket at Union Station. I remember those old Dutchmen standing there on the streets in New Athens and watching me leave. As far as they were concerned, once you crossed the Kaskaskia River, you were leaving the United States.

I said good-bye to all of them, got on the bus, and never looked back.

The Journeyman

To be honest about it, I never was a very good baseball player. I'd probably be worth only $250,000 a year or so nowadays, which is about what you have to pay extra men, defensive specialists, and pinch-hitters. That's what I was in the big leagues. I was always one of those guys people said had "great potential."

But I got in eight years, which is a lot more than most guys ever do. I had a lifetime batting average of .257, and it would have been a lot higher if baseball had outlawed left-handed pitchers and off-speed breaking balls. I couldn't hit left-handers worth a damn, and the slow curveballs and screwballs ate me up.

Toward the end of my career, in 1962, *Sport* magazine did a feature article on me as part of "the changing character of baseball." I was supposed to represent the platoon player, the guy who only plays in certain situations. Today they'd have called me a "role player." My role was to play against hard-throwing right-handers, to hustle and play good defense. If I was managing me, that's just how I would have used me.

But I studied the game and studied it hard. I was on the bench a lot of the time, so I had plenty of opportunity for it. When I was with the Orioles in 1961 and 1962, I spent a lot of time on the bench with a couple of other platoon guys named Dick Williams and Darrell Johnson. We'd talk baseball, about what we'd do if we ever became managers. We all did, of course, and the three of us have managed in eight World Series, so I guess we must have learned something.

I tried to learn something from every manager I ever played for, and that wasn't easy to do with a few of them. I always hustled, I always played hard and fundamentally; I played the game right. In all the years I played, I never missed a sign once. I wish I could say that about some of my players today.

I retired after the 1963 season, and in December of that year I took a job scouting for the Kansas City A's. One of the first things I had to do was go to Dallas for a baseball banquet. A sportswriter named Gary Cartwright, who's now a semi-famous novelist and magazine writer, did a column on me for the *Dallas Morning News.* Cartwright wrote the epitaph for my playing career:

> Whitey Herzog was one of those journeyman players you always heard of but were never sure where. You knew he was either a baseball player or the emcee of a kiddies' TV program.

The train called "The Rocket" took me from St. Louis to McAlester, Oklahoma, in June, 1949, to join a team called the Rockets in the Class D Sooner State League. The train didn't seem like a rocket as it crawled across Missouri into Oklahoma. I was seventeen years old, 5' 10" tall and 150 pounds of piss and vinegar, and I couldn't wait to get to McAlester and show them a thing or two. I got a break right away when I drew Vern Hoscheit as my first professional manager. He showed me a thing or two.

In 1949, the Yankees had made Vern the manager of the McAlester Rockets, and they knew what they were doing. In those days, a minor-league manager had to be the father-figure for a bunch of teenaged kids who'd never before been away from home. He also had to be the trainer, the clubhouse boy, the bus driver, the traveling secretary, and sometimes, he had to be a player, too, because there were only seventeen guys on the team.

Hoscheit was very good at his job. He could teach every phase of the game, and he was just hard enough to make everyone a little scared of him. He really taught me what being a professional baseball player is all about. It was tough that year because the Rockets were the worst club in a bad league. Only one guy hit over .300 in the whole league, and that was Pete Runnels, later an American League batting champion. I led our club with a .279 average and didn't make an error in the field. The only thing Vern did wrong was try to make a pitcher out of me. He needed a left-hander, so he stuck me out on the mound one day in practice and stood in the box with a bat. I couldn't find the plate and wound up hitting him in the head.

"I told you I wasn't a pitcher," I said.

The Yankees sent me back to McAlester in 1950, and I really caught fire. That's when I learned something else about Vern Hoscheit: he could build you up when you needed a boost, but he could also take you down a notch when you got a little too cocky. After sixty games that season, I had 120 hits and was hitting .446. We had a doubleheader one day and I got six doubles, and man, I thought I was something.

On the way back to the hotel, Vern said to me, "When you get dressed, come on in to see me. I got something to tell you."

Well, I thought my ticket had been punched. I knew for sure the Yankees had taken notice of me and were going to move me up to their club in Joplin, or the one in Grand Forks. I hustled into my room, threw on some Levis and a T-shirt, and ran down to Vern's room.

"Here," he said, throwing a ring of keys at me. "I got a dinner date. Get the bus and drive the boys to town."

I was crushed. Of all the things that have happened to me in baseball—getting fired in Texas, getting fired in Kansas City—this still ranks as my biggest disappointment, driving the damned bus to town after getting six doubles.

I spent the whole year in McAlester and wound up hitting .351. The Yankees put me on the roster of their Class A Binghamton, New York, club for spring training. We trained in Orangeburg, South Carolina, and that was a weird experience—the first time I'd ever been in the Deep South. The color barrier had been broken in the big leagues by then, but not in Orangeburg. You'd meet a black person on the street, and he'd bow and move out of your way. It was uncomfortable.

Bill Skiff was my manager that spring, and I can't say that he was the greatest judge of talent I've ever seen. There were thirteen outfielders in camp, and they kept only four, sending out me and eight other guys. Of the four they kept, none of them ever played in the big leagues. All nine of us who were sent out made the majors, if only for a cup of coffee. Two of the nine, Bill Virdon and Bill "Moose" Skowron, became stars.

Skowron, Virdon, Lou Skizas, and I were all optioned to the Norfolk team in the Piedmont League. I only got into five games there because they didn't need two center fielders, and Virdon was a lot better than I was—and later proved it in the big leagues. Hell, I knew he was better than I was even then. Besides, he and I were good friends, and we still are. They sent me down a rung to Joplin, where I played center field and first base and hit .285. I started hitting with a little more power and got ticketed for the Double A club in Beaumont, Texas, the next year.

◇   ◇   ◇

I wasn't ready for the pitching in the Texas League. The manager there in Beaumont was Harry Craft, who took a real liking to me. Harry had been a great defensive outfielder but a poor hitter, and I think I reminded him of himself. He kept me in the starting lineup until June, even though I was hitting under .200. Then he had to send me down to Quincy, Illinois, in the Three-Eye League. That spring eventually paid off, though, because in 1958 Harry was managing the Kansas City A's when the Washington Senators put me on waivers. Harry picked me up, which prolonged my big-league career long enough to qualify under the pension plan. In baseball, you never burn any bridges. You never know when a guy you're pissed off at and never want to speak to again will wind up being your boss in some other place. Besides, Harry was right to send me down.

I played pretty well at Quincy, but I knew my baseball career was about to get interrupted when I got my draft notice in midsummer. Still, I hung in there and was hitting .289 in August when the manager, Paul Chervinko, called me in one day. He told me I was supposed to get to Milwaukee in a hurry to join the Yankees' top farm club, the Kansas City Blues. A couple of the Blues' outfielders had been hurt, he said, and they needed me by game time the next day.

Well, I just flat didn't believe him. It didn't make sense. I'd had my draft notice already and the Yankees surely didn't think I was the solution to Kansas City's problems. So I said, "Right, Skip," and then I went to bed. I'd been around too long to fall for that.

The next morning, Chervinko sees me at eleven o'clock and says, "What the hell? Why aren't you on your way to Milwaukee?"

I knew from the expression on his face that he wasn't kidding. I grabbed my stuff, threw it in the trunk of my '42 Ford, and took off from Quincy for Lambert Airport in St. Louis, about 130 miles away. Halfway there, the Ford blew up: no oil in the crankcase, and it threw a couple of rods. I coasted into a service station, sold the car for twenty bucks, hitchhiked to St. Louis, caught the plane to Milwaukee, and made it there by game time.

And then I didn't play for a week. Blew up my car, made a fool of myself, and rode the bench. Life in the minor leagues.

When I finally got to play, I hit a hot streak, getting a double, three singles, and three walks to get myself on base seven straight times. I started a couple of games in center field. The Blues wanted me to petition the draft board to get my induction date moved back a couple of weeks so I could play in the Little World Series with them. I didn't want to do that. I've always figured that if you've got something to do, you might as well go ahead and do it and get it over with.

◇ ◇ ◇

So, on the 15th of September, 1952, I was inducted into the Army at Camp Crowder, Missouri. I had a hell of a two-year hitch. They made me an engineer and assigned me to an armored division at

Fort Leonard Wood down in the Missouri Ozarks, where I played baseball for two years. We had a damned good team—the Fort Wood Hilltoppers. We won the National Baseball Congress tournament in Wichita in 1953, and I hit .483 with 6 home runs and made the All-America team. Eddie Kasko and Jerry Lumpe were also on the team, and they both had pretty good careers in the major leagues.

By 1954 I had made corporal, and the Army gave me my first managing job. I guess I was a soft touch. We had a doubleheader scheduled on the 4th of July that year, but it was hotter than hell, and we all wanted to go up to St. Louis to see the Cardinals' doubleheader. So we snuck out that morning, turned the fire hoses on, and soaked the field. We told the captain we didn't have any idea how it happened and took off for St. Louis.

I also found time to get married while I was in the Army. Made time, actually. I went AWOL on Armistice Day in 1952, snuck home, and got engaged. I'd known Mary Lou all my life. She'd grown up down the street and around the corner from me, been just a year behind me in school. She was working in the public information office at Scott Air Force Base outside of Belleville, but after we were married in February of 1953, she put in for a transfer to Fort Leonard Wood. That worked out pretty well. She was in the PIO office, writing press releases and stories about our baseball team, so I always got plenty of publicity.

◇ ◇ ◇

We went home to New Athens after I got out of the Army on September 14, 1954. I got a job working for the A.O. Smith Company in Granite City and played ball with the New Athens town team. Then the Yankees decided I needed to play winter baseball, so they sent me to Navajoa in the Mexican state of Sonora. What an experience that was.

Mary Lou was pregnant by then, so she stayed with her parents. This was just as well, since I was sick most of the time. I'd never been out of the country before, and I just couldn't get used to the water down there. All I drank was Nescafé, Orange Crush, and cerveza—Mexican beer. I spent more time on the can than I did on the ball field. Eventually, I got over it, but when I got home I got sick all over again because I couldn't get used to American food.

The manager at Navajoa was one of the greatest teachers I've ever met in this game, a man named Hub Kittle. Like a lot of great baseball men, Hub never played in the big leagues. He spent his life in the minors, coaching, teaching, driving the bus, and selling the tickets. I finally got him to the majors in 1981, when I made him pitching coach with the Cardinals. He did a super job for us, but he's a guy who likes to bullshit. You've heard of guys who tell you how to build a watch when you ask them what time it is? Hub would give you the history of timekeeping. It got so some of the veteran pitchers couldn't stand to listen to him anymore. They were bitching all the time, making fun of him. Some of them wouldn't have been in the big leagues if Hub hadn't worked with them to get them there, but still they were all over him. After the 1983 season, we gave him a job working with the young players in the system and double-checking prospects; and he still does a hell of a job. One thing about the Cardinal organization—we take care of our own.

Baseball ought to do something for guys like Hub, who spend their whole lives working their asses off in the bushes turning raw kids into big-league ballplayers. The great teachers are part of the foundation of the game, yet nobody ever recognizes them.

When Hub got hold of me at Navajoa, he knew I couldn't hit the curveball or a high fastball, so he had me out on the field every day, throwing curveballs and high heat at me. He almost drove me crazy. Like most young players, I didn't have the sense to know I should be working on my weaknesses instead of my strengths. Young pitchers ought to work on their strengths, but position players and hitters need to work on the things they don't do well. I learned that from Hub, but he had to drill it through my thick skull.

I left Navajoa in a hurry in late January, after I got a phone call from Mary Lou's folks telling me that she'd gone into labor. I flew all day and all night and finally got to the hospital in Red Bud, Illinois, at seven in the morning of February 1. My daughter, Debbie, had been born the night before, and I don't think Mary Lou has ever quite forgiven me for missing the birth of our first child. It ain't easy getting from Navajoa, Mexico, to Red Bud, Illinois, and thirty years ago, it was damned near impossible.

◇   ◇   ◇

I only had a couple of weeks at home because the Yankees wanted me at their rookie camp, which is where I fell under the spell of Charles Dillon Stengel. Of all the managers I've ever played for, Casey had the most influence on me, even though I never really got to play a regular season game for him.

Casey took a liking to me, spent a lot of time with me at that rookie camp. I was one of the fastest guys in the camp—I finished only a half of a stride behind Mickey Mantle in the 60-yard dash —so Casey decided to teach me baserunning. He'd been a great baserunner as a player, and he liked to teach baserunning as much as he liked to talk, which was plenty. With me, he had someone he could teach and talk to at the same time. Later on, after he'd retired as manager of the Mets and I was director of player development there, he'd follow me around spring training, talking all the time.

Casey called me in right before the regular camp started for the big club. "Now Herzog," he said, "you're a good ballplayer. . . . You want to play. . . . You got a good swing . . . fair arm . . . run the bases well . . . so I'm going to send you to Denver."

Some guys might have been disappointed at being sent out after that kind of buildup, but not me. I knew Casey was gambling on me because he liked me. My stats didn't qualify me for Denver, which had replaced Kansas City as the Yankees' top farm club after Kansas City got a big-league club in 1955. But Casey not only sent me there, he told the manager, Ralph Houk, that he wanted me in center field. I knew then that I was never going to play center field for the Yankees. Mantle was the same age I was. What's more, I had begun to figure out that I was never going to be good enough to make the Yankees at any position, and Casey knew that, too. But he liked me, and he wanted me to do well and learn as much as I could. Ol' Case.

He sure did me a favor by letting me play for Ralph Houk. Of all the managers I've ever seen, Houk is the best at handling people and keeping his players happy. I had a pretty good year for him, too. I hit .289, hit 21 homers, and drove in 89 runs. Denver is a great place to play if you can't hit a curveball. The ball doesn't break so much in that mile-high air. If they ever get a big-league franchise in that town, they'd better load up on fastball pitchers.

Mary Lou and I loved Denver. The people there were all so great to us, and what a sports town it is. Great people and great sports fans. We stayed out there after the 1955 season, and I worked with the Denver Brick and Pipe Co. We even went back after the 1956 season, when I played in Washington. We've now got a place out in Dillon, Colorado, where we ski in the off-season. If I ever give up managing, I wouldn't mind being associated with a big-league club out there as a consultant. I'd like to help those people get started right in the big leagues.

I had such a good year there in 1955 that the Yankees put me on the big-league roster in the spring of 1956, even though I was still having trouble with curveballs at low altitudes. The Yankees had a great club in 1956; it was a thrill just being around those guys in spring training. I'm a realist, though, and I knew there was no way I was going to make that club.

I didn't do much in camp. One day we were playing the Tigers at their place in Lakeland, and I hit what should have been a double off the right-field wall—only, I tripped over first base and sprained my ankle. Lying there in pain, I looked up and saw Casey's face.

"Well, I'll be goddamned," he says. "You've been playing baseball all your life, and you still don't know where first base is at."

A few days after that, on Easter Sunday, April 1, 1956, I went to Easter services with Bobby Richardson and Tony Kubek. When I got back to the hotel, Bob Fishel, the club PR man, said the old man wanted to see me up in his suite. When I got up there, I saw that Casey had already been celebrating Easter with a few drinks. He was rambling on.

"Well, Herzog," he kept on saying, "you're a pretty good ballplayer, but you're not as good as the feller I got."

I knew he meant Mantle, and I couldn't disagree with him. Mick only won the Triple Crown that year.

I kept wishing that Casey would get to the point, and, finally, he did. He told me I'd been designated as the player to be named later in the trade the Yankees had made earlier to get Mickey McDermott from the Senators. The last thing Casey said to me that day was, "Go over there and have a good year, and I'll get you back."

He probably would have, too. The Yankees did just about anything they wanted in those days. But I never had that good year, and I never wore the pinstripes in Yankee Stadium. In my heart, though, I was always a Yankee. I never got over the fact that they'd traded me, even though I knew they had to.

Still, it's funny. Through the years—even when I was managing against his club—George Steinbrenner, the Yankees' owner, has always been good to me. He'll write me or call me or send me a telegram, congratulating me and telling me I'm the second-best manager in baseball—second to whomever is working for him at the time. I like George, but I don't know that I'd want to work for him.

◇   ◇   ◇

The 1956 Washington Senators were a horseshit baseball team, which made them no different from most other Senators clubs since Walter Johnson stopped pitching. We finished 59–95 that year. The only thing that kept us out of last place were the Kansas City A's, who were even worse than we were. The only good part about being with the Senators was that they were in the major leagues. I'd finally made it.

Charlie Dressen managed that club, and he was one of the greatest optimists I've ever met. Everybody on the club knew we were horseshit, but Charlie would call a meeting every day and say, "Get me a run early, keep us close till the seventh, and then I'll think of something." He always thought he could win. He never gave up. He had a reputation as a tough guy, a real disciplinarian, but that man's heart was mush.

Charlie never thought much of my ability as a player, but for some reason he decided to make me his pet. He got up at a banquet that year to introduce the team, and when he got to me, he said, "Every manager has a pet, and mine is Whitey Herzog." It embarrassed the hell out of me.

I played 117 games that year, hit .245, and played the hell out of center field. The Senators had Jim Lemon in right and Roy Sievers in left, two of the worst outfielders in the American League, so I had my work cut out for me. Dressen told me to catch anything I got to because he never knew what would happen if Lemon or Sievers tried it. One day in Chicago, we got beat 18–4 in the first game of a doubleheader. I don't think I had a single putout, but I still ran about 40 miles, backing up right and left, shagging balls off the walls.

Charlie came up to me after the game and asked, "Do you think you can make another one?"

I said, "What the hell? I didn't come to the big leagues to watch." So I started the second game, damned near out of gas, but I stole home off Howie Pollet and we won, 2–1.

It was in Washington that I met one of the great baseball characters of all time, Clinton Dawson Courtney. Old Scrap Iron. Courtney was the catcher on that club, and he and Dressen would go round and round. It was like a menagerie. I've never seen a manager and a player go at it like those two would.

Dressen was obsessed with Scraps and the things he did. He was always trying to figure what Courtney was up to. We were barnstorming our way north from spring training in 1956, playing the Cincinnati Reds in small towns, getting on the train each night and going wherever we were supposed to be the next day. Dressen would be playing bridge in the club car, but he was always worried about what Courtney was doing. And for good reason.

We had a Cuban outfielder on the team named Carlos Paula

who couldn't speak English worth a damn and played poker even worse. Every night, Courtney and a couple of other guys would get Paula into a poker game and clean him out. They'd play pot limit, meaning you could raise whatever was in the pot. They'd let Paula win a hand every now and then, when there wasn't much in the pot, and then clean him out on the big pots.

Dressen found out about it. He knew Paula was making only about $6,000 a year and had about six kids down in Cuba. So Dressen went up to Scraps one day and told him, "I know what you guys are doing to Carlos. He's cashing a $200 check from the traveling secretary every other day. He can't afford that and neither can we. You can play, but I want a quarter limit on the raises."

Well, the next night we're rolling down the track, and Charlie's up playing bridge in the club car. Late that evening, right before we're supposed to turn in, Charlie comes wandering back, and there's Scraps and the guys playing poker with Carlos Paula—and there's about $88 in the pot, which would be pretty hard to do with a quarter limit. Cash all over the table. Scraps looks up and sees the look on Charlie's face.

"Well," he says, real cool. "I'll raise that two bits."

Dressen reached down, took the cash off the table, gave it to Paula. He fined Courtney $250 and he gave that to Paula, too. That was the end of the poker games.

Scraps wasn't much of a con man because he wasn't smart enough, and he wasn't the smartest ballplayer you ever saw, either. He never did get the hang of flashing signs to the pitchers. All he knew how to do was put down one finger for the fastball and two for the curve. If a runner got on base, he'd never put down two; he always wanted the heater so he could handle it better if the guy was stealing. Clint could throw—and he was real proud of how hard he threw the ball back to the pitcher—but let a guy get on second base, and Clint was in trouble. He couldn't figure out how to change signs to keep the runner at second from stealing the signs and relaying it to the hitter. Scraps would get confused.

One day we were playing Detroit, and they were beating the hell out of us by thirteen runs or something. They were all sitting on the fastball like they knew when it was coming, and then they were smoking it.

Charlie finally said to Courtney, "Scraps, are you sure you're changing signs on them when they get to second? They're hitting some pretty good pitches."

Courtney said, "Sure, Charlie. I'm using the second sign. Whatever sign I flash second is the live one."

"Well," Charlie said, "Don't you think they might have figured that out by now?"

Scraps was in the dugout, taking off his gear and shaking his head. He said, "Now Charlie, don't you worry. There's no way they can get the signals from old Scraps, because I slip 'em down there when they ain't looking."

Another afternoon we were playing Kansas City, the only team we ever had a good chance of beating. The A's had the bases loaded, and Joe DeMaestri was at the plate. He tapped back to the pitcher, who fired to Courtney to get the force at home. Scraps gave it a great big first baseman's stretch, looking real sharp, and then walked the ball to the mound and gave it back to the pitcher. Dressen was in the dugout going crazy because the A's went on to score six runs with two out.

When we got back to the dugout, Charlie was climbing all over Courtney.

"Scraps," he said, "for Chrissakes, a grade-school kid knows the catcher's got to go back to first with that ball and get the double play."

Courtney got all pissed and said, "Well, shit, Charlie. If you're so goddamned smart, why didn't you holler at me and tell me where to throw it?"

The strange thing is that as goofy as Scraps was, he had ambitions to manage after he retired, and he managed in the Braves' chain when Paul Richards, his buddy, was running the Braves. As crazy as baseball is, Scraps might have made it to the big leagues as a manager if he hadn't been so nuts about ping-pong; he loved to play. He never had much of a slam, but he could get back almost everything hit to him. He was playing on a hot afternoon in Rochester, New York, in 1975 and dropped dead of a heart attack.

You don't have guys like Courtney in baseball anymore—you don't have the characters, the nicknames. Everybody's too serious today. Most of them are college-educated, and they're all so damned intense, trying to make a buck, all hung up on security. They're so serious they don't get fun out of the game the way we used to. I don't think players today realize the fun we used to have playing baseball—how much pure fun it is just to be a ballplayer.

Hell, even the minor leagues were fun. People talk about the hardships of the minor leagues, with the bus rides and all. It didn't mean anything to us. We didn't know any better. We'd buy two Red Dot cigars for fifteen cents, wine-dipped and all, get off the bus, go to the movie house, and get a box of popcorn for lunch. Play pool, shoot snooker. Then we'd go to the ballpark and hang out five ropes. We were ballplayers, and that's all that counted. We didn't worry about money; it wasn't enough to worry about. In those days, if you didn't make it in baseball, you knew you could probably make as much outside of baseball. Nobody knew what their roommate was making in those days, and nobody cared. They just wanted food on the table and a chance to play the game.

◇　◇　◇

And not only don't today's players have as much fun, I don't think they play as hard today as we did back then. They're not as hard-nosed as we used to be. They grow up without their mommas and their daddies ever scolding them, ever kicking them in their ass. Oh, there are exceptions, of course, but you hardly ever see anybody run into a wall, unless it's a guy like Freddy Lynn, who's made a career out of running into walls. Today's ballplayers won't play hurt as often as we did back then. They're all worried about their futures, by which they mean their future earning power, yet I suppose they can't be blamed for that.

However, I've managed players making a million dollars a year who haven't put out at contract time. I've managed young players making $150,000 or $200,000 a year who've never really had a good year in the big leagues, but claim they're unhappy because they're not making as much as the guy at the next locker. If they have a horseshit year, do they get a salary cut like we used to? Hell, no. We double their money and give them a five-year contract. And then what happens?

Time and again I've seen a guy sign a long-term contract and get lazy. He won't go full speed until the final year of his contract, when he's trying to make an impression. Not everybody does this, of course, but on the average, I'd say players work harder when they are hungrier.

I'm not one of those ex-ballplayers who say players today aren't as good as they were when I played. And I don't resent a dime of the money they're making. Players were getting screwed long before free agency came along. Mantle, for example, got a raise when he won the Triple Crown in 1956. When he didn't win it in 1957, they wanted to cut his salary, even though he hit 34 homers and batted .365.

I will say again, though, that we had more fun playing the game than they do now, and we played it harder. Even on the Washington Senators.

◇   ◇   ◇

What a terrible, terrible team we were. Calvin Griffith, who had taken over ownership from his uncle Clark Griffith, had scheduled us only for night games in the old Griffith Stadium, which was a slum within a slum. I had to look in the papers to make sure I was still in the big leagues.

Bad as things were for us in 1956, at least I had a halfway decent rookie year. When spring training started in 1957, people kept talking about my great potential. Wherever that potential was, it didn't show that year. I started spring training in a slump, and it just got worse. Burt Hawkins, one of the writers who covered the team, wrote: "The twenty-three-year-old Whitey is potentially a future star, but he's hitting southpaws as if he's swinging with a wet noodle."

Mary Lou saw that and hit the ceiling. "How could he say that?" she asked me.

"He's said it because it's true," I said.

After thirty-six games I was hitting a cool .167, so the Senators sent me to the minor leagues . . . the Miami Marlins. They told me I'd start to hit and be back in ten days. But I didn't get back at all that year, even though I was hitting .330 on July 31, the last recall date. After that, I just got down in the dumps. I had your basic bad attitude. My average slumped, and then, in late August, I got the first of a bunch of bad injuries which helped shorten my baseball career considerably.

While we were playing Columbus, it started to rain like hell. I was on second base when Don Landrum singled, and I decided to try to score in case the game was rained out. The catcher, Don Kravitz, was blocking the plate, so I tried to bowl him over. I wound up with a dislocation and fracture of my left shoulder—my throwing arm. I was through for the year.

The only good thing about my brief career in Miami in 1957 was that I got to play with the immortal Satchel Paige. The Marlins had signed him as a late-inning relief pitcher, mostly as a gimmick to boost attendance; they kept a rocking chair in the bullpen for him. But old Satch still had enough life in his arm to get out some guys in that league. He told everybody that he was forty-nine years old, but a conductor on the train told me one night that Satch had to be at least sixty-two.

He was quite a character. He called me "Wild Child," which is the same thing he called every other young player on the team. We called him "Q"—after the time we got into a spelling bee with him. Satch wasn't the greatest speller in the world, but he liked to think he was. We'd get into spelling games on the bus or the train, and Ol' Satch would be bragging. One night he got the word "cucumber."

"Cucumber," Satch said. "Q–U–. . . ."

Satch couldn't spell, but man, could he throw. He had the greatest control of any pitcher I've ever seen, regardless of age. He'd warm up with a gum wrapper. He'd take a piece of Wrigley's Spearmint (his favorite chew), pop it in his mouth, and then lay the wrapper on the ground. That would be his home plate, and from 60 feet 6 inches he'd be over the wrapper nine times out of ten.

The Marlins once had a distance-throwing contest before a night game. Landrum and I had the best arms of any of the outfielders. We were out by the center-field fence, throwing two-hoppers to the plate. Ol' Satch came out, didn't even warm up, and kind of flipped the ball sidearm. It went 400 feet on a dead line and hit the plate. I wouldn't believe it if I hadn't seen it.

We were on the road in Rochester one night, screwing around in the outfield. They had a hole in the outfield fence just barely big enough for a baseball to go through, and the deal was that any player who hit a ball through there on the fly would win $10,000. I started trying to throw the ball through the hole, just to see if I could. I bet I tried 150 or 200 times, but I couldn't do it, so I went back to the dugout.

When Satch got to the park, I said, "Satch, I bet you can't throw the ball through that hole out there."

He looked out at it and said, "Wild Child, do the ball fit in the hole?"

"Yeah, Satch," I said. "But not by much. I'll bet you a fifth of Old Forester that you can't throw it through there."

"Wild Child," he said. "I'll see you tomorrow night."

So the next night Satch showed up for batting practice—first time in his life he'd ever been that early. I took a few baseballs, went out to the outfield, and stepped off about 60 feet 6 inches, the distance from the mound to home. Satch ambled out, took the ball, brought it up to his eye like he was aiming it, and let fire.

I couldn't believe it. The ball hit the hole, rattled around, and dropped back out. He'd come that close, but I figured it was his best shot.

Satch took another ball and drilled the hole dead center. The ball went right through, and I haven't seen it since.

"Thank you, Wild Child," Satch said, and then went back into the clubhouse.

If Satchel had been able to play in the big leagues for twenty or twenty-five years, he would have retired the record book. I'm just glad I got to know him a little bit.

◇　◇　◇

I went back to Navajoa in the winter of 1957–58, got my shoulder back in shape, and tore the hell out of the ball. I had one month there that may have been the greatest month I ever played. I finished it off by hitting two homers to win the pennant for us on the last day of the season. I reported to spring training in great shape, with a great attitude, and had a hell of a spring. I think I was 25 for 41 in the Grapefruit League. But I was looking over my shoulder all the time.

The Senators had made a big trade with the Red Sox over the winter and had picked up center-fielder Albie Pearson. Pearson was a hell of a player and a big fan favorite because he was only 5′ 5″ and weighed 140 pounds. "The Mighty Mite" they called him. Well, the Mighty Mite had a mighty bad spring, and I had a great one, so the writers were speculating that I'd start ahead of him on Opening Day. Which shows what writers know. The only thing I did on Opening Day was catch the first ball of the season which President Eisenhower threw out.

Ike had been president long enough—and had thrown out enough first balls—that the players had a book on him. The book on Ike was that he liked to show off, really air it out, and throw it high and hard. So when the time came for the players to line up for the first ball, I shoved my way forward, jumped, and caught it.

Then I sat down—and I didn't hardly get up for a month. The Senators didn't get Pearson to sit him on the bench. I only got to bat twice during the first month of the season. Then they put me on waivers. On May 17, my old friend from Beaumont, Harry

Craft, picked me up for the Kansas City A's. One way or the other, I've been a Kansas Citian ever since.

◇　◇　◇

Kansas City was awfully good to me, both on and off the baseball field—especially when considering the shape that the franchise was in. The A's had left Philadelphia in 1955 and were trying for a new start in Kansas City. However, the owner, Arnold Johnson, didn't have much money, so every time he got a good ballplayer, he'd trade him to the Yankees. It was like the Yankees were still operating a farm club there. Johnson gave away Roger Maris, Ralph Terry, and a bunch of other guys who helped the Yankees win pennants. The commissioner should have done something about it, but commissioners have always been partial to the New York clubs.

I had a pretty good year playing for Harry Craft and the A's. I was a platoon player again, a role player. I'd go into left field for Bob Cerv in the late innings, and I backed up Vic Power at first base. I did a pretty good job as a pinch-hitter, too. But the big thing about 1958 for me was that I finally got my feet a little bit on the ground. I came to the realization that I was never going to be a star in the big leagues, but that I might still have a pretty good career if I hustled, kept my nose clean, and did the things that I do best as well as I could.

I mean, what the hell? We can't all be Mickey Mantle, can we? It's a tough thing for a ballplayer to come to grips with the limits of his talent. I've read a poll somewhere which said that more than half the men in America think that if they were given the right breaks and training, they could have become professional athletes. It's a nice dream, but that's all it is. Professional baseball players are the top 1 percent of all the boys in America who have played the game. An even smaller percentage makes it to the big leagues, and a small fraction of a fraction become stars. At some point, you have to discover where you fit in. For me, it came in Kansas City in 1958. It was the first time I figured I belonged in the big leagues and the first time I knew what my role would be.

As a manager, I look for guys who will be content with being extra men. I tell them straightaway that they're not going to be starting, that they're going to have to be content with playing defense and pinch-hitting, or that they'll be called in from the bullpen to get just one guy out. Too many managers make the mistake of stringing guys along, making them believe that if they work hard enough they can be regulars. Both the manager and the player know, deep down, that this will never happen, but they keep the illusion alive. All this does is breed unhappiness and dissension. The best guys you can have on your team are guys who know what their roles are and are content with them.

With all this in mind, I bought myself a right-handed catcher's mitt and reported to spring training the next year, in 1959, volunteering my services as an emergency catcher. One of the hallowed traditions of baseball is that catchers have to throw right-handed, although the reasons for it aren't all that strong. I knew in spring training that if I was going to stick in the big leagues, I was going to have to be so damned useful that it would pay them to keep me around. I could already play all three outfield positions and first base, and if I could catch, too—if only a little bit—it would help the club. A catcher, by the nature of his position, gets hurt more than any other player. If I could catch, the club wouldn't have to carry three catchers on the roster in case two guys got hurt in the same game. Also, the manager would be able to pinch-hit for a catcher in the eighth or ninth, knowing I could fill in if I had to. It sure as hell never hurts to let the manager know you're versatile.

So I brought my mitt to spring training and caught during exhibition games, warmed up pitchers, and did a lot of interviews with writers who were looking for an off-the-wall story. It didn't hurt me one bit; in fact, the club gave me an extra thousand bucks the next year just because of my attitude and enthusiasm. Got me all the way to $11,000 a year.

But, most important, it helped me stay in the big leagues. I got into the lineup on a semi-regular basis in June, and I was having a pretty good year by my standards. I was hitting over .300 on June 9, when we went into New York for a series with the Yankees.

Yogi Berra chose that day to drive a ball into the right-field stands, and I chose that day to give it a Fred Lynn try. I jumped over the concrete wall and landed about four rows deep in the seats; the ball landed in my glove.

It was, if I do say so myself, a hell of a big-league play. Unfortunately, it was also the one play that did more than anything else to cut short my big-league career.

I wound up with a deep bruise on my right thigh. Since we were leaving for Boston that night, I didn't get the leg iced down like I should have. The next day it was so sore that I couldn't stand the pressure of one finger on it. I sat out a couple of days, but then Craft asked me if I could play. Although I was still pretty sore, I was also aware of how shaky my job was. I went back out to right field, and sure enough, someone hit a looping fly ball into short right field. I came in for it, second baseman Jerry Lumpe went out for it, and we had ourselves one fine collision. His knee hit me right on the thigh, and that was the end of my season. I was hitting .293 at the time, but the leg just wouldn't get well.

It turns out that sometimes, with a deep bruise, pieces of calcium form around the injury. Calcification is what it's called, and I had it bad. Every step I took hurt, and it hurt all winter long. I kept on trying to heal it with rest, but it wouldn't come around. So I started the 1960 season in pain. Every time I took a good swing, I'd land on the leg, and it would start to hemorrhage around the calcification. Yet a player like me couldn't afford to ask out of the lineup, so I hung in there. I was hitting around .300 at the All-Star break, but the pain just kept getting worse. The doctors told me that they couldn't operate on it until the little pieces of calcium solidified, so I played in pain and waited it out.

One of my major achievements that season was hitting into the only all-Cuban triple play in baseball history. It makes a great trivia question. In the third inning of a game on July 23 at Washington, Bill Tuttle led off the inning with a single, and Lumpe singled behind him to move him to second. I'm up next, the count goes to 3-2, and the runners are moving on the next pitch. I line it back to Pedro Ramos, the pitcher, who throws it to Julio Bec-

quer at first to double off Lumpe. Becquer fires it to Jose Val-
divielso, the shortstop, who tags out Tuttle. We lose the game, 8–3,
and the top half of the *Washington Post* sports section the next day
shows a giant picture of the whole thing. Unless Fidel Castro lets
Cuban players in the big leagues again, my record is going to stand
forever.

By late August, the pain in the leg was too much to bear, so the
club sent me to Johns Hopkins Hospital in Baltimore to see Dr.
George Bennett, one of the most renowned orthopedists in the
country. He told me that little pieces of calcium had broken off
around the bruise.

"How have you been able to stand up?" he asked me. "If you
don't get this operated on, you'll be crippled the rest of your life."

I went back to Kansas City and had the surgery on August 31.
I was in the hospital for three weeks, then the doctors told me to
go out, play golf, take therapy, and work the hell out of the leg.
By spring training of 1961, the leg was all right.

◇   ◇   ◇

The same could not be said of the Kansas City A's. Arnold Johnson died that winter, and his widow sold the club to the legendary
Charles O. Finley of Gary, Indiana, and Chicago, Illinois, and
other points on the compass. Charlie Finley and I were destined
to have many a go-around, but not for a few more years.

When Charlie bought the club, he brought in Frank Lane, one
of the great wheeler-dealers in baseball, to be general manager. In
late January, Frank wheeled and dealed me to the Baltimore Orioles. I was disappointed at first because Mary Lou and I liked
Kansas City and were building a home there, but I wasn't the kind
of ballplayer who could pick his spots. I knew the Orioles had a
good club, and I thought it would be interesting to play for a good
club for a change.

Besides, I was kind of flattered by the deal. In exchange for me
and Russ Snyder and the traditional player to be named later, the
A's got five guys from the Orioles, including my old buddy Clint
Courtney. Scraps was later returned to the O's as the player to be

named later, thus becoming one of the few guys in baseball history to be traded for himself. This was only fitting, since Scraps was one of a kind.

The 1961 season was a good one for me. I got into 113 games and hit .291 as a platoon player. And for the first time, I got to find out what it feels like to be in a pennant race, or at least kind of a pennant race. The Yankees won 109 ball games that year with one of the best clubs I've ever seen, with Mantle and Maris chasing Babe Ruth and with Roger finally catching him. We won 95 games, which would be enough to win in a lot of years, and finished third behind the Yankees and the Detroit Tigers. Still, we were in the race for a long time and had some big games with the Yankees in September. My leg was OK—not what it had been before the injury, but OK. My shoulder was all right, and the whole year kind of rejuvenated me. I might have hit .305 that year if it hadn't been for Gene Conley, a big right-hander who pitched for the Red Sox and also played in the NBA for the Celtics. I was 0 for 23 against him. That big sucker cost me some money. The next year, on Opening Day, I hit a single, double, and triple off him.

Even though I hit well that year, I wasn't satisfied with the way I played the game. I played dumb ball, trying to do things with my legs that I couldn't do any more. I didn't have the quickness, didn't have the good burst of speed to turn on. I remember telling myself about halfway through the season, "Just when you learn how to hit, you can't run anymore."

So I started using my head a little more and was a pretty good player from then on.

The manager at Baltimore for most of 1961 was Paul Richards, the Wizard of Waxahachie, Texas. I learned a lot from Paul, some good and some bad. He had a reputation as a genius when it came to strategy and handling pitchers, and he did everything he could to foster that reputation. He'd never talk directly to a player; he'd always tell one of his coaches, "Go tell Whitey to play right field."

Richards was smart, all right—smart enough to play golf half the time and still have the owners think he was the hardest-working guy in baseball. One of the things he was always saying was, "When you have dumb people working for you, don't have them work a whole day. Let them work half days, and then they only screw up half as much."

But he did have a way with pitchers. He'd get hold of guys at the ends of their careers and teach them the palm ball as an off-speed pitch. He'd get a couple of years out of them and then do the same thing with other players. Offensively, he was what I call a "safety-first" manager, meaning he didn't hit-and-run and didn't steal bases. With runners on first and third and nobody out, he'd order the batter to hit the ball on the ground, content to give up the double play if it got him a run. Defensively, he wanted his outfielders with green paint on their backs. We had to play so deep that if a ball was hit over our heads, it was in the seats. He always wanted to force the other team to get three hits to score a run. I didn't care much for the way Paul played baseball, but he thrived on it. He relied so much on good pitching that he felt if we could hold the opposition to three runs or less, we'd win most of the time.

Richards left the Orioles before the year was over to take the general manager's job with one of the expansion teams, the Houston Colt .45s. Billy Hitchcock, a fine southern gentleman, took over as the Orioles' manager in 1962. Billy was truly a nice man; too nice for his own good, too nice to be a major-league manager. I enjoyed playing for him—he knew his baseball, his strategy was sound. But the man never wanted anybody to be mad at him, and one of the sad facts about our game is that it's just not possible. If you've got a nice guy as manager, somebody will always take advantage of him. On our team, that somebody was James Edward "Diamond Jim" Gentile.

Diamond was a free spirit, a big, hot-headed, left-handed–hitting first baseman; he'd hit 46 homers in 1961, including five grand slammers. He was scared to death of Richards, but when Paul went to Houston, Diamond turned himself loose. He dumped all over Hitchcock, the team's discipline went to hell, and we weren't the same ballclub. I got into ninety-nine games and hit .266, but the club finished seventh.

I went back home to Kansas City, finished the work on the

house I'd been building, and played with the kids. Debbie was going on eight at the time; David had just turned five, and Jimmy was just learning how to walk. I worked in the construction business and refereed basketball games, trying to keep bread on the table, all the while wondering how many years I had left in baseball. The answer was one.

◇   ◇   ◇

During Thanksgiving Week, I was traded to the Detroit Tigers along with catcher Gus Triandos for a young catcher named Dick Brown. As soon as I heard the news, I knew I was in trouble.

I considered myself one of the better ballplayers in the league by then, at least at what I did. I prided myself on playing in a hundred or so games as a platoon player. I could pinch-hit, and when I got hot, I'd play regularly for a week or two. But Detroit didn't need a guy like me. In Detroit, the four positions I could play were manned by All-Stars: Norm Cash, a batting champion, was at first; Al Kaline, who's now in the Hall of Fame, was in right; Billy Bruton, a fine defensive player and a solid left-handed hitter, was in center; and Rocky Colavito, a home-run hitter, was in left. I figured I wouldn't get to play there unless someone had a bone sticking out of his body. And that's just the way it turned out.

The good thing about playing for the Tigers was meeting Bob Scheffing, who later became one of my best friends in baseball. Bob managed the club until May, when he was replaced by my old pal, Charlie Dressen.

The bad thing about playing for the Tigers was that I almost died before spring training was over. Mary Lou and I were down in Lakeland, where the Tigers train. I got up one morning to go get the newspaper. When I came back into the apartment, I was real, real dizzy. I started throwing up and couldn't hold my head up—it would just nod and roll. Mary Lou loaded me into the car and drove me to the ballpark, and the trainer drove me to a hospital. The doctors told me a virus had settled into my nervous system and that I might need to stay in bed for six months. They explained that it was a sort of inner-ear infection which affected my balance and orientation. They kept me flat on my back for two weeks, then I had to leave the hospital.

I should have gone on the disabled list for the year, but I had to play—or at least try to.

Lord, I was messed up. I couldn't even play catch. I'd go out to shag fungoes, and the balls would almost kill me. I gradually got better, but I knew I'd never be any good again as a player. I only went to bat fifty-three times and hit a mean .151.

About the only time I got to hit was in batting practice, so I started counting batting practice home runs just to keep my interest up. I hit precisely 299 and was rained out of my chance for 300 on the last day of the season.

I went to Charlie Dressen at the end of the season and told him I'd better go on the voluntarily retired list. Dressen had been awfully nice to me, but he hadn't played me, and I couldn't blame him. He told me I could stay on as a coach, but I figured it was time to call it quits and do something else for the rest of my life.

So I said good-bye to major-league baseball. Or so I thought.

Apprenticeship

The biggest difference between baseball today and the way it was when I played is the money. I never made more than $18,000 per year playing baseball, which is about what the Cardinals pay our shortstop, Ozzie Smith, every day and a half. Money makes a difference in so many ways. One of them is that if today's players get some help and don't throw away their money, not only don't they have to work during the off-season, but they don't have to worry about what they're going to do when their careers are over.

I don't know whether that's good or bad. It's good, I guess, that a guy can make a living and set himself and his family up for life with ten or fifteen years of playing ball. But it's bad, I think, because it isolates guys from the real world.

When I played, I always went home and got a job in the off-season: working in a bakery, or the brewery, or as a laborer. When I played in Denver, I sold bricks in the off-season for the Denver Brick and Pipe Co., and I was a damned good salesman, too. I liked the job—liked it so much that I went back out there after my first big-league season and sold bricks for another winter. I'd do anything to put bread on the table, and as our kids started coming along, we needed more and more bread. Even when I was in the big leagues, I'd work five days a week in construction during the off-season, and I never turned down the time-and-a-half on Saturdays or double-time on Sundays. I would referee basketball games fifty nights a year, sometimes doing two games a night. I had an off-season PR job with the Armour Meat Company in Kansas City, too, pushing meat and signing autographs.

The job I liked the most was refereeing basketball games—the White Rat as a zebra. A lot of big-league umpires won't believe this, but I have a whole lot of sympathy for them because I know what their jobs are like.

I started reffing basketball in southern Illinois in 1957 and kept after it when we moved to Kansas City. I got a reputation as one of the best referees in the area, and I used to be assigned to all the top high-school matchups and the tournaments. Then I moved up to small-college ball. I thought nothing of driving all night to make $75 and expenses.

I used to work a lot of games with a guy named Jack Fette, who now sells sporting goods in Kansas City. He's also an official in the National Football League—and an outstanding one. Jack could have been a great major-league umpire. He worked Triple-A ball when I was with the Kansas City Blues, and he was a terrific umpire, although he had one of the worst cases of rabbit ears I've ever seen. If anyone so much as whispered at him from the bench or the stands, he'd kick him out. Jack's a super guy, a man who'd give you the shirt off his back, but he's a different person when he has stripes on.

One time we were reffing a game at Rockhurst, a small Jesuit college in Kansas City, and someone was sitting at the top of the stands in this little old gym, yelling, "Call the foul, Fette. Call the foul."

Jack blew his whistle, came over to me, and said, "Who's that clown rooting for?"

I said, "I think he's for Rockhurst, Jack."

"O.K.," Jack said, "watch this."

So we gave the ball to a kid, and he tossed it in—no contact made or anything—yet Jack blew this terrific blast on his whistle and called a foul on a Rockhurst player. He took the ball, turned around to the guy in the stands, and yelled, "There's your foul, loudmouth."

Another time we were working the finals of the All–Air Force Basketball Tournament at the old Richards-Gebauer Air Base outside of Kansas City. It was a morning game because everyone had to get back to their squadrons. We were working a hell of a game—you can always tell when you're reffing well because you're on top of everything, everything's working smooth. The crowd was real, real quiet—maybe because we were reffing well, maybe because it was so strange to watch basketball in the morning, or maybe they were all a little hung over. Jack couldn't stand it.

He came up to me and said, "It's too quiet. We've got to rile them up a little bit."

So he started antagonizing them. He'd call, "Blue ball!" when it should have gone white, or "White ball!" when it was supposed to go blue. The crowd was going crazy. I thought we were going to be killed.

A lot of refs get reputations as "homers," which means they're afraid of the home crowd so they give all the tough calls to the home team. Not Jack. He developed a reputation as a "roader," and it got so bad that almost nobody would hire him to work a home game for them. One time we were working a game at Northeast Missouri State in Kirksville, and Jack called five technical fouls in the first five minutes of the game. We were running up the floor, with Jack as the inside official, when he blew his whistle and came running out to me, yelling, "I got two! I got two!"

"Two what, Jack?" I asked.

"Two T's," Jack said. The crowd went crazy. We needed a police escort after that one.

Another time, he was working a Bradley University game in Peoria, when one of the coaches got all over Fette for not throwing the jump balls high enough. The next time there was a jump, Jack took the ball and threw it so high it hit the scoreboard clock. He turned to the coach and asked, "High enough for you?"

Jack Fette. What a guy. I wish he was umpiring in the American League. He'd have given Billy Martin and Earl Weaver fits.

◇   ◇   ◇

Between refereeing basketball and working construction and selling bricks and pipe, Mary Lou and I were putting away a little money for the day when we'd buy our own home. We didn't know where we were going to settle down, but when we did, we wanted a nice house, so we saved for it.

We spent $2,100 on a used house trailer in 1955, and for three years, that was our house, no matter where we were calling home. We lived in it in Denver, and then we towed it east after I got traded to Washington, and we lived in it there. We towed it back west in the winter and back east in the summer. In 1958, when I got traded to Kansas City, we gave up on the trailer. We had two kids by then, and the trailer seemed to be shrinking. Baseball is murder on families if you haul them all over the country. So we decided to put down roots right where we were. Kansas City was a nice town, and people there were good to us. It was time to start thinking about school for the kids, so we decided to stay there. That's still where I call home, and the house we live in is the one I built with my own hands.

I got a job there after the 1958 season with a commercial construction company owned by a couple of guys named Alex Barkett and Tudi Patti. Lord, those two were good to me. Mary Lou and I always had enough to make ends meet and educate our kids, with a little left over. And I liked construction, so much so that I even went back to school to get better at it. I went to a technical engineering school for two winters, studying drafting and blueprints, trigonometry and geometry. It was amazing how much better I was at school when I was paying for it myself—I carried a 99 average one semester. I figured that whenever my playing career ended, I'd just go to work full-time for the construction company. I practiced by building my own house in Independence.

I hired the skilled craftsmen, the carpenters and plumbers, to rough it out, and I did all the labor work and finished it myself.

I mixed all the mortar, stacked all the bricks, built the scaffolding. Eighteen thousand bricks are in that house, and I stacked every one of them. It's not beautiful, but, by God, it's practical. I'd never sell it—too much of my own blood is invested in it.

Some of my teammates who lived in town would come over and help out—guys like Bill Tuttle, Norm Siebern (who lived across the street), and Roger Maris, (who lived down the street and around the corner). This was in 1961, mind you, the winter after Roger broke Babe Ruth's home-run record. I had this national celebrity stacking bricks for me. The only trouble was that Roger and I looked a little bit alike in those days, and people kept coming up and asking if I was him. I'd tell 'em, "No, but I wish I was."

You meet a lot of people in baseball, and you make a lot of friends. But I'd have to say that of all the friends I made in the game, Roger was one of the best. As close as we were, our wives were even closer. He and Pat and Mary Lou and I stayed up late an awful lot of nights, playing pinochle. He was a different kind of guy than I am; he didn't warm up to a lot of people. But once he got to know you, you couldn't ask for a better friend.

The last time I talked to him was right before the sixth game of the World Series in 1985. He'd been fighting lymph cancer for years, and he told me that day that he didn't figure he'd be on this earth much longer. Mary Lou and I were out at our place in Colorado when he died at the end of the year. We got in the car and drove to Fargo, North Dakota, where he was buried, and I was a pallbearer at his funeral.

A bunch of Roger's old ballplayer friends were also at the funeral: Mickey Mantle, Whitey Ford, and Clete Boyer from the Yankees, Bob Allison from the Twins, Mike Shannon from the Cardinals. We sat up late after Roger's wake, talking baseball. Those Yankees were good-time Charlies when they played, and they haven't changed; so we closed the bar.

"You know," Mantle said that night, "of all the guys I played with, I thought Roger would outlast us all. We'd be out late, boozing and carrying on, and he'd be back at the hotel, taking care of himself."

For Roger to die as young as he did—at fifty-one—after the suffering he went through during his last two years, was a hard, hard thing for me to bear. I know there's not much sentiment for Roger to be in the Hall of Fame because he supposedly didn't establish himself over a long number of years. But there was nobody better during the years I played ball. I played with him and Al Kaline both, and I couldn't tell you who was the better player. Yet Al's in the Hall of Fame, and all Roger has is an asterisk after his name.

Roger won back-to-back MVP Awards in 1960 and 1961, playing on one of the greatest teams of all time. Maybe I'm prejudiced, but I think Roger Maris belongs in the Hall of Fame.

◇   ◇   ◇

Anyway, with Roger's help, I finished building my house. We'd settled into Kansas City so that when my playing career ended, I was set. Hank Peters, the minor-league director for the A's, had offered me a job in scouting, but I had decided I was through with baseball. I was only thirty-two years old—plenty young enough to start a new career. I liked construction, and I was good at it—good enough that Barket and Patti said they'd pay me $16,000 a year to be a superintendent for their company, the Metropolitan Construction Co. That was more money than people were making in the minor leagues, more than most Triple-A managers were making. So in the fall of 1963, I came home from Detroit and started work. And I mean work—ballplayers work hard, but most of them don't know what real work is.

Construction is tough, and there's so damned much involved. That first winter, we had a job pouring twelve-inch concrete slabs for heavy machinery, and sometimes we'd pour 110 yards of concrete a day, pour it even in the wintertime, when you had to build fires and put blowers around the slab to keep it from freezing. Naturally, someone had to get up in the middle of the night to go out and check the blowers, because if they went out, the whole job was shot. Naturally, that someone was me.

It was hard, but I could stand it. If hard work had been the only problem with construction, I'd still be doing it. What got me was the union rules. I was running a concrete gang with about thirty-three laborers out of the union hall in Kansas City, and one Friday afternoon, after most of the work was finished, the general superintendent on the job—a man named Hank Dahlke—told me to lay off twenty of them because we didn't need so many guys anymore.

Well, there were only about four of the guys who were any good at all. The rest of them were screw-ups who were only good for spotting trucks and holding surveying flags. In construction, the good workers get the dirtiest jobs because the lazy ones just screw them up. Baseball players have a hell of a union, but if someone isn't doing the job, you can still get rid of him. Not in construction.

I figured I could get around that. I called the whole gang in and laid them all off. Then I went around quietly to the dozen or so best workers and told them to be back on Monday morning and they'd get their jobs back. When word of this got back to the union business agent and stewards, they were all over me. They were out on the job, raising hell, waving their arms, threatening to throw up pickets. They said either I took the guys as they came out of the union hall, or I took nobody at all.

I couldn't take that. I went to see Hank and told him, "I don't believe I want to fight this the rest of my life. I don't need a business where you have to fire good guys and keep the dogs." And I quit.

I got in my car and drove over to the old Municipal Stadium in Kansas City, where the A's had their offices, and I asked to see another guy named Hank—Hank Peters, who now runs the Baltimore Orioles. He is one of the finest men I've ever worked for as well as one of the finest men I've ever known. He is bright, intelligent, always in complete grasp of the whole situation. He put together the A's teams that dominated baseball in the early seventies, and then he went to Baltimore and built champions over there, too. Players like him, owners like him. I've always thought he'd be a hell of a candidate for baseball commissioner, and I've never understood why his name didn't come up.

I went to see Hank that winter morning, still dressed in my

construction clothes. I told him what I'd done and asked if the job he'd talked to me about was still open. Hank gave me the job right away, but said he could pay me only $7,500 a year. That was about a third of what I'd made the year before from baseball and construction, but I swallowed hard and took it. Mary Lou thought I was crazy, but she knew I had to do it. A gambler would say I was "betting on the come," and I guess I'd have to say I won that bet.

◇　◇　◇

All of a sudden, I was a big-league scout, even though I didn't have the slightest idea how to go about scouting. Joe Bowman, the A's scouting director, taught me the ropes. He took me around the Midwest territory, which was my assignment, and introduced me to all the bird dogs—the part-time guys who work for the team. I received a lot of help from other scouts, particularly those who worked for the Dodgers. They didn't have to help me, particularly in those days, before the free-agent draft was started and scouts competed directly for the same talent. But they did help me, and I've always been grateful.

Scouts are some of the most misunderstood people in baseball. Everybody thinks of them as washed-up ballplayers sitting in the sun in golf hats, holding notebooks and radar guns. What they don't see is all the work that goes into it—all the driving, all the plane rides, all the nights in motel rooms, all the checking and cross-checking, and all the crap they have to take from the front office. A good scout has to love baseball an awful lot.

Even with all of the changes in the game, it has remained a constant that the most successful teams are those with the best scouts. If you don't scout well at the pro as well as the amateur level, there's no way your team can be successful. Scouts are still the foundation of any baseball organization.

But scouts are funny; they think there's a whole lot more to evaluating baseball talent than there really is. Some of them told me it would take me eight years to learn how to scout, which is a lot of nonsense. Some guys can scout for twenty years and never learn how to do it right because they never learn to stick their necks out. That's never been a problem for me. I figure all you can do is figure out the things you can figure out, forget about the things you can't, and forge ahead.

In my first year as a scout, I signed twelve ballplayers for a total of $125,000 in signing bonuses. I had a big territory, one with an awful lot of talent in it. I worked it hard, and I was lucky. Charlie Finley, the A's owner, was always swinging back and forth between spending too much money and too little. The year I started scouting, he was spending a lot. He'd made a lot of money in his insurance business in Chicago the year before, and it was either spend it on ballplayers or pay it to the government. I signed those twelve guys for Finley, and seven of them eventually played in the big leagues. Any scout will tell you that's a hell of a year, especially for a rookie.

Scouts are also a little like fishermen; every scout has a story about the one who got away. In my case, the one who got away was a young man named Don Sutton, who has now won more than 300 ball games in his major-league career. When I first saw him, he had two years of college under his belt and was a terrific semi-pro pitcher. I scouted him hard, and at the 1964 National Baseball Congress tournament in Wichita, Kansas, I had him in my hotel room, ready to sign an A's contract for $16,000. What a bargain he would have been.

But Finley wouldn't go for it. He'd already signed three pitchers that year for more than $75,000 each: he had given Catfish Hunter and Blue Moon Odom $75,000 each, and Skip Lockwood had signed for a hundred grand. Finley knew that the rules then required all of the big bonus babies to be protected on the big-league roster, or else they could be drafted by another club for $8,000. And Charlie knew he couldn't protect them all.

I knew that Hunter, Odom, and Lockwood were all good prospects—they all became fine big-league pitchers, with Hunter as one of the finest pitchers of his era—but I thought then that Sutton had a chance to be better than all of them. I figured we could give Donnie his $16,000, take a look at him, and even if we lost him in the draft, we'd still get back $8,000. I told this to Hank Peters when I called him from my motel room.

"Charlie won't go over $10,000," Hank told me. "I'm sorry."

"Listen," I said. "This guy's got two years of college, and he's got as good a chance to be a big-league pitcher as anyone I've ever seen. Let me talk to Charlie, will you?"

Finley called me, and I begged him. I knew he was crazy about nicknames—he loved Catfish and Blue Moon and Skippy, and he almost took a flyer on a kid named Soprano Crawford, who later signed with the Dodgers. Later on, he tried to get Vida Blue to change his name to True Blue—that's how crazy Finley was. So when I got him on the phone, I asked him to hang on a minute, and I turned to Sutton.

"Goddamn, Donnie," I said. "Don't you have a nickname? I could get you the money if you had a snappy nickname."

Sutton shrugged and said, "Heck, I don't care. Tell him anything you want. Tell him my name is Pussyface Sutton if you want, just get me the money."

I said, "Charlie, I've got a kid named Pussyface Sutton you can get for $16,000."

But not even Charlie Finley was that crazy, and I lost Don Sutton. I went out and told Burt Wells of the Dodgers that he ought to sign him. It took Burt two weeks to get the money from his front office, but they eventually signed Sutton, and he became a great one.

About a year and a half after that, I was coaching for the Mets when Sutton came to New York with the Dodgers. I think he'd been something like 25–6 in the minors, and the Dodgers brought him up to the big club. Sutton told the New York press that the third-base coach for the Mets had him signed for $16,000, but that Charlie Finley had nixed it. Finley denied it, of course, saying he never denied any scout any money. We got a big laugh out of it. Just think how good the A's would have been if they'd had Sutton in the early 1970s, along with Hunter and Blue and Odom and Rollie Fingers. They won three World Championships as it is, but if they'd had Sutton, they might never have lost a game.

Finley was a real crackpot. He did some crazy things to the game, some of them harmless—like when he tied a white mule named Charlie O in the bullpen at the stadium in Kansas City, or when he dressed the A's in yellow and green uniforms—and some of them not so harmless. It was Finley who brought about free agency when he let Catfish Hunter off the hook at the end of the 1974 season. Charlie started thinking he was a genius after he moved the A's to Oakland and they started winning. But it was people like Hank Peters who built those teams. Once they got the players in the system, Finley fired all the good people and surrounded himself with people who wouldn't talk back to him. I don't think he ever appreciated the work that people did for him. I know he didn't appreciate me.

◇ ◇ ◇

After I scouted for Finley in 1964, Peters asked me to join the coaching staff in 1965 and work with the young talent they had signed. The bonus-baby rule meant you had to keep a lot of kids on the twenty-five-man big-league roster, or risk losing them for $8,000 in the draft. We had eight of them on the roster in 1964, which was ridiculous. You can't win with that many kids around, but Charlie didn't care about winning. He knew he was going to move his team out of Kansas City, and he was building for the future in Oakland.

Building for the future is nice if you don't mind screwing the fans—and Charlie didn't mind—but you have to have someone around to teach the kids baseball. The trouble was that the A's didn't have any coaches at the big-league level who could—or would—work as instructors.

Mel McGaha was the manager that year, for a while at least. He couldn't get along with the players, or coaches, or the press—so he only lasted until the middle of May. He was replaced with Haywood Sullivan, one of Charlie's bobos, but a good guy nonetheless. Finley had hired some other pals, like Luke Appling, Eddie Lopat, and Gabby Hartnett, to be his coaches, and they didn't seem interested in getting out there in the afternoon sun in

Kansas City and working with the kids. So they told me to do it.

Every day when we were at home, I'd be out there with the kids: Sal Bando, Rene Lachemann, Rick Monday, Joe Rudi, John Sanders, Chuck Dobson, Catfish Hunter, Blue Moon Odom, and Skip Lockwood. We'd do fundamentals until they were blue in the face, and then I'd throw batting practice. I worked their tails off. And when the game started, I'd sit on the bench and talk baseball with them. I was also the first "relief coach" in baseball history. During doubleheaders, Hartnett and Appling would be too tired to coach the bases both games, so I'd coach first base in the first game and third in the second. I was doing all of this for $10,000, which was $15,000 less than the other coaches were making.

At the end of the year, we went on a western road trip, and Finley invited my wife to go along on the charter. When we got back, he sent us a bill for $92 for her plane fare. Here I was making only ten grand a year, and her trip didn't cost him a penny, yet he sends me a bill for ninety-two bucks. I paid the damned thing, but at the end of the year I went in and asked for a $2,500 raise. He turned me down. However, the next thing I know, I'm reading in the paper where Finley is bragging about me, telling people how I am the best coach he's ever had. So I got him on the phone one day and really started to chew him out. Mary Lou came up and asked who I was talking to like that, and when I told her, she turned pale. I didn't care. Finally, I said, "I tell you what, Charlie. You just get that damned mule to coach for you, because I quit."

The first thing I did when I hung up was to call Joe McGuff, then the sports editor at the *Kansas City Star* and one of my all-time favorite people. I told Joe what I'd done, and that Finley would be calling to tell him that he'd fired me. Sure enough, Charlie got on the phone, trying to tell people he'd run me off. But McGuff protected me; he really wrote some nice articles. Joe knew Charlie was getting ready to move the A's anyway, and he didn't care much for the man. He had a lot of company. Even today, I run into guys I worked with for Finley, and we sit around and tell stories. Kind of a Charlie Finley alumni club. We always marvel at how lucky Finley was. The man had a knack. In 1967, with the seventh choice overall in the draft, he took a kid pitcher named Brian Bickerton, who never made the big leagues. Then on the second round, they took another pitcher, a left-hander named Vida Blue. Once Vida arrived, the A's were off and running, at least until Charlie tore them apart.

◇   ◇   ◇

I'd told off Finley, so I was out of work again. I had turned down an offer the year before to become baseball coach at Kansas State University, because if you're in baseball, the big leagues are the only place to be. But now, without a job, I couldn't be so choosy.

I called Lee MacPhail, another of the great people in baseball, whom I'd met when I was in the Yankee chain. Lee was then running the Orioles, and I told him I needed a job. He hired me to manage the Orioles' Double-A club in Elmira, New York. I said I'd see him in the spring and went off to spend the rest of the winter working in construction again.

I really figured at that point that I'd make a career in the minor leagues. I didn't think I'd ever make a major-league manager, but Mary Lou and I had talked it over and decided we could be happy in the minor leagues. We'd sure as hell never get rich, but I enjoyed working with the young kids, and it's really a pretty good life for a baseball man.

But one day that winter, I was out on a construction job when I got a call from George Weiss and Bing Devine, who were running the New York Mets. They wanted me to come coach third base for them. Well, any job in the big leagues is better than any job in the minors, as far as I'm concerned, but I told them I couldn't take it unless MacPhail released me from my promise. Lee said he hated to lose me, but he gave me his blessing, and I went off to spring training with the Mets. That one phone call from Weiss and Devine really turned my life around.

◇   ◇   ◇

Boy, what a year I had in 1966. If there's one thing I can say about my career in baseball with absolute confidence it's that I was the greatest third-base coach who ever lived. I still think it's the most fun job in baseball. You're right on top of the game, involved in all the plays, flashing signs, moving runners along. I took a look at the Mets' records from 1965 and saw that they'd struck out something like 1,150 times, which told me one thing: if I had a chance to wave a guy home, I'd better do it, because chances were nobody was going to drive him home from third. As Dick Young wrote in the *New York Daily News,* "Hold a Met at third and the next thing you know, you're taking his glove out to him."

I've had some real good third-base coaches working for me, people like Chuck Hiller and Hal Lanier, but I still think I was the best. I owe it all to Casey Stengel, who worked with me day in and day out in those Yankee rookie camps. Casey loved to coach baserunning: cutting the bases right, getting a good walking lead off third, being ready to haul ass when the ball was hit. I've taught it to the Mets and to every ballclub I've had since then.

I had a pretty good deal working in New York that year. I shared an apartment with Kenny Boyer, who'd been a big star with the Cardinals and was winding up his career as the Mets' third baseman. We were about the same age, even though I was a coach and he was a player. Kenny later went on to manage the Cardinals —in fact, he was the man I replaced in 1980. We shared our apartment with Roger Maris and Kenny's brother, Clete. When the Mets were on the road, Clete and Roger had the place, and when the Yankees were on the road, Kenny and I took it over. Try telling a big-league ballplayer today that four guys lived in the same place.

Wes Westrum was the manager of the Mets that year—a fine baseball man, but not the kind of guy who ever took the bull by the horns. I made it a point to be aggressive, and I got a lot of help from the New York writers. They knew I was always good for a story, which Wes and none of the other coaches ever were, so when guys like Dick Young or Jack Lang needed an off-day story, they'd come to me.

If there's one thing that did more than any other to help my career along, to enable me to make the money I'm making today, it's the treatment I got in 1966 from the New York writers. I had eight or nine really nice articles written about me that year, and there's nothing in baseball more influential than the New York press. The writers told me they'd make a big-league manager out of me, and they sure as hell did.

The only problem was that New York was a hell of a long way from home, and the Mets never played in Kansas City. I guess I must have been pretty homesick because when Finley tried to hire me back at the end of the year, I said I'd go. He'd made Eddie Lopat his general manager, and Eddie tempted me bad. He said he'd pay me more than the $12,000 the Mets had paid me, plus I could live at home. I hadn't signed a new contract with the Mets yet, so I was free. There had been some stories in the paper about how Westrum was jealous of all the attention I was getting, and some of the writers were boosting me as his successor. I didn't think that it was the best situation in the world for either me or Wes, so I jumped at Finley's offer.

When Bing Devine, who'd taken over from Weiss as general manager, got wind of it, he called. "What are you going back to Finley for?" he said. "Last year you told him to get the mule to coach for him."

"Bing," I said, "it's very simple. He's going to pay me more money to live at home than you're paying me to live in New York."

"Well, I'm not going to let you go," Bing said. "What will it take to keep you?"

I figured a minute. I'd never made more than $18,000 a year, so I said, "Twenty thousand plus expenses."

"You got it," Bing said. "You're going to work directly for me, as my special assistant, and we'll get you home every now and then."

He was as good as his word, and always has been. Bing had been general manager of the Cardinals and had built the World Championship club they had in 1964 before running afoul of Gussie Busch somehow. Then he'd gone over to the Mets, worked for Weiss a year, and had taken over in time for the 1966 season. He was a twenty-four-hour-a-day baseball man, the kind of guy who'll call you at any hour of the day or night. He ran me all over the country, scouting free agents, scouting big-league clubs and the high minor leagues, looking for ballplayers who could help the big-league club. I was on the road seventy out of ninety-three days at one point, but Bing was also the kind of guy who'd send you home for three or four days to see your family. If I was in the middle of the country scouting, Bing would call and tell me to go home for a few days. He'd call me there when he needed me.

I learned a lot in that job in 1967. It was my first taste of being involved in high-level trade talks, yet the people in the organization reached the point where they relied more and more on my judgment about who to sign and who to get rid of. But I missed being in uniform, coaching and working with the young players. Bing sensed that, and in September, he got me and Bob Scheffing, who was director of player development, to switch jobs.

In baseball, the director of player development assesses the talent in the system and decides who should move up and who should move down. It requires some coaching, getting on the field to see who can cut it and who can't. I hate to keep being modest, but I was probably the best player development man who ever drew a breath. Two years after I took the job, the Mets won the World Series, and we did it with young players whom I had rushed through the system. Our scouts had come up with some good young players. The free agent draft had gone into effect in 1965, and because the Mets were always finishing at the bottom, they were getting some high draft choices. I moved them along as fast as I could, and cleaned house of all the old, stagnant guys in the system. We went with kids at all levels and pushed them hard. The thing really blossomed.

The only real problem in working for the Mets was working with M. Donald Grant, who was club president, the one who ran the team for Mrs. Joan Payson, the owner. He was a stockbroker, a guy who didn't know beans about baseball but thought he did. I've run into guys like Donald Grant a lot in my career, and everywhere they show up, they're trouble. Sometimes they're owners, like Finley or George Steinbrenner of the Yankees, who figure that it's their team and, by God, they'll meddle if they want to. Sometimes they're buddies of the owners, or club executives who have no background in baseball. But they figure, "Hell, I always wanted to be a baseball player, so I'll just pretend I know what I'm doing."

Second-guessing the manager or the general manager is a time-honored American tradition, and I've got no quarrel with it. It keeps radio talk-show hosts and sports columnists employed, and most of the time it doesn't do any harm. I love to listen to people call up the radio shows and talk about why I should have taken a pitcher out earlier, or why I should have pinch-hit so-and-so, or why I should trade two of my minor-league pitchers and a hot-dog vendor for Dwight Gooden. Baseball is a game almost everybody has played at some time or the other, which qualifies most of them as experts in their own minds.

The thing these people don't understand is that most of us in the big leagues didn't just ride into town on a turnip truck, as my buddy Norm Stewart, the Missouri University basketball coach, puts it. We've spent our lives in baseball, and unless we're real, real stupid, we've managed to learn a few things along the way. No manager likes to be second-guessed—I go out of my way to avoid second-guessing my fellow managers, but it comes with the territory. I figure that being second-guessed is part of the territory, and I don't mind it—as long as I don't have to pay any attention to it. That was the problem with M. Donald Grant. We had to pay attention to him.

◇   ◇   ◇

Grant had his "pets," and no argument on earth could convince him that they weren't worth keeping. One of his pets was a left-handed pitcher named Don Shaw—"my Donnie Shaw," Grant called him. He won a total of thirteen games in the big leagues, but Grant was convinced he was a great prospect. In the winter of 1967–68, we went down to Mexico for the winter meetings and had a deal all set with the White Sox. We were going to give them Shaw and outfielder Tommy Davis for Tommy Agee, a young outfielder everyone in the Mets' organization was hot for. Gil Hodges, who'd replaced Westrum as manager, wanted him. Bing, Scheffing, and I all wanted him, and we had the deal set. But Bing said we'd have to wait until Grant flew in to approve it.

The deal leaked to the papers, and when Grant hit town, he was furious. "How could you think about trading my Donnie Shaw?" he asked.

And he killed the deal. We eventually got Agee anyway, but Grant's decision cost us a good man—Bing Devine. "I don't really believe they need a general manager around here," he told me.

And he went back to the Cardinals. He asked me to come with him, but I didn't think I could afford to do that. I'd already jumped Finley to go to the Mets, and I'd backed out on the Orioles the year before. I didn't want to get a reputation as a guy who wasn't loyal, so I told Bing no thanks. He went back to St. Louis, got in on another pennant winner, and eventually got fired there again. He spent some time with the Expos and then went back to St. Louis with the football Cardinals. We see each other, and I still look to him for advice. Bing is a guy who cares about you, and he's been awfully good to me.

When he left the Mets, they made John Murphy the general manager. John was a fine man, but his nickname was "Grandma" —he just couldn't seem to make a decision. That was fine with me, since I moved right in to make all the tough ones for him. All Murphy really cared about were the bonus babies and the big pitchers. He let me run the organization pretty much as I wanted. One morning in spring training, I released about $400,000-worth of bonus babies without bothering to check with him. Players like Steve Chilcott, who the Mets had taken in the draft ahead of Reggie Jackson, and Les Rohr, who they'd made the second pick in the country in 1965.

"Oh my God," John said when I told him what I'd done. "Tell me you really didn't do that."

"Yeah, John," I said, "I can't look at them any more. We're better off getting them out of here. They're just taking up space.

We've got to get this organization moving. If any of them ever make the big leagues, you can have my job." None of them ever did.

The next winter I did something else that almost cost me my job. I unloaded Don Shaw. The National League was adding two teams, one in Montreal and the other in San Diego, and we all had to give up some players. Gil Hodges had suffered his first heart attack, and with him in the hospital, nobody wanted to decide whom to protect and whom to throw into the draft. I put Shaw on the draft list. And I can still hear Donald Grant telling us, "Don't lose my Donnie Shaw."

I said, "Listen, if I'd seen that kid pitch in college, he never would have been here. If we can get them to pay us $200,000 for the privilege of drafting him, we're going to be miles ahead."

As the draft proceeded, we lost Dick Selma, Jerry Morales, and Larry Stahl, but I still had Shaw hanging out there and refused to take him off the list. I also had Eddie Kranepool, a first baseman who was one of the Mets' first bonus babies and another one of Grant's pets, on the list. Finally, on about the fourth or fifth round, Montreal took Don Shaw. I looked down the table in the draft room, and there was John Murphy, red as a beet.

He came over to me and said, "All right, you got rid of Shaw. But you'd better get Kranepool off the list, because if Grant loses both Shaw and Eddie, you and I are both going to get fired."

"John," I said. "Nobody is going to take Eddie Kranepool. They're all smarter than Donald Grant. And even if they do draft him, we're better off playing kids like Kenny Singleton or Mike Jorgensen. Trust me."

But John got worried and took Kranepool out of the pool. Maybe he was right. Eddie played another eleven years for the Mets and spent eighteen years in the big leagues. He had a lifetime average of .262, so he wasn't as bad as I thought he was. Maybe I was just trying to get to Grant. He sure as hell got to me.

The next year was 1969—the year of the Miracle Mets. I still don't know how we won the World Championship, but we did. I've still never seen a young pitching staff that could equal the one we had that year: Tom Seaver, Jerry Koosman, Gary Gentry, Nolan Ryan, Tug McGraw, and the others. The players who won the championship were all in the Mets' system before I got there, but I like to think I helped move them along, put them in a position where they could play in the big leagues as quickly as possible. I got a lot of satisfaction out of the World Series. I'd been in baseball for twenty years, and that was the first time I was associated with a championship team.

The club had a celebration in the Diamond Club at Shea Stadium after the Series, and I went up to congratulate Gil Hodges. He jumped out of his chair and said, "No, Whitey, I want to congratulate you. I really appreciate all the things you've done since I got here. Everything you've told me about a ballplayer has been true, and you've never been wrong on an evaluation. You're more of the reason we're the champions than anyone else."

It was one of the finest compliments I've ever received in baseball.

◇   ◇   ◇

The Mets went to pieces after that. John Murphy died of a heart attack the winter after we won the World Series, and Bob Scheffing replaced him. Scheff, who died in 1985, was another of those super guys you find in baseball. I had played for him when he managed Detroit in 1963, and he'd been good to me that year, when I was having so much trouble. He knew baseball front and back, but he was just too nice a man to be an effective general manager. He just wasn't forceful enough to deal with Don Grant, and the Mets went downhill very quickly.

Under Grant, the Mets were absolutely paranoid about money. Even when we were finishing ninth and tenth in the league, you could walk into the front office and ask, "How are we doing?" and the people there would tell you how many people we were drawing instead of whether we were winning or losing. They all cared more about profit-sharing and bonuses than they did about building a ball club. They didn't seem to care that the Mets were the laughingstock of baseball as long as they made money.

We made a terrible deal with Montreal, giving up three fine young players—Tim Foli, Mike Jorgensen, and Ken Singleton—for Rusty Staub. Rusty was a great hitter, but Lord, he was slow, and you have to be crazy to give up three starters for one player, no matter how good a hitter he is. Right after that deal, we traded Nolan Ryan and three other guys to the California Angels for shortstop Jim Fregosi. We made crazy deals like that, bringing in veteran players, because Don Grant didn't like minor leaguers. Overall, we traded eleven prospects, and the only guy we got who was any help was Rusty Staub.

Here I was, busting my tail to develop young players, and Don Grant says he doesn't trust minor leaguers, that we needed big names. We had guys in our system who could have helped the Mets dominate baseball in the 1970s—players like Foli and Jorgensen and Amos Otis—and we gave them up.

A baseball team is like an organism which is constantly changing, one cell replacing another. You hang on to the old players too long, and rot sets in. That's what happened to the Mets. We looked around, and the team we had counted on for the future wasn't there any more.

The Mets won the pennant again in 1973, with a club that was only three games over .500. They took the A's to seven games before losing the World Series, but I think they gave up too much for that one year of glory. It was a long time before they even got close to winning again. And by then I was long gone, trying to beat their brains out.

Joe McDonald, whom I later brought over to the Cardinals, succeeded Scheffing as general manager in 1974, and he had a tough time of it. Mrs. Payson wasn't putting any money into the team, so Joe had to operate on a shoestring. He got a lot of the blame for the Mets' collapse, but I don't think it was fair. His only fault as a general manager is that he's a tough negotiator and is tight with the owner's money. Nowadays, it looks like the only way to keep your job is to throw away money and forget about arguing with the agents and players. If you win, you win. If you don't, you don't. It doesn't make much difference to the owners so long as they get their names in the paper, and the general manager can always blame the manager if things go wrong. Count the number of general managers who get canned, and then count the number of managers who get fired. You'll see who the scapegoats are.

One thing I learned during the seven years I spent with the Mets is that the whole organization has to work in harmony if things are to go right. You can't give a manager horseshit players and expect him to win. You can't acquire or develop good players unless everyone in the front office is thinking alike, or unless there's one strong personality in charge. And that's hard to have happen unless you've got ownership that's willing to put ego aside and let the baseball people do their jobs. You don't find an organization like that very often, but when you do, it's usually flying pennant flags.

◇   ◇   ◇

Having learned all that, I still wanted to become a big-league manager. He's the man who can make it all happen. If he's a strong enough guy, a take-charge person, he can sometimes influence the whole organization.

But I knew I'd have to manage in the right kind of organization to succeed. I wanted one with some stability and some sense of purpose, some place that would give me a decent chance to build a winner. That's why I turned down the first three managing jobs which were offered to me.

Two of them came from Finley, and I knew enough about him to know he wasn't the kind of guy I could work for. If he'd still been in Kansas City, I might have taken a shot at it just so I could live at home. But he had moved the club to Oakland in 1970, and there was no way I was going to work for Charlie Finley and live on the West Coast (the A's managed to do pretty well without me). The other job I was offered was with the Cleveland Indians, a franchise that was in chaos then and is just now coming out of it.

When Gil Hodges had his second heart attack and died in April of 1972, I really hoped I'd get a chance to manage the Mets. I knew the personnel in the organization better than anyone. But the ink was barely dry on the newspaper obits for Gil when Grant hired Yogi Berra. For some reason, Grant always thought a former Yankee or Dodger should manage the club. Grant's people even ordered me to stay away from Gil's funeral just so there wouldn't be speculation that I'd be the new manager. I've never forgiven them for that.

I finished the year as player development director, even though I was frustrated and bored with the job. It sometimes took three years to find out whether or not I'd made a mistake. A manager can find out in three seconds. So I put out the word that I was looking for a manager's job.

Meanwhile, down in Arlington, Texas, Ted Williams wanted out as manager of the Texas Rangers. And who could blame him? His club had won 54 and lost 108 in 1972. Ted recommended me as his replacement. He called me and said, "I really think we can do fifteen percent better next year?"

I said, "Fifteen percent of fifty-four or fifteen percent of one hundred and eight?" and he just roared. I took the job anyway.

One thing about me: when I make a mistake, it's a dandy.

Rangers, Angels, and Royals

Bob Short, the owner of the Texas Rangers, and Joe Burke, his general manager, had talked to me during the World Series in 1972 about taking over the club from Ted Williams. They'd also talked to Tom Lasorda, then a coach with the Dodgers, and Billy Hunter, who was then coaching with the Orioles. I drew the short straw. So, after the Series, Short and Burke snuck me into Dallas and signed me to a two-year contract to manage the club. And then, at my first press conference as a big-league manager, they opened the floor for questions.

"Whitey," someone said, "you've been in the National League for a lot of years, but I'm sure you've seen most of the Rangers play before, or at least you've looked at the roster. What are your first impressions of your new team?"

Now, there's two ways to deal with a question like that. The first one is to bullshit your way through it, talk about the great potential on the team or the fine veteran leadership that could, with a few breaks, make you into a contender. The second way is to be honest. I figured I might as well get off on the right foot.

"To be honest about it," I said, "this is the worst excuse for a big-league ball club I ever saw."

I think our performance during the 1973 season bore me out.

I managed this juggernaut to 47 wins and 91 losses. The only thing that saved me from managing a team which lost 100 games is that I got fired on September 8. I think the best way to describe my career with the Texas Rangers is as "a learning experience." A lot of character got built that year.

Man, we were bad. The Rangers were in their thirteenth season by the time I took over in 1973, and you could chalk up the season to unlucky number thirteen—except for the fact that they had never been any good. They'd been formed in 1961 as the Washington Senators when my old boss, Cal Griffith, moved the original Washington Senators to Minnesota to become the Twins. The original Senators hadn't been any good, and the new Senators weren't any good either. People didn't go to see either team play.

When Short, a trucking millionaire from Minneapolis, moved the Senators after the 1971 season, he became the most hated man in Washington, D.C., which is quite an accomplishment. He always ran his club on a shoestring. He hired Williams, figuring that some of Ted's ability might rub off on his players. But the Senators still couldn't win, and they didn't draw, so Short moved them to Arlington, Texas, on the turnpike between Dallas and Fort Worth. I guess he was hoping that new surroundings would help him make money, but the first rule about making money in baseball is you've got to win, and the Rangers have had trouble with that part.

Ted Williams was the only first-class thing about the franchise. However, with his eyesight, he could read the handwriting on the wall better than anybody. He recommended me for the job, and I always tell him I'll never forgive him for it.

◇   ◇   ◇

When I arrived at spring training in 1973 and looked at the "talent" the Rangers had, I knew we were in trouble. I'd never seen such a motley assortment of has-beens and never-wases. Williams, like a lot of great players, wasn't much of a teacher. The game comes so easy to guys like Williams and Mickey Mantle and Willie Mays that they can't understand just how hard it is for a man of lesser abilities to play. I think of a man like Bob Gibson, a Hall-of-

Fame pitcher for the Cardinals who later became a pitching coach for the Mets and the Atlanta Braves. Gibby wanted all the pitchers to throw like he did. Very few people can do that.

As manager of the Senators/Rangers, Williams just rolled out the bats and balls, and expected his team to be as motivated as he was. As a player, the only part of the game Teddy liked very much was hitting, so about all the team did every day was take batting practice.

The whole organization was screwed up, from their player development to their managing and marketing. As bad as the Senators and Rangers had been, they'd been in pretty good position every year for the draft. But they'd wasted a lot of their choices and hadn't stressed fundamentals enough to the good young talent they'd drafted. So that spring we spent hour after hour working on fundamentals: bunt plays, pickoffs, rundowns. The players were amazed and kept talking about how much baseball they were learning. I'd just shake my head.

Three weeks into spring training, I knew I was doomed. The biggest part of managing is handling your pitching, and we didn't have any to handle. We started the season with five starting pitchers, and by June I'd replaced every one of them. What we really had was a chance to win about two of every ten games we played, and .200 baseball just doesn't cut it. Our pitching was gawdawful.

It got a little better in June, when Bing Devine, who was back in St. Louis, did me a favor and let me have Jim Bibby, a big right-handed pitcher who was unhappy with the Cardinals because he wasn't getting enough work. Bibby won nine games for us that year, which made him our ace. At 6' 5" and about 235, he was such a fearsome sight out there on the mound that a lot of guys never got the bat off their shoulders.

We had a lot of decent pitching prospects on the club—high draft choices—but most of them needed a lot of seasoning in the minors. Short was like Charlie Finley, though. If he paid big money for someone, Short wanted him to produce right away. By the end of June, though, I'd finally convinced him that we had to send a couple of his young phenom pitchers—right-handers Pete

Broberg and Don Stanhouse—down to Triple-A for a while. I
called up Del Wilber, who was managing our Triple-A club in
Spokane, and told him I was sending him Broberg and Stanhouse
—and that he should work the hell out of them.

"Don't worry about that," Del said. "They'll get all the work
they need down here."

"Del," I said, "how big a lead have you got down there?"

"Fifteen games."

"Well, that ain't enough with these guys."

Two weeks later, I called him back. "You were right," he said.
"I've pitched those guys eight times, and they've lost every one of
them. Our lead is down to three games."

Stanhouse eventually became a pretty decent pitcher. Earl
Weaver, who had him with the Orioles for a while, called him
"Full Pack" because every time Stanhouse pitched, Earl smoked
a whole pack of cigarettes. Other people called Stanhouse "Stan
the Man Unusual," which explains a lot.

◇   ◇   ◇

The big pitching story for the Texas Rangers in 1973 was a young
man named David Eugene Clyde. In fact, the story of David Clyde
is a nutshell version of the story of the Texas Rangers under Bob
Short's ownership. I still feel bad about the part I played in what
happened to David Clyde.

Bob Short was a fast-buck artist, a man who would do anything
for a buck, a man who never had a long-term plan in his life. He
had no earthly idea how to run a baseball team. With him, it was
profit and loss and day to day. There were times when guys ap-
peared on the waiver wire—players who could help our club—and
we couldn't claim them because we couldn't come up with the
$25,000 waiver price.

Bob Short read all the stories in the Texas newspapers about
David Clyde, who was a hotshot left-handed pitcher for a high
school in suburban Houston. And Short decided that the Rangers,
who had first pick in the June draft that year, would select David
Clyde and pay him a big signing bonus to keep him from going to

college on a scholarship. This wasn't in itself a bad idea; Clyde was a hell of a young pitcher. At eighteen years of age, he already had an outstanding major-league fastball. The only young pitcher I've seen come along who was as good as David Clyde was at that tender age is Dwight Gooden of the Mets. If Clyde had been brought along carefully, as Gooden was, he could have had an outstanding major-league career. He might still be pitching in the big leagues instead of being a footnote in a trivia book.

But Bob Short couldn't see the long-term potential. All he saw was the short-term possibilities for making a few bucks. So, after we drafted Clyde, Short told me he wanted him to start a couple of games. Just two games, he said, and then we could send him out. I went along with it. What the hell? Even one week out of high school, David Clyde was still better than most of the other guys I had.

For one month, Clyde was the best pitcher on my staff. He won three or four games right away, and every time he pitched at home, we'd draw 25,000 extra people. Short was delighted. I'd tell Bob it was time to send David out, but he'd say no, just one more start. Pretty soon the hitters caught up with David and started sitting on his fastball. Also, he started running around with some of the older guys; he wasn't taking the best care of himself. He finished the season at 4–8, came back the next year (after I was gone), and hurt his arm. He was never much after that, and it's a tragedy. He might have taken the Rangers to a couple of pennants if they'd taken care of him.

◇   ◇   ◇

Although that was typical of the way Short ran the Rangers, I kind of liked the man. He had your basic heart of gold. He was always flying in his private plane between Dallas and his home in Minneapolis, and if we had a day off coming up, he'd offer to take me along and drop me in Kansas City so I could spend the day at home. I wound up getting along with him better than I did with Joe Burke. That was an unfortunate situation.

Joe was as good a businessman as I've ever met in baseball; he didn't pinch pennies, but he was pretty tight with nickels. However, he wasn't a very good judge of ballplayers, so we were bound to clash sooner or later. It happened when we had a chance to unload two pitchers to the Red Sox in exchange for Sonny Siebert, a pitcher I liked a lot. I wanted to make the deal, but Joe said Sonny's salary—he was making about $80,000 at the time—was too high.

"What the hell?" I told him. "The other two guys are making forty thousand each and can't do as much for us as Sonny."

"Nope," Joe said. "You just can't give up two guys for one."

So I started going around Joe to talk directly to Short, which wasn't the best way to do business. Later on that year, a couple of weeks before I got fired, Burke quit and went to work for the Kansas City Royals. He later became general manager there; and, in fact, it was Joe who hired me to manage the Royals in 1975. He knew what happened in Texas wasn't my fault.

I still regret getting fired down there. Of all the places I've been since I quit trying to play baseball, Texas is the only one where I didn't help bring home a winner, and it bugs me. I think if I ever left the Cardinals and wanted to stay in baseball, I wouldn't mind going back to Texas and see if I couldn't rectify the situation. I loved the people in Dallas and Fort Worth, and I still feel like I owe them something.

I think I could have done it if I'd stayed. We had all the young kids, and if we'd gone about the job systematically, I think we'd have won the division in three or four years. I had the team running more, playing sound fundamental baseball. We were scoring runs; the team was shut out twenty-six times in 1972, but in 1973, we didn't get shut out until the eighty-first game of the season.

Our problem was pitching, but I was working on that, too. I'd begun negotiating the deal that eventually brought Fergie Jenkins to the Rangers, and I had an agreement to bring Buzz Capra over from the Mets during the winter. I could have won with the Texas Rangers; I sure as hell couldn't have done any worse than the guys who came in there after I left. All we needed was time, patience, and the discipline to build a sound organization with a systematic plan—although I can see now that it would have been impossible as long as Bob Short owned the club. Time, patience, and discipline were not in his vocabulary. A few days after Burke left, Short called me in on a Saturday morning and offered me the general manager's job.

"Bob," I said, "I appreciate the offer. But I came here to manage the club and bring you a winner, and I want to finish the job."

"Whitey," he said. "I appreciate hearing that. I want you to know you're the best manager I ever had."

The next morning, he announced that he'd hired Danny O'Brien to be general manager, so evidently he'd had Danny in mind when he'd talked to me the day before. Before the game that afternoon, Short and I were shooting the breeze in the dugout when someone came up with the news that the Detroit Tigers had fired their manager, Billy Martin.

"How the hell can they fire the best manager in baseball?" Short said to me.

I forget what I said, but what I thought was, "Oh, shit. Here we go."

Sure enough, a couple of days later, I got a call from some friends in Kansas City who told me they'd been playing golf with Billy, and he told them that Short had talked to him about taking over as manager. That prepared me for Friday, when Short called me in and fired me. He told the press that he'd made a mistake in hiring me in the first place, and that, with Billy Martin, he was bringing in the best manager in baseball.

Well, that pissed me off. If he wanted to fire me and bring in Billy, that was fine. Managers are hired to get fired, as Billy knows better than anyone. But to get ripped as a "mistake"—six days after being told I was the best manager Short ever had—that burned me up. It worked out all right, though. Billy took the club I'd built to a second-place finish in 1974, but then he got canned in 1975 and took over the Yankees—for the first time—which started a legend.

As for me, I moved on to the California Angels as a third-base coach. And it was there that I began a relationship with one of the greatest men I've ever met—the Cowboy, Gene Autry.

◇   ◇   ◇

Like any other kid, I'd seen a bunch of Gene Autry's cowboy movies when I was growing up. Later on, I heard stories about how rich he'd become in real estate and radio and television out in Southern California. I knew he'd bought the expansion Angels in 1961 and that he wanted a winner more than anything in the world. But I really never knew the man until I got to spring training with the Angels in 1974. The Angels train in Palm Springs, California, which isn't too shabby.

Mary Lou stayed back in Kansas City while the kids were in school, but Bobby Winkles, the manager, and the other coaches had their wives and families out in Palm Springs. It meant that I was left pretty much by myself after the work was done for the day. The only other guy in that situation was Autry, so he and I would get together for a few drinks and dinner almost every evening. Even after the season started, he'd ask me up to his box after the ball games for a few belts, and we really got to be close—so close, it got to be embarrassing.

Autry had a big dinner for the team in Palm Springs one night and invited a bunch of corporate people, big sponsors for the television games. There were people from General Motors and from Budweiser, and they had their wives with them. After dinner, Autry got up to introduce all the coaches and players. And when he got to me, he said, "Now I want to introduce our newest coach, Whitey Herzog. He got his ass fired down in Texas last year, but he really didn't deserve it. On the other hand, two years ago, I got the gonorrhea—and I didn't deserve that either."

This was a mixed audience, so the joke really didn't go over that well, but I could barely talk I was laughing so hard. Autry didn't care. The Cowboy is a go-to-hell guy.

He told me one day, "You know, we owners have got to be the

dumbest goddamned people in the world. I just spend and spend all this goddamned money for ballplayers, and what do they ever do for me? Now you take my horse Champion. He made me a millionaire, and when he died, a guy came to me and wanted to stuff him and mount him in the lobby of my hotel on the Hollywood Strip. I asked him how much it would cost, and he says, 'Fifteen hundred dollars.' I said, 'Bury the son of a bitch.' "

Another time we were having a couple of drinks in the pressroom and talking about the Watergate scandal, which was big news at the time. The Cowboy knew President Nixon pretty well because Nixon was a big baseball fan; he came to a lot of the Angels' games when he was in San Clemente.

"You know," the Cowboy said, "I should have realized on Opening Day in 1974 that this country was fucked up with Tricky Dick in charge."

I asked, "Why's that, Cowboy?"

"Well, he came to brunch in my owner's box at the stadium, and then went downstairs to my field box to watch the game. When he gets there, he sees my wife and says, 'Hello Dale. How's Trigger?' "

◇   ◇   ◇

I had such a good time with the Angels that it was almost possible to forget the troubles we were having on the field. Winkles, who'd been a legend as the baseball coach at Arizona State, was trying to make it as a big-league manager. He was a hell of a good guy, as was the general manager, Harry Dalton. But I think I got off on the wrong foot with them the first day in spring training. They were talking about how they thought they really had a chance to win a pennant.

"No way," I said. "Not with the crew we got here."

We had the nucleus of a pretty good pitching staff, with hard throwers like Nolan Ryan, Bill Singer, and Frank Tanana, but the rest of the team was just a bunch of sandblowers. We had a pretty good young center fielder in Mickey Rivers, and two good young infielders in Jerry Remy and Davey Chalk, but when Singer and Chalk went down with injuries in midseason, we started going right down the drain, and Winkles got fired. Harry Dalton is a fine baseball man, but he tends to overrate the talent he's got. When we didn't win, he figured it couldn't be the talent, so it had to be the manager. It works like that a lot of the time, which is the great occupational hazard of being a manager.

I was named the interim manager and ran the club for four days. We split four games, but I kept Tanana out of the rotation, saving him for Dick Williams, the new manager. Dick had won a pennant with the Red Sox in 1967 and two straight World Championships with Finley's great Oakland A's teams in 1972 and 1973. He was the right guy for Autry to bring in because he needed a big-name manager in a market where he was competing with the Dodgers.

But when Dick arrived, not even Tanana could help him. He lost his debut, and then we lost about nine more games in a row. The Cowboy couldn't stand it. He came storming into the club-house after we'd lost our tenth in a row, spotted me, and said in a real loud voice, "Goddamn. I think I hired the wrong manager."

I finished that season coaching third base for Dick, who's one of the best managers I've ever seen, and I loved every minute of living in Southern California. So did Mary Lou and the kids, who came out after school was over. My daughter Debbie, who's bilingual in Spanish, got a good job as an interpreter at Disneyland, and she met her husband, Kirk, there. So a lot of good things happened to us in Anaheim.

We've liked just about everywhere we've lived in baseball. The kids were all good students, and the principals at their schools always told me travel was the best thing in the world for kids, so they saw a lot of the country.

Autry gave me a three-year contract to coach for him, at more money than most managers were making at the time. So, when the 1975 season opened, we figured we could live quite happily in the California sunshine. We figured the only place we'd be better off was back home in Kansas City, but that job wasn't open at the time.

◇   ◇   ◇

However, it soon came open. The Angels were playing in Baltimore during the fourth week of July, staggering along to what would be a sixth-place finish in the division. I got a call there from Joe Burke, who'd taken over as general manager in Kansas City. The Royals weren't playing badly at the time—they were four games over .500—but for some reason, the fans were all over Jack McKeon, who'd been manager there since 1973. Early in the season, Jack had had troubles with Steve Busby, his best pitcher. That got calmed down, with Burke later standing up in the clubhouse and giving McKeon a vote of confidence, which is usually the kiss of death for any manager. Six weeks later, Jack got fired. (Later on, when I was with the Cardinals, Jack landed in San Diego as general manager of the Padres, and he and I did a lot of business together.)

For all his quirks, Joe Burke is a fair man. As I've said, he knew what had happened to me with the Rangers in 1973 hadn't been my fault. I'd been worried that my one year there might have screwed up my chances of ever managing again, so I'll always be thankful to Joe for giving me a second chance. I flew into Kansas City and accepted the manager's job on a one-and-a-half-year contract. Autry let me out of a contract that still had two and a half years to run because he knew how much the Kansas City job meant to me.

It was just the perfect situation. My home is two miles from the ballpark, so I got a chance to live there year-round for the first time in ten years. It made life easy, made it a pleasure to do the job. I inherited a good young team that was just getting ready to blossom, a team that played in a big, Astro-Turf ballpark which was made to order for the way I like to play baseball.

Of all the expansion teams that have come into baseball since 1961, the Royals and the Toronto Blue Jays did the best job of building their clubs. They put the money into player development and tried to avoid the quick fix of paying big money to players who are over the hill. It's tough to do it like that because it means you lose money for five or six years and the fans get impatient. But if you have patience and hire the right people, then give them the authority to build the club, it pays off. The Royals' first year was 1969, and they were awful for those first few years. But by the time I got there, they were on the verge of success. I think I had something to do with putting them over the top.

I'd been a popular player in Kansas City and a popular coach. I got along with the writers and the fans. The people in Kansas City like it when one of their own succeeds, and they were rooting for me all the way. What a great deal it was, and it was made all the greater when the team caught fire after I took over.

The Royals had a twenty-two-year-old third baseman named George Brett, then in his second year of big-league ball, who became the best player I've ever managed and one of my best friends in baseball. If every player approached the game the way George does, it would sure make managing a lot easier. He's always on time, always hustling, always ready for extra work. When he's in a slump he still hits .300, but he goes out and takes extra hitting anyway. When he's hurt, he comes to the park early, fills the whirlpool, and treats himself. The toughest thing about managing the Cardinals against the Royals in the 1985 World Series was rooting against George Brett. I told our guys to walk him every chance they got.

Playing next to George was Fred Patek, a fine little shortstop, and playing first base was a big young kid named John Mayberry, who could hit the ball nine miles. We had two good young outfielders in Amos Otis, whom I'd had in the Mets system, and Jim Wohlford. Hal McRae was our designated hitter, and he hit like the position had been invented for him. The only older guys on the club were the second baseman, Cookie Rojas, and the right fielder, Vada Pinson.

I watched the club play for a couple of weeks and then made my first moves. I benched Rojas in favor of a young player named Frank White and started platooning Pinson with a kid named Al

Cowens. I took a lot of heat over those moves, especially my benching Rojas. He had been a great favorite of the fans, a real hustler and a great guy. But in Frank White, I had a kid whom I thought would become one of the greatest second basemen in the history of the game—and I was right. I've never seen a second baseman with the range he has, and he developed into a very good hitter.

When I made those moves, it seemed like the team just took off. They really changed the ball club, like making a major trade for two regulars without giving up anyone. We wound up winning 91 games, finishing second behind another great Oakland team. The Royals had been four games over .500 when I took over, and we finished twenty games over. The fans really got behind the team, and we drew more than 1.1 million people.

◇   ◇   ◇

Any manager who thinks he can ignore the attendance figures is on his way to becoming an ex-manager. I don't think anyone ever came to a ball game to see a manager, unless it was to see Casey Stengel or maybe Leo Durocher. But fans pay good money for tickets, and when they do, they expect to see entertaining baseball and they expect the players to look as if they're interested in the game. I'm proud of a lot of things I've accomplished as a manager, but the one thing I'm proudest of is that attendance has increased everywhere I've gone. The fans aren't coming out to see me, Lord knows, but my players hustle, they steal bases, and we try to make things happen. I think that's all most fans really expect, and if you can give them a winner every four or five years, they'll back you.

When I got to Kansas City, they were lucky to draw a million people a year. When I left, they had drawn over 2.2 million two years in a row, and that was unheard of in a metropolitan area of 1.3 million people, the smallest market in the big leagues. The promotion and marketing people were trying to take credit for it, but the only thing that really sells tickets is W's. You win, you draw. Simple as that.

I had a tough time selling that idea in Kansas City. I never really got along with Ewing Kauffman, the owner of the club; and his wife, Muriel, hated my guts. People would tell me they'd overhear the Kauffmans at the country club arguing about me in public, saying I was getting too much credit for the club's success and how they should get rid of the son of a bitch.

I was never sure of what I'd done wrong. I do know that Kauffman had liked McKeon a lot and couldn't understand why the fans hadn't liked Jack the way he did. The fans liked me and he didn't, and he couldn't believe his tastes were that bad. I think his wife was jealous of me. My picture was on billboards and posters and in the newspaper—not hers or Ewing's—and I guess she couldn't stand that.

Kauffman is a multimillionaire who made his fortune in the pharmaceutical business. Even though his drug company, Marion Laboratories, is a major firm in Kansas City, a lot of people had never even heard of him when he stepped forward and bought the expansion franchise in 1969. But after that, he became one of the best-known and most beloved men in Kansas City. He and Muriel loved to stand up in their private box, wave to the fans, and hear them cheer. Those fans were awfully bitter about Charlie Finley's abandoning them, and Kauffman became their hero.

In addition to some terrific tax advantages, that's the great attraction that owning a sports franchise has: instant celebrity. A man like Ewing Kauffman builds a great company and a huge fortune, and the public doesn't know who he is. But let him become a franchise owner, and he's the biggest man in town.

I guess that's why I rubbed him and Muriel the wrong way. When I got to town and the club began winning, I was getting most of the credit. Ewing used to come around and bitch, "With the club you've got, we should've won a long time ago." Why he kept me around as long as he did, liking me as little as he did, I'll never know, except for the fact that we kept winning.

◇   ◇   ◇

The winning began in 1976. As soon as we got to spring training in Fort Myers, Florida, I knew we had a hell of a shot at our division. The players seemed to know it, too. Finley's run was about over in Oakland. He'd screwed up and lost Catfish Hunter to the Yankees, and Reggie Jackson had let it be known he was finished with Finley after the year. Charlie went ahead and traded Reggie to the Orioles just before the season started. Without those two guys, the A's were in trouble, and our team figured on knocking them off.

If we lacked anything, it was catching. We had three catchers, though not one was what you'd call a star. But they were good enough. We later traded one of them, Fran Healy, to the Yankees for a left-handed pitcher named Larry Gura, who became a good pitcher for us.

We had the damndest bunch of no-name pitchers you ever saw. Steve Busby, our ace, was out with a shoulder injury that later ended his career. Dennis Leonard, who later became a twenty-game winner, was just coming into his own. Paul Splittorff, Andy Hassler, and Gura gave us pretty good left-handed pitching, and Al Fitzmorris became a dependable starter. Marty Pattin became a valuable spot starter and reliever.

We didn't have a hoss in the bullpen until Mark Littell, a rookie, started coming through for us. He was a big, raw-boned country kid who could throw it through a wall. I flip-flopped righties and lefties in the bullpen until the eighth or ninth, and then let Littell come in and scare the shit out of hitters with his fastball and hard slider. It wasn't the greatest bullpen in the history of baseball, but it did the job for us. We jumped off to a great start and were twenty games over .500 by the All-Star Game.

Then we started having injury problems. Three of our starters went down at the same time. So we made a trade for Hassler and Gura, and Pattin came through. We were able to hold on and win by two games over Oakland. The fans went crazy, and even the Kauffmans were happy.

The season ended on a sour note, though. On the last day of the season, Brett, McRae, and Rod Carew of the Twins were all within one point of each other for the batting title. As luck would have it, we were playing the Twins. Carew went 0 for 3. George got a couple of hits, including an inside-the-park homer on a ball that the Twins' left fielder, Steve Brye, let drop in front of him. McRae came up, needing one hit to win the batting championship, and hit a one-hopper to short for an out. He charged Gene Mauch, the Twins' manager, accusing him of ordering Brye to help Brett because George is white and Hal is black.

It was ridiculous, and I told Hal that. He was always very sensitive about the racial issue. But he's also a hell of a good guy who only knows one way to play—and that is hard. It was an ugly way to end the season. And the playoffs got uglier.

The Yankees had won the Eastern Division to set up a big-town vs. small-town playoffs in which the big town was the big favorite. Still, I liked our chances a lot—until Amos Otis broke an ankle on the first play of the first game. He'd hit eighteen homers in the regular season, but with him out, our outfielders had a grand total of seven homers between them, four of them inside-the-park jobs. I had to switch Cowens to center field from right field and put McRae out in right. McRae was barely adequate as an outfielder, but the big difference between him and Cowens was that Al is six inches taller. That fact, plus the fact that our bullpen finally caught up with us, doomed us in the playoffs.

We split the first four games with the Yankees, who most people figured would sweep us three straight. In the fifth and deciding game, we got a lead, blew it, and then Brett got us a 6–6 tie with a three-run homer in the eighth. It came down to the ninth inning, and the people in Yankee Stadium—those polite, well-mannered fans—began to throw bottles and start fires.

I brought in Littell, figuring he was the guy least likely to throw a home-run ball. He'd only given up one home run in 108 innings all year long. But he threw a fastball that Chris Chambliss, their first baseman, turned on and hit to deep right center. Hal McRae went to the wall and jumped for it, giving it all he had, but the ball went just barely over his glove. If Cowens had been there, we might have been in the World Series. Hal missed it by six inches, and so did we.

◇   ◇   ◇

I went in a couple of weeks later to see about a new contract. I was looking for a two- or three-year deal and figured that the way the club had played, I deserved it. Ewing Kauffman didn't see it like that.

"But you lost the playoffs," he said.

I tried to explain that I couldn't help that. At least I'd won him a division championship and put a lot more fans in the park. But he knew how much I liked the job, how much I liked living at home, and insisted that he never gave managers more than a one-year contract. I signed it, but I wasn't very happy about it.

These days, with players all getting multiyear contracts, it's just not fair to ask a manager to work on a one-year deal. It's one thing that we get a hell of a lot less money than the players; managers are easier to find than players. But when the players know that a manager is on a short contract, it makes it easier for them to stir things up. They know that if there's trouble, the owner is a lot more likely to get rid of the guy on a one-year deal than a guy on a three-year deal. I would later have a chance to find that out firsthand.

But at the time, things were all right. The club came out swinging in the spring of 1977, acting as if we had something to prove. We'd made a major trade over the winter, getting Darrell Porter from the Milwaukee Brewers. He gave us the solid catching that we'd lacked the year before, and I liked our chances a lot. The A's were in chaos, the Angels were spending money on free agents but weren't getting anywhere, and I thought if we played anywhere near the way we were capable, we could win the division without a lot of problems.

And yet even I was surprised at the way that 1977 Kansas City club played. I still think it was the best team I've ever managed, and I think we had the best club in baseball that year. We stayed almost entirely free of injuries and only made one roster change all year long. We struggled at the .500 level through the early part of the season; we were only three games over .500 at the end of June. But around the All-Star Game, we started playing very, very well. The Twins put a move on us, and in late August, their manager, Gene Mauch, said he didn't think any club in the division had the horses to pull away.

All we did after he said that was win sixteen in a row, the longest winning streak in baseball in twenty-four years. Then we lost one and won the next eight in a row. We won twenty-four out of twenty-five and put on the greatest stretch drive in the history of baseball. We wound up winning 102 games, more than any club in baseball that year, and the people in Kansas City went crazy. Brett and Cowens each hit .312, and Al drove in 112 runs. McRae hit .298 with 21 homers and 92 RBIs. We had four guys hit over 20 homers, and we played in a big park. Dennis Leonard won 20 games for us; Jim Colborn won 18, including a no-hitter; and Splittorff won 16. We were a sight to behold. The only guy who didn't play up to par all year long was Mayberry. He'd hit 34 homers in 1975, dropped to 13 the next year and only got back to 23 in 1977. I figured something was wrong, but the shit didn't hit the fan until the playoffs.

◇   ◇   ◇

Once again it was us and the Yankees, me against Billy Martin, our no-names against all those big names in New York. They had an outstanding club. That was the year when George Steinbrenner, their owner, had added Reggie Jackson to the stew over there, and Reggie had a great year for them. The man was born to play in New York. George had Billy and Reggie and Catfish Hunter and Ron Guidry. He had Graig Nettles playing third and hitting 37 homers for him. He had Mickey Rivers running everything down in center field and hitting .326. He had Sparky Lyle in the bullpen with 26 saves. It was quite a cast of characters.

But if I could have had my choice of players on that club, I would have taken Thurman Munson, the catcher. He could throw, he could hit, he was aggressive and took charge of the game the way a catcher should. He hit .308 for the Yankees in 1977 with 18 homers and 100 RBIs. I haven't seen many catchers who do the job offensively and defensively as well as he could. It is just a great,

great tragedy that he was killed in a plane crash in 1979. The man was on his way to the Hall of Fame.

The playoffs opened in New York that year. I sent out Paul Splittorff after the Yankee crew, and he won the first game for us. The Yankees took the second game behind Guidry, and then we came home. Leonard pitched a four-hitter and we were sitting pretty. Reggie Jackson, Mr. October, had only one lousy hit in the three games. The Yankees were ready to pack it in and go home. And then disaster struck.

We'd played a night game on Friday, to win Game Three. Game Four was scheduled for early afternoon Saturday to accommodate the television people who wanted to show a football game in the late afternoon. I told our players that batting practice was optional, so those who wanted to could sleep a little longer. John Mayberry dragged in real late, but I put him on first base anyway, which was my big mistake.

He missed a couple of throws and dropped a pop-up to hand them a couple of runs. He kept striking out, missing the ball by about a foot each time. I finally sat him down in the dugout and asked what the hell was wrong. The man couldn't even talk, and I knew what was wrong. The trainer got John out of the ballpark, into Kauffman's limo, and the chauffeur drove him home. We lost the game, of course, and then I made another mistake by lying to the press. I told them that Mayberry had a toothache and was in a lot of pain, so he'd taken painkillers, which had made him dizzy.

The truth was he'd been out real late the night before with his brothers, who'd come down from Detroit, and God only knows the kind of stuff they did. It must have been a hell of a party. It's just a damned shame, because John Mayberry was actually a wonderful young man. I always loved the way he played. The only thing he ever wanted to know was whether he was in the lineup or not, and then he'd go out and play the best he could. What a great first baseman he was—a big, big man who could dance around out there like Vic Power and use his hands like a surgeon. But he'd done something that I couldn't live with: you don't show up not ready to play. Not on my team.

The whole team knew what had gone on, but we went out the next night and hit line drives all over Royals Stadium. We'd get runners on, and some guy would smoke one, only somebody would run it down and catch it. We got three runs in the first and had the bases loaded with two out and Porter at the plate. He hit a shot to center field that looked like it would put the Yankees away for good. But Rivers went back and climbed halfway to the moon to haul it down. It should have been a three-run triple, but it was the third out.

Still, we had a 3–2 lead going into the ninth inning, and we should have been home free. I brought in Leonard, who'd pitched so well in the third game, to get me three outs. Billy responded by sending Paul Blair up to pinch-hit. I have to believe that if Dennis Leonard faced Paul Blair fifty times, he'd get him out forty-eight times. But Dennis jammed him with a pitch, and Paul blooped one off the handle of his bat for a single. Roy White came up next and fouled off about a half-dozen pitches before drawing a walk.

Now they had runners on first and second, so I decided to bring in Gura. I've gotten second-guessed a lot for that move, but I wanted my best fielding pitcher in there to try to get the runner at third if they bunted. Instead, Rivers hit a ground ball about six inches past Frank White, who was playing in close at second, and we're screwed. They got a couple more bloop hits, including Mr. October's second hit of the series, and we lost 5–3. The Yankees went on to beat the Dodgers in the World Series, and Reggie made up for his lousy performance in the playoffs by hitting .450 with 5 homers, including three in the last game.

Those last two games were my toughest two days in baseball, but I learned a couple of things. First, if at all possible, get yourself a great relief pitcher. The big difference between us and the Yankees in the two playoffs was that Billy could bring in Sparky Lyle, and I had nobody nearly that effective.

The second thing may be more important: don't lie to protect a ballplayer. They're big boys, and if they screw up, let them explain it. When I covered up for Mayberry, it just caused more trouble. The players knew what the deal was, but the public didn't. When there's two versions of the truth, you can't win.

So when I went in to negotiate a new contract—Kauffman again told me I'd lost the playoffs and he'd give me only another one-year deal—I insisted that they had to get rid of Mayberry. I said it was him or me, and I really didn't care which way they went. I told them that if John came back, it would undermine my authority and show the players that management wouldn't back me on discipline. Kauffman and Joe Burke assured me that they'd trade Mayberry and back me to the hilt.

◇   ◇   ◇

Some hilt. They diddled around in the off-season and only came close to trading Mayberry once. We were going to send him and Andy Hassler to the Mets for pitcher Jerry Koosman. If Mayberry had had his act together, the Mets would have made that deal in a minute.

Come spring training, the club reported to Fort Myers, and John Mayberry doesn't say a word to me all spring. I went to Burke and said, "Look, you told me he wouldn't be on the club."

"We told you we would try to move him. We tried."

I got pissed off then and called him and Kauffman liars, which didn't help my standing with them, but, as I say, my standing wasn't all that great with them in the first place. I knew if I ever lost the division, they would run me off anyway.

"Look," I said. "I told you before it's him or me, and I mean it. Either he's out of here or I am."

So they finally moved him, sold him to Toronto. Then the first time the Blue Jays came into Kansas City, Mayberry came to bat and Kauffman stood up in his box and gave John a standing ovation. Showed me up in front of all the fans.

The Mayberry situation really set in motion all the factors that eventually led to my being fired in Kansas City. Before we shipped him to Toronto, some of the black players on the team wanted to have a team meeting and vote on whether John should stay or not.

That would have been great. Democracy is a wonderful system of government, but it doesn't work on a baseball team. Next thing you know, we'd have been voting on who to bring in from the bullpen.

My vetoing the meeting and vote idea angered the black players, who thought I was being prejudiced because I wanted to play Clint Hurdle, a white kid and a rookie phenom, at first base. One thing led to another, and after the season started and Mayberry was gone, I found myself getting heat from the National Association for the Advancement of Colored People, saying I was prejudiced because I didn't have a black coach on the team.

I said, "No kidding, I don't have a black coach? I didn't know they were all white. I never thought of that. The only thing I care about my coaches is that they work hard and do the job."

The whole situation festered all year long, but we still played pretty good baseball. The division was weak enough so that we were able to win the championship, even though we won ten fewer games than we had the year before. Clint Hurdle turned out to be a disappointment, and I wound up platooning John Wathan and Pete LaCock at first base.

It's interesting what happened to Hurdle. He came in with a ton of publicity, had his picture on the cover of *Sports Illustrated* before he'd played ten games in the big leagues. He was a big, handsome, strapping kid with a ton of potential, but he never lived up to his billing. He didn't apply himself well at all, and his work habits were atrocious. George Brett sort of adopted him for a while and tried to drill some sense into his head, but Clint had some personal problems and even washed out of the big leagues for a while.

Then something happened . . . maybe he grew up. He climbed back, worked hard, turned his life around, and, like me, even learned how to catch a little bit. He caught on with the Mets as a backup catcher, and finally, after the 1985 season, we bought his contract and brought him over to the Cardinals. Clint Hurdle ought to be a lesson to a lot of guys—it takes a hell of a lot more than talent and a big-league uniform to be a big-league player.

Nobody on our club in 1978 had the same kind of year he'd had the year before with the exception of Amos Otis. That was kind of ironic, since it was A.O. who was most pissed off at me. I wouldn't care if they were all upset if they played like he did. Late in the season, another controversy broke out when I fired Charlie Lau, my hitting coach.

McKeon had fired Charlie at the end of the 1974 season, and I'd brought him back as soon as I was hired. Charlie had done a good job as a hitting coach and had some strong disciples on the club in Brett and McRae. He wasn't as good as he thought he was, though. He had everyone laying back on the ball and hitting ground balls, even big guys like Brett and Cowens. People get the wrong idea about me sometimes—I don't hate home runs. I like 'em. I love 'em. If a guy is capable of jacking it out of the park, more power to him. But with Charlie, it got to the point where guys couldn't hit the ball out of the park even in batting practice.

That wasn't my big problem with Lau. The big problem was that he was working for the players more than he was working for me. He wouldn't get with the program. A little clique was forming around him, and the team was dividing. So I fired him. That stirred up things even more, with people saying I got rid of him because I was jealous of his publicity. Bullshit. Why would I be jealous of a guy who turned a .260 hitter into a .300 hitter? The whole thing came down to: Who was running the club?

We had an awful lot of injuries in 1978, including, at one point, three-quarters of our infield. We got great pitching, though, with Leonard winning 20 games again and Splittorff getting 19, and we hustled ourselves back into the playoffs. But it only took the Yankees four games to get rid of us this time. They'd beaten the Red Sox in a one-game playoff to win the Eastern Division, and their club was even better than it had been the year before. Billy and Reggie had gone round and round, and then Billy'd been fired and replaced by Bob Lemon. Lem won forty-eight of the sixty-eight games he managed and blew us away in the playoffs. He not only had Sparky Lyle in the pen, but Goose Gossage had come over to the Yankees that year, too, and he was fearsome.

We had the series tied at one game each, when in the third game, Brett hit three homers—and we still lost. After that, I knew we were screwed. I knew that 1979 was going to be trouble.

◇   ◇   ◇

Sure enough, it was. It began with my annual contract dispute with Kauffman. The club had won the division three years in a row, and we'd drawn two million people for the first time in the club's history, but that still wasn't good enough to get me a long-term contract. Ewing was just waiting for us to lose the division so he'd have an excuse to get rid of me. We obliged him in 1979.

We hit great, scoring 851 runs, but we pitched awfully, giving up 816. Willie Wilson, our young left fielder, hit .315 and stole 83 bases. Brett had his usual great year, and Porter had the greatest year I've ever seen a catcher have. He hit .291, drove in 112 runs, and hit 20 home runs. And yet they gave the league's Most Valuable Player Award to Don Baylor of the Angels, a designated hitter. How can a DH be the MVP? He only plays half the game.

But the pitching was pure horseshit, and we won only 85 games, finishing three behind the Angels. I was happy for the Cowboy because he finally had a winner after spending all that money. But I wasn't all that happy since Kauffman finally had the excuse he needed to get rid of me.

He had some allies. Some of the players were still pissed at me for firing Lau and were working behind my back, taking shots at me in the newspaper. I kept my mouth shut. I knew I was history, anyway, and I didn't want to start some useless kind of feud. If ownership didn't want me, didn't appreciate what I'd done, to hell with them. I'd go somewhere else. I'd had it with Kauffman and Burke by then, anyway. In all the years I'd worked there, they'd never once invited Mary Lou upstairs to sit in their warm, enclosed boxes. She'd be out there in the rain or the snow and the cold, and they'd be sitting up there, acting as though we weren't good enough for them. I'd won three division championships for them, helped to put more people in the park than they'd ever dreamed of seeing, yet my wife and I weren't good enough.

They called me in and said they wanted to make a change. I said adios, and that was it.

The first guy who called me was the Cowboy.

"Goddamn, Whitey," he said. "I'm awful sorry to hear that you got fired, but I can't say I was surprised."

I asked why.

"Well," he said. "I had the unfortunate experience of sitting with Muriel Kauffman at the All-Star Game luncheon last summer, and I asked her how my old friend Ewing was getting along, and she said fine. And then I asked how my old friend Whitey was.

"And she says, 'Who gives a shit?' "

Autry offered me a job—a good job—paying good money. Two years before, he had offered me a million dollars over a five-year period—double what I was making in Kansas City as manager—just to be a consultant. That was right after Mayberry had pulled his stunt, and I figured I kind of owed it to Kansas City to try again. I tried, but it didn't make Ewing and Muriel happy.

I told the Cowboy thanks for his offer, but I still wanted to manage. His team had just won the division under Jim Fregosi, so Autry didn't need a manager. I said I'd just loaf a while and see what developed.

I didn't get to loaf for very long.

Building a Champion

The spring of 1980 was awfully strange. It was the first spring since 1949 that I didn't have a job in baseball. In fact, I didn't have much of any kind of job at all. The weird thing is that I wound up making more money while I was out of work than I'd ever made before in my life.

I made a beer commercial—probably the least remembered of all the beer commercials ever made. I can't even remember whether I was on the "Tastes Great" side or the "Less Filling" side. "Pays Great, Less Work" as far as I was concerned. Part of the job was being one of the sports people who went around the country promoting the beer by playing in golf tournaments. Between golf tournaments and fishing tournaments, I saw a lot of the country in the eight months I was out of work, and I made a minor fortune doing it. I lost the job later that summer when I went to work for Anheuser-Busch.

I went to Florida in the spring of 1980 more out of habit than anything else. I played in Jackie Gleason's golf tournament and saw some of my old friends and players from the Royals. One thing about baseball is that you make an awful lot of friends, and it doesn't make any difference what team you're with, because sooner or later you change teams. Uniforms change, but the friend-ships don't.

One guy I didn't get to see, but should have, was Darrell Porter, who was having a tough, tough time of it. I knew what he wanted to talk about because over the winter I'd heard that he had been seen doing drugs and acting crazy in Branson, a resort town in the Missouri Ozarks. I was surprised. I don't know how anybody could have had the kind of year Porter had in 1979 and be on drugs, but that's the way it was. With booze and pills and cocaine, he had himself a hell of a problem.

It worked out all right, though, because the day after Darrell and I tried to get together, he went to Joe Burke and asked for help. He spent a few months down in a rehab center in Arizona, came back to the Royals, and had himself a good year, all things considered. Hell, with the drugs he was taking, just being alive constituted a good year.

I followed his progress pretty closely because I knew 1980 was the last year on his contract with the Royals, and I figured I might need Darrell Porter down the road somewhere. Managers always need good catchers, and I knew I was going to be a manager again pretty soon. Let's face it: the way managers are hired and fired these days, no one was going to let a guy who'd won three division championships sit around twiddling his thumbs. Everybody else in baseball knew it. I think it was Sparky Anderson who told a newspaper guy, "We all better be on our toes, because Whitey's sitting over there in Kansas City waiting for the first one of us to fall on his ass."

I was in the position of being able to be choosy about where I went next. The jobs in Texas and Kansas City proved to me that you have to be careful about whom the owners are and where the money is coming from. The job with the Mets had shown me how important the organization behind the manager is. Besides, I knew I wasn't going anywhere until the middle of May, which was when the Major League Players' Association had set a strike date. No owner—not even the dumbest one—was going to pay me and the guy I replaced not to manage at the same time. I told Mary Lou we might as well relax and enjoy ourselves because we weren't going anywhere until the strike deal was settled. We went off to Lake Powell in Arizona and did some fishing.

◇   ◇   ◇

While we were there, John Claiborne, the general manager of the Cardinals, called to ask my opinion of some ballplayers. That was something I'd been doing as a favor to John for a while, anyway. He and I went back to my Mets days, when we both worked for Bing Devine.

John also asked me this time whether I'd like to go to work for the Cardinals on a contract basis, as a talent consultant. I told him I didn't want to get tied up with something like that, but I'd be happy to give him my opinions when he asked for them. After I hung up the phone in the hotel room, I made a bet with Mary Lou that as soon as the strike thing was settled we'd be on our way to St. Louis.

And that's exactly what happened. The players and the owners decided to extend the contract for the remainder of the 1980 season, and it wasn't even three weeks after that when the Cardinals contacted me. I was off playing in a golf tournament—being out of work was pure hell—at the Tan-Tar-A resort at the Lake of the Ozarks. They called me off the course to take a phone call, and I knew it was either bad news or a job offer.

It was Lou Susman, Gussie Busch's lawyer, telling me to drop whatever I was doing and get to St. Louis because Gussie wanted to see me. I had a pretty good idea what he wanted. The Cardinals had a whole bunch of high-priced ballplayers who were playing poorly. Kenny Boyer, my old buddy from the Mets, was managing, and they were running all over him. That was about the only running they were doing, too.

The first thing I asked Susman was whether Kenny knew they were contacting me, and he said no.

"Goddamn," I said. "I don't want to be taking the man's job before he even knows about it."

"You just get up up here and don't let anybody know about it," Susman said. "I'll take care of notifying Boyer right away."

Well, he took care of it all right. It was a Saturday when he called me, and he sent Claiborne to Montreal, where the Cardinals had a doubleheader scheduled with the Expos the next day. John's plane got delayed in New York by bad weather, so he didn't arrive in Montreal until the first game of the doubleheader was over. That's when Kenny got the word—between games of a double-header, just when he was least expecting it.

Susman had wanted me to leave Tan-Tar-A right away, but I had a dinner to go to that night, a dinner for Buddy Blattner, a former player and sportscaster who is one of the best-known base-ball people in Missouri. I knew if I didn't show up for the dinner someone would figure out what was going on. So I waited until the dinner was over, snuck out of Tan-Tar-A, and drove the 150 miles to St. Louis. I checked into a hotel under an assumed name—real cloak-and-dagger stuff—and the next morning I drove out to meet Gussie Busch.

◇　◇　◇

Gussie has three or four homes, but when he's in St. Louis, he stays at a place called Grant's Farm. It's the Busch family estate, and it is sprawled over hundreds of acres in south St. Louis County. Ulysses S. Grant farmed on the land before the Civil War, but the Busches don't raise anything on it except Clydesdales and money. They've got horses, exotic animals, a petting zoo, and a tourist center with train rides through the woods. Gussie lives in the main house, a big French Renaissance mansion. He lives like a German beer baron, which I suppose he is.

So that's the kind of place I drove to that Sunday morning, to meet with the Baron of the Manor, who was then eighty-one years old, and his secretary, Margaret Snyder. She had worked for the brewery for something like forty years before he married her and made her the fourth Mrs. August A. Busch, Jr. He's got so many kids from his first two marriages that I can't keep them all straight, but only one of them has anything to do with the Cardinals. That's

August A. Busch III, the first son of the second marriage and the chairman of the board of Anheuser-Busch Companies, Inc., the holding company that runs everything. Including the Cardinals.

Lou Susman was there that morning, too, and he did most of the talking. He's been Gussie's lawyer for years, along with being one of the most successful corporate lawyers in Missouri. He looks like a corporate lawyer: tall and distinguished-looking, always impeccably dressed, just the right amount of gray in his hair. He served for a couple of years as the Democratic National Committeeman from Missouri, and he still raises millions of dollars for people like Ted Kennedy. He's a big pal of Tom Eagleton, who was the senior U.S. Senator from Missouri for years. Before Susman was Gussie's attorney, Eagleton's father was. Things tend to be very tight in St. Louis.

After we talked about the Cardinals job in general, Susman told me they were prepared to offer me a one-year contract to manage the club at $100,000 a year, which is about what managers were making in 1980. The salary was OK by me, but not the one-year term.

"I'll tell you what," I said. "If you want to give me a one-year contract, then you'd better get someone else to manage. I just went through that in Kansas City. I won three division championships, missed a fourth by three games, and still got fired. A couple of ballplayers with long-term contracts went to the general manager and whined, and I got fired. It was cheaper for them to fire me, on a one-year contract, than it was them. I don't want that to happen again. I want some hammer."

Susman looked at Gussie, who said in that gravelly voice of his, "You're right. I'll give you a three-year contract."

That's the way he ran things, even when he was eighty-one years old. One man in charge, no committees, no crap. Fish or cut bait. I wondered where he'd been all my life.

So Kenny Boyer, who would die of lung cancer a couple of years later, got fired, and I flew to Atlanta to take over the club on June 9, 1980.

I made only one promise when I took over the Cardinals. I said we would hustle and bust our tails, or else I'd find people who would. I don't have a whole lot of rules as a manager, but one thing I insist on is that players run as hard as they can all of the time. That was going to be a new experience for some of the Cardinals' players.

◇   ◇   ◇

The 1980 Cardinals had three of the ten highest-paid players in the major leagues: shortstop Garry Templeton, first baseman Keith Hernandez, and catcher Ted Simmons. So there was some talent there. They could hit, but they couldn't run, and those who could run wouldn't. It sometimes took four base hits to score a single run. Also, there was nobody in the bullpen who could be counted on. In a big ballpark like Busch Stadium (most of the other parks in the National League are big as well), two things are absolutely critical: speed and a good bullpen. And we had neither one.

I managed the club that summer for seventy-three games, or until August 29, when I turned things over to Red Schoendienst, one of my coaches, and moved upstairs to the general manager's office. We won thirty-eight of those seventy-three games, climbed out of last place, and got within seven games of first. Then Templeton suffered a broken thumb, and I knew without Garry we weren't going anywhere. He was the heart of the ball club, which shows how bad off we were.

I've never seen such a bunch of misfits. Nobody would run out a ball. Nobody in the bullpen wanted the ball. We had guys on drugs—and another guy who sneaked off into the tunnel between innings so he could take a hit of vodka.

A couple of weeks after I took over, Gussie called me up to his office in the stadium and growled, "Well, what have I got?"

"Well, Chief," I said. "You've got a bunch of prima donnas, overpaid SOBs who ain't ever going to win a goddamned thing. You've got a bunch of mean people, some sorry human beings. It's the first time I've ever been scared to walk through my own clubhouse. We've got drug problems, we've got ego problems, and we ain't ever going anywhere."

"You really think it's that bad?" Gussie said.

"I know so. We ain't going to win with this sorry bunch. We've got to do some housecleaning."

"Well," Gussie said, "keep me posted."

That was easy enough for him to say, but it wasn't all that easy to do. I was the manager, all right, but between the manager and the owner there are layers of club executives, PR men, and lawyers. It wasn't easy to get to Gussie then, and later it became almost impossible. They were all scared to death of him on the one hand and protective of him on the other. The man was eighty-one years old and not in the best of health. But Gussie was a tough old bird—"The Big Eagle," they called him—and I knew he wanted to keep his hand in.

One day shortly after I arrived, I was having lunch with Bing Devine, and I told him the trouble I was having in getting to Gussie. Bing gave me a great idea.

"Listen," he said. "You've got a hell of an advantage. You drink. So does Gussie. Claiborne doesn't drink, and neither did I when I was general manager. But I always wondered what would have happened if I'd just gone out there to drink with him. Try it. Just call him up and tell him you're coming out for a few beers."

So I tried it. I'd call him up and say, "Chief, what are you doing?"

He'd usually be getting up around noon—he'd stay up late playing gin with his buddies—so he'd say, "I'm having my breakfast."

"Great," I'd tell him, "I'm coming out to have a beer and a braunschweiger sandwich."

And that's what I'd do, all the time talking baseball with him, telling him what I wanted to do with the club. Sometimes I'd bring him some fresh fish, which he loved, or some headcheese, which a friend of mine in New Athens made. We'd sit and eat sandwiches, play gin and drink beer. I'd always call to go out there on the spur of the moment because if I called a day ahead of time, it seemed like he would always have company.

It was the first time in my career as a manager I'd had good,

The best-looking guy at New Athens High.

Scoring after a home run for the Ft. Wood army team. *(U.S. Army photo)*

The 1953 National
Baseball Congress
Champions. I'm at the
top right. To my right
is Eddie Kasko, a
pretty fair big league
shortstop and manager.
(U.S. Army photo)

Taking issue with an ump in
Denver, 1955. *(David C.
Snyder, staff photographer,
Denver Post)*

The dude, 1955. *(Photo by David Mathias)*

Mary Lou, Debbie, and I enjoy trailer living at its finest, 1956. *(Photo by David Mathias)*

Ace flyhawk of the Denver Bears, 1956.

Dancing my cares away in 1957, when I was with the Senators and had a lot of cares. *(Photo by Don Wingfield)*

With the Miami Marlins, 1957.
(*Jay Spencer,* Miami News)

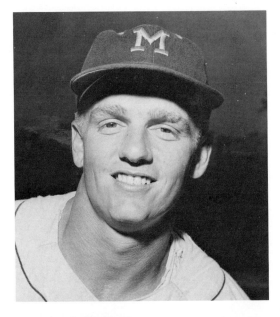

My friend Roger Maris and my
son David on the day Roger tied
Babe Ruth's home run record in
1961. *(Herb Scharfman)*

With the Kansas City A's, 1960.

Haywood Sullivan tags me out, 1962. *(AP wirephoto)*

With Casey Stengel, the greatest manager I have ever known.

With Bob Short, the day I made my worst mistake in baseball, taking over as manager of the Texas Rangers. The sport jacket was another mistake. *(UPI)*

Gussie Busch introduces me as the Cardinals' new manager, June 1980.

A familiar pose—getting between Joaquin Andujar and an umpire. This time Jerry Davis was throwing me out for arguing a balk call. Joaquin and Darrell Porter don't look all that upset, but I was. *(St. Louis Post-Dispatch)*

The day Bruce Sutter made me a genius by signing
with the Cardinals. *(UPI)*

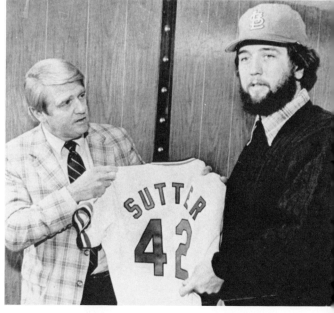

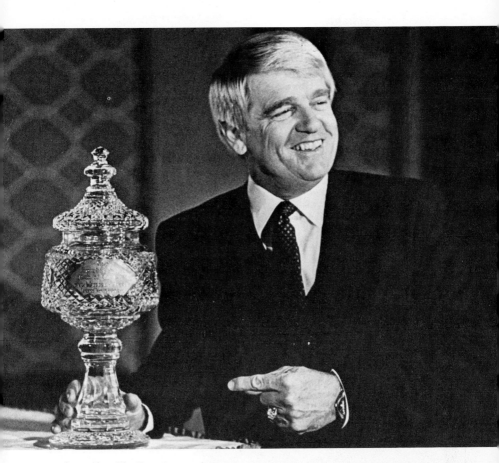

Accepting *The Sporting News*'s Man of the Year Trophy in 1982. (*Sam Leone,* St. Louis Post-Dispatch*)*

With George Brett, who's not only the best player I have ever managed but one of my best friends, too. *(AP Laserphoto by James A. Finley)*

With Mary Lou, 1985.

Making a point to Tom Lasorda before the 1985 playoffs. I was probably telling him to pitch to Jack Clark. (*J. B. Forbes,* St. Louis Post-Dispatch*)*

Dick Howser and I before the 1985 World Series. *(AP Laserphoto by Rusty Kennedy)*

With my grandson, John. The white hair runs in the family. *(AP Laserphoto by Rusty Kennedy)*

solid access to the owner of the club, the man who could give me the authority to make the decisions I needed to make. That was absolutely critical to the success we would enjoy in 1981 and 1982. I knew we were going to have to do major surgery on the Cardinals' organization, and if you're performing major surgery, you sure as hell don't want to have to call a committee meeting to decide what to cut. Gussie had decided I was the guy he wanted to cut on his team, so in late August, he gave me even more authority by making me the general manager.

The club had fired John Claiborne in early August, then Lou Susman went on the road conducting a big search for a new general manager. In the meantime, nobody was minding the store. I came in one day and found out that the San Diego Padres had put Rollie Fingers on the waiver list, and we hadn't put a claim in for him. Teams put guys on the waiver list all the time, which is what you have to do if you want to trade them during the season. Most of the time they really have no intention of getting rid of them, but unless another club puts a claim in for them, they can be traded. I sure as hell didn't want Fingers traded, especially to another club in our division. I wanted him stuck in San Diego, where we might have a chance to make a deal for him over the winter.

So I asked around to find out who was supposed to be watching the waiver wire, and I found out that Susman, Cary Blaze, and Jim Baines were. I asked why we didn't put a claim on Fingers and was told that he was making too much money.

"Jeez," I said. "He's only making $125,000 over there. That's why he's raising hell. Don't you read the papers?"

I couldn't believe it. I knew I was in big trouble if that kind of thing continued. A day or two later, when Susman was off in New York interviewing candidates for the general manager's job, Margaret Snyder called to ask me out to Grant's Farm. I went out there that evening, and Margaret said, "Mr. Busch really likes you because you don't give him any doubletalk and you tell it like it is. He wants you to be general manager of the team so he can get some straight answers."

I asked for some time to think about it. I didn't really want to be a general manager. They have to spend all their time in the office, summer and winter, talking on the phone all the time, dealing with agents, some of whom are jerks. A general manager's job is nothing but putting up with bullshit and bullshitters, day in and day out.

On the other hand, I knew that unless we got someone in that office I could work with, I was going to be in trouble anyway. I thought about it for a couple of days, then I called Gussie and told him I'd give it a shot.

"But," I told him, "I want the understanding that I can go back to managing if I want to, or I can do both jobs, or I can do one or the other."

"Great," he growled. And that was all the understanding we needed.

◇　　◇　　◇

So I turned the club over to Red Schoendienst on August 29, and I hit the road. The minor-league season was about over, and I needed to see what kind of help we had available on the farm. One thing I've never understood is why major-league general managers feel they have to sit around an office in a big-league ballpark all the time, seeing the big club play eighty-one home games and then going on the road with them, too. If they can't see everything they need to see in forty games or so, they're pretty bad off.

They ought to be in the minor leagues, evaluating talent, or in other big-league cities, looking for people who can help. There's two reasons why they don't do that. One, it's a lot more comfortable sitting at home, playing big shot, and two, most of them have never had a jockstrap on in their lives and wouldn't know a big-league ballplayer if they saw one.

I left the office to my secretary, Judy Lovelace, who was the only one who knew what was going on anyway, and I went out to look at the kids. The trouble was they weren't kids—most of them, anyway. The Cardinals had a bunch of twenty-four- and twenty-five-year-olds in the minor leagues. By baseball standards, that's middle-aged. If a player hasn't made it to the big leagues by then, odds are he'll never make it. The hardest thing for a baseball executive to do is to tell a kid that he's never going to play in the big leagues, especially when the kid has spent five or six years rattling around in the minors. When I was player development director with the Mets, I always tried to make a decision as soon as possible. I'd tell a kid to go home, get a job or continue his education, and not waste the best years of his life riding buses in the minors.

In 1980, the Cardinals had a bunch of veteran minor-league players in their farm system. The teams were winning minor-league pennants, but they weren't producing ballplayers for the big club. If that isn't a stupid way to spend money, I don't know what is. We only had a handful of prospects: a second baseman named Tom Herr and a couple of right-handed pitchers named John Stuper and Andy Rincon. I figured we'd have to force-feed those three into the big leagues and clean out the rest of the bunch.

I went back to St. Louis and drew up a master plan of what I wanted to do, the kind of team I wanted to build to accommodate the ballparks we played in. In baseball today, geography is all-important. In the National League, you've got a whole bunch of big ballparks—ten, to be exact—where it's hard to hit home runs. Our park in St. Louis, where we play eighty-one games a year, is the toughest hitter's park of them all. The fences are 383 feet from home in the power alleys, and the center-field wall is 414 feet away. Busch Stadium was built right near the Mississippi River, and the hot, heavy air in the summertime is death to fly balls. The first time Casey Stengel ever saw the place, at the All-Star Game in 1966, it was 110 degrees on the field. Someone asked Casey what he thought about the brand-new place, and he said, "It sure holds the heat well."

Only two of the twelve parks in the National League are hitter's parks: Chicago and Atlanta. The other ten are big parks, and six of them, including Busch Stadium, have artificial turf. In a big park, especially one with fake grass, you have to have team speed —speed on the bases to take advantage of balls hit on the turf, and speed in the outfield to cut off balls before they skip through on the turf to the wall. If you're managing in Fenway Park or Wrigley Field, you can wait for a guy to hit a three-run homer. But in our place—and in a lot of other places around the National League— you take your runs one at a time and hope for more. Hit the ball on the ground and run like hell. Steal a base, sacrifice, push the runner along, first-to-third them to death. I use the squeeze bunt as much as any manager in baseball, but in our park, it makes sense to give up an out for a run.

That's why the bullpen is so important these days. With runs so hard to come by, you absolutely have to have guys in the pen who can come in with a one-run lead and get you six outs. The other thing you need is a catcher who can throw. The other teams are trying to manufacture runs, too, and the best way to do that is to steal bases.

The team we had in 1980 had no speed to speak of outside of Templeton and the rookie second baseman, Ken Oberkfell. Most of the guys were so slow it took them two trips to haul ass. The bullpen was a disaster waiting to happen, and the catcher was Teddy Simmons, the kind of player they invented the designated hitter rule for. Teddy is a switch-hitter with a lifetime batting average near .300, but he gave up a lot of passed balls and he couldn't throw worth a damn.

Baseball is a game of odds. The good relief pitcher who gets you six outs can cut the other team's chances of scoring from twenty-seven to twenty-one. The catcher who can throw forces a team to give up an out by sacrificing the runner over from first. Nobody ever bunted with Simmons catching. They'd steal, and then have three chances instead of two to get the guy home from second. So the master plan called for us to get a good catcher, and the one I had in mind was Darrell Porter. And then I wanted a top reliever, a door-slammer, someone like Rollie Fingers or Bruce

Sutter. And, finally, I wanted to clean out the leadfoots and get us some guys who could run.

◇   ◇   ◇

I took my plan to a big meeting at the Anheuser-Busch brewery in south St. Louis, a huge conglomeration of brick buildings which always smells like malt and hops. Gussie was there, of course, and so were Susman and Mrs. Busch and the top brewery executives and lawyers, including August Busch III, the chairman of the board. What I was proposing to do was a big enough deal that I wanted everyone to hear what I had to say.

I told them that what we had to do was something that hadn't been done very often before. We needed to rebuild the entire organization systematically to bring it into line with modern base-ball geography. We'd have to do it within the confines of modern baseball economics, too, without breaking the bank, and by navigating our way around all the lawyers and agents and guaranteed contracts and through the whole maze which makes it so hard to make a deal. And we wanted to do it fast, so we could play interesting, competitive baseball right away and put people in the stadium.

They listened to what I had to say, and they gave me the green light. The only thing that young August asked was that if we signed a high-priced player like Darrell Porter, we unload a big contract in return. That was reasonable; baseball teams have budgets, too.

I knew it wasn't going to be easy, but I also knew there was no way we were going to win unless we tried it. If it didn't work, I'd be fired. But, hell, with the bunch we had, it wouldn't take long to get fired anyway, so I had nothing to lose. I hired Joe McDonald, who'd been general manager of the Mets, to be my assistant. And together we went to work.

I went to the playoffs and World Series and started sounding out people about deals. I usually avoid those kinds of meetings just because there's so much useless bullshit involved. But I had to see certain people just to get things rolling. Back home, Joe Mac was on the phone all day long, and between us, we contacted just about everyone who had anyone who could help us. We were willing to move just about anyone. The only player I really wanted to keep was Garry Templeton, who had as much ability as any player I've ever managed.

I'd hate to guess how many hours Joe and I spent on the phone that fall. I bet I talked to Jack McKeon, the general manager of the Padres, seventy-five times, and probably at least that many times to Bob Kennedy, who was then running the Cubs. Each time you'd call, you'd get a little closer, or find out a little more, or propose different packages. It was frustrating.

About the only thing we got settled that October was who the next field manager of the Cardinals would be. Me. I knew Gussie really wanted me to take both jobs, so one day I drove out to Grant's Farm and told him I'd try it.

"Chief," I said. "I'll tell you what. We're losing money here already, so I'll do both jobs, and I won't even ask for more money. The only thing I ask is that if I ever want to give up one of the jobs, you'll say OK."

"Fine," Gussie said, and all of a sudden I was a one-man band. I probably had more authority and more autonomy than any one man in baseball. But it wasn't doing me any good because I couldn't get anything going. Then, at Thanksgiving, we got a big break.

Darrell Porter had declared for free agency in Kansas City. His agent, Frank Knicely, called me and said the Royals hadn't made an offer yet. I wanted Porter a lot. He'd been a fiery guy, a leader, a guy who handled pitchers well, and he threw well enough to keep baserunners honest on the rug in Kansas City. The big question mark was drugs. Darrell had spent part of the 1980 season being treated for drug and alcohol abuse, and you never know how a player will respond to that. But knowing Darrell as I did, I was sure that if he said he was OK, he was OK.

Darrell, who made his home only a few miles from mine in the Kansas City suburbs, was going to be married over the Thanksgiving weekend. So a few days before that, I sat down with Knicely and found out what he wanted—$700,000 a year and a five-year contract. I said that it sounded like an awful lot of money to me, and Knicely pointed out that we were already paying a catcher we didn't want, Simmons, $667,000 a year, so why not pay $33,000 more for a catcher we did want? I said I'd think about it.

One of the things I thought about was that I already had a pretty good catcher sitting on the bench, a kid named Terry Kennedy. He was twenty-four at the time, a gung-ho kid, a fine hitter who came from good baseball stock. His dad is Bob Kennedy, then the Cubs' general manager. You can't overlook that part. A kid who grows up around baseball learns something. Maybe it's attitude, or work habits, but it's definitely a plus. One thing about Terry Kennedy: he was a smart kid. He looked around St. Louis and saw Simmons catching in front of him, and knowing how popular Teddy was in St. Louis, he put two and two together and knew he'd never get a chance to catch in St. Louis. He came to me and asked to be traded to someplace where he'd have a chance to start and make some good money. I'd have done the same thing if I were him, and so I told him I'd try to oblige if the right deal came along.

About a week after I met with Darrell's agent, I was sitting in my office, having just about decided that we had no chance of signing Darrell. I knew that his home was in Kansas City and that he liked it there. If all things were equal, he'd just as soon stay with the Royals. Just about then, Knicely called and asked us to make a firm offer. I knew what he was up to: he wanted us to make an offer that he could take to the Royals and use to force their hand. It was one of those games that agents play, which is another reason I don't like agents. I didn't want to play that game because I knew that if the Royals matched our offer, I'd lose him.

"I'll tell you what," I said. "We'll give you $200,000 up front as a signing bonus, $500,000 for the first year, and $700,000 a year for the four years after that. No loans, nothing fancy. That's the deal, take it or leave it, because after I hang up the phone, the offer is withdrawn."

Well, that got his attention. He told me Darrell was out on a cruise ship somewhere on his honeymoon. What if he tried to reach him and got right back to me. I said fine, but unless I heard from him that afternoon, the deal was off. He wound up reaching Darrell by ship-to-shore telephone or something, and Darrell OK'd the deal. Once we got him off the boat, we agreed not to announce the signing until the first day of the winter meetings, which were held in Dallas that year during the second week of December.

In the meantime, I'd talked to Simmons and his agent, LaRue Harcourt, about the possibility of Teddy's moving to first base. We already had the best first baseman in the league in Keith Hernandez, but I figured that if we had Darrell catching, Simmons at first, and Hernandez in left field, we'd have three very good bats in the lineup—and I could always move Keith in to play first in the late innings if we had a lead. As good a defensive first baseman as Keith is—and he's the best I've ever seen—I had no doubt that he'd have been a great outfielder, too. I talked to him about it, and he said if that's what it took to get the help we needed, he'd play anywhere I wanted him to.

So, as I packed for the winter meetings, that was the plan: Porter catch, Hernandez in left, and Simmons at first. That way we could try to trade Kennedy and another prospect, a first baseman named Leon Durham, to get the relief pitching we needed.

◇　◇　◇

I got to Dallas and we announced the Porter signing right away, on Sunday night. It seemed to open the floodgates. Suddenly, all the groundwork that Joe McDonald and I had done in October started paying off. This was kind of surprising, since the winter meetings are usually nothing but a lot of eating and drinking and bullshitting. Guys like to go there and talk about making deals, but very few of them have the guts, or the authority, to make them.

McKeon called, and we finalized the deal we'd been talking about with the Padres, agreeing to announce it the next day. We got Rollie Fingers, catcher Gene Tenace, left-handed pitcher Bob Shirley, and a catching prospect named Bob Geren. We sent them

Terry Kennedy—whom I'd come close to sending to Cincinnati for relief pitcher Tom Hume—and five other guys who didn't figure in my plans or whose salaries I was trying to unload. Fans often don't understand that sometimes, when you give up a lot of players to get a couple, you're doing addition by subtraction.

So there I was on Monday morning, with the great relief pitcher I needed, but not the one I really wanted. The guy I was really after was Bruce Sutter of the Cubs. I hadn't given up on getting him, but with Fingers in the fold, I knew I had some insurance in case the deal didn't come off.

As it happened, I ran into Fingers in Dallas, and he told me he would have no objection to working in the same bullpen with Sutter.

"Rollie," I said, "what happens if you're pitching with two outs in the bottom on the ninth, one out away from a save, and a left-handed hitter comes up? What if I decide to bring in Sutter because a right-hander with a split-finger fastball has a better shot of getting the hitter out than you do with your slider? I take you out and you lose the save."

Rollie had to agree with me that two right-handed closers in the same bullpen would never work. I knew that if I got Sutter, Fingers was gone. I'd already talked to Billy Martin, who was between stints with the Yankees at the time and was managing in Oakland. Billy said he'd be very interested in Fingers if I got Sutter and agreed to give us a starting pitcher if we made the deal for Sutter. That was one possible market for Fingers, and I knew there'd be others. But first I had to get Sutter.

I knew the Cubs wanted to move Bruce because he'd nicked them for $700,000 in an arbitration dispute the year before. However, Bob Kennedy knew how badly I wanted him, so he was trying to take us to the cleaners. I don't blame him. The Cardinals and the Cubs are big rivals, playing in the same division and all, and Bob knew that by giving us Bruce, he might be cutting his own throat.

Kennedy wanted three top prospects: Durham, who I knew was going to be a great player; Tom Herr, the kid at Louisville who was going to be my second baseman, and Ty Waller, a young outfielder.

The first word when making a deal is to avoid giving up prospects, kids you've trained and invested a lot of money in, because you never know how good a prospect will become. Instead, you try to move a player who has reached his peak, so you don't wind up giving away more than you know. In this case, I wanted to keep Durham and Herr and give up Ken Reitz, a fine-fielding third baseman but a streak hitter and maybe one of the slowest runners I've ever seen. I figured on moving Ken Oberkfell from second to third and playing Herr at second. Obie could do everything Reitz could do, plus run, and Reitz was making way too much money for what he was providing. I kept trying to find a package where I could keep both prospects and move some of the older guys, but Kennedy kept saying, "No Durham, no Sutter."

Finally, I reached a compromise with Kennedy. He agreed to give us Sutter if we would give him Durham, Waller, and Reitz. The only hangup in the deal was that John Claiborne, for reasons I'll never understand, had given Reitz a no-trade clause in his contract. A lot of fans think players want no-trades because they want to stay in dear old St. Louis or wherever, but the truth is that most of the time, they only want the right to be bought out of their no-trade. A no-trade clause is actually an asset you surrender to the player and then have to ransom back, like a penalty clause. I don't like them because they restrict what I can do with a player, and I especially don't like them with fringe players like Ken Reitz.

The no-trade clause was holding up the Sutter deal as we announced the Fingers deal on Monday morning. Later that night, we finally agreed to pay Reitz his fifty grand so we could trade him to the Cubs, and I finally had Bruce Sutter.

Reitz turned out to be a bust in Chicago, and Ty Waller didn't last long, either. So the trade actually turned out to be Leon Durham for Bruce Sutter. As good a player as Bull Durham has become, I'd make that deal again. Relief pitchers like Bruce Sutter are worth their weight in gold—sometimes more, as I found out four years later.

I was pretty proud of myself. Two days before, I had no relief pitching, and now I had the greatest bullpen in the history of the world. I had Fingers to trade, either for a prospect to replace Durham or another starting pitcher. I had the catcher I wanted, and better speed.

Then I found myself with a brand-new problem. Right after we announced the Sutter deal, I was walking through the hotel lobby, and whom do I run into but LaRue Harcourt, Ted Simmons's agent. He told me that Teddy had changed his mind about playing first base. He'd started thinking about trying to replace Keith Hernandez and was afraid that, compared with Keith, he might embarrass himself in the field. He was right; he probably would have. I could just see Hernandez, out in left field, laughing into his glove when Simmons got his feet tangled up at first base or missed a throw from Templeton, who didn't have one of the world's most accurate arms.

So I went back to my room and thought about it. I thought Simmons would hit enough to make up for his defense. But he was a proud man who'd played a lot of years in St. Louis, and I didn't want to see him hurt.

Even so, his changing his mind really pissed me off. I'd made all those trades predicated on Ted Simmons playing first base, and it wouldn't be easy to trade him. He had more than ten years in the big leagues—all of them with the Cardinals—so under baseball rules he had the right to veto any trade. I knew it would take a ton of money to buy out that veto, but in the back of my mind, I thought it might be a good idea. We'd already started cleaning house, so we might as well go ahead and finish the job.

I liked Teddy. He is bright and intelligent, and he played hard for me in 1980. If the National League had the designated hitter rule, he would have died a Cardinal.

I knew the fans would be all over me—the consensus in St. Louis at the time was to trade Hernandez if we had to, but to leave

Simmons alone. But Teddy couldn't catch—at least, not on my club—and he wouldn't play first, so he had to go. As far as I was concerned, he traded himself.

◇   ◇   ◇

I started thinking about putting together some kind of package with Fingers and Simmons, getting them both out of the National League so they couldn't bother us. I figured I might as well make it a hell of a package, so I threw in Pete Vuckovich, too. He was a big right-handed pitcher, a mean-looking, surly son of a gun who was coming up on the last year of his contract. He'd been the Cardinals' best pitcher for the previous two years, but I didn't think we were going to sign him again. We'd just signed Bob Forsch, another right-hander, to a five-year deal, and I knew Vuke would want the same kind of deal that Forsch had gotten. I didn't want to get tied up in a five-year deal with Pete Vuckovich. He didn't keep his body in shape, and he didn't take very good care of his arm. I just didn't think he'd last five more years. On the other hand, he had a good chance to be very good for another couple of years, so I didn't want him hanging around the National League.

I went to the managers' breakfast in Dallas and asked around, to every American League club I knew needed relief help and a DH. Only two clubs, the Oakland A's and the Milwaukee Brewers, showed any interest at all in Ted Simmons. Everyone else was scared of his contract, scared of how much it would take to buy out his no-trade, and scared of his defense. Harcourt said Simmons wouldn't play in Oakland because it was too far from his home in St. Louis, so that pretty much narrowed my options. I went to Harry Dalton, the Brewers' general manager, and Walter Shannon, their chief scout, and I asked them one question. "How'd you like to win the pennant next year?"

They said they'd like that fine.

"Well," I said, "I've got a deal for you. Rollie Fingers, the best relief pitcher in baseball. Pete Vuckovich, who can win you fifteen to twenty games, especially if Fingers is there to finish for him.

And Ted Simmons, who can catch one-hundred games for you and DH the other sixty-two and be the best designated hitter in the history of the world."

They asked what it would cost them, and I told them: Sixto Lezcano, because I needed a right-handed–hitting outfielder; Lary Sorensen, because I needed another right-handed starting pitcher if we moved Vuckovich; Dave LaPoint, a left-handed pitcher they had in Triple-A, and one more guy. David Green.

Well, that last name got them. At the time, David Green was rated as the best prospect to come along in a long, long time. He was a big, fast, hard-hitting outfielder from Nicaragua who could do it all. He was absolutely the key to the deal because we needed a prospect to replace Durham.

All of the people in the Milwaukee organization had been waiting for Green to develop, and now that he was almost ready, they didn't want to part with him. And yet they knew I wasn't lying when I told them I was offering them a shot at the pennant right away. I really put them between a rock and a hard place when I put a Friday noon deadline on the deal. I'd heard from George Steinbrenner, who said he wanted Simmons for the Yankees and didn't care how much it would cost to buy out the no-trade clause.

The Brewers' people called all kinds of meetings, made all kinds of phone calls. They went to Simmons and asked him how much it would take to buy out his no-trade, and Teddy told them $750,000. Harry Dalton called me and asked how much of that the Cardinals would be willing to pay.

"Not one red cent," I said. "Either you take him or we'll ship him somewhere else."

Harry couldn't risk calling my bluff because he sure as hell didn't want Simmons winding up with the Yankees or one of the other powers in his division. He went back to his people and met some more. The deadline came and went; they called and asked for an extension. That evening they finally called and made the deal.

It turned out to be a great one for them. Fingers saved twenty-eight ballgames for them in the strike-shortened 1981 season and won the Cy Young and Most Valuable Player Awards in the American League. In 1982, Vuckovich, who'd won fourteen games the year before, won eighteen games, and then he won the Cy Young Award. Simmons took a while to adjust to American League pitching, but then he got on track and hit 23 homers and drove in 97 runs, helping the Brewers win the pennant.

On the other hand, David Green was mostly a bust. We brought him up to the Cardinals in 1982 after his last year in the minors, and while he showed flashes of greatness, he could never put it all together. He had all kinds of personal problems and we finally gave up on him. We sent him to San Francisco before the 1985 season, and they gave up on him after that year. He wound up back with the Brewers in the spring of 1986, but they cut him loose, too. Despite all of that, he had more raw ability than any young player I've ever managed. What happened with David Green is just a shame.

But that's the way it goes. You make a deal based on your best judgment at the time, on your needs at the time, and on your best guess about what will happen down the road. If it works, fine; if it doesn't, you can't kick yourself. The writers and the fans will do it for you.

The Simmons deal turned out to be a great one for the Brewers for two years, and then it went sour. Fingers and Vuckovich both had arm trouble, and Simmons tailed off badly. On our side, Lezcano and Sorensen turned out to be fringe players, and we traded both of them after the 1981 season. Dave LaPoint, a big, kind of flaky left-handed change-up pitcher, turned out to be the best player we got in the deal, and he helped us a lot for three years. Then we sent him and Green to the Giants in return for Jack Clark, which turned out to be one hell of a deal for us. But you never get any guarantees. You pays your money and takes your chances, and overall, I like what we did in Dallas that December.

What a week that was. Baseball people still talk about it. We made three major deals at a time when you weren't supposed to be able to do that kind of thing any more. The writers made a big deal out of it, calling me a riverboat gambler. I bet every paper in the country used the same headline: "Whitey Shuffles the Cards."

What most of them didn't realize is that Joe McDonald and I didn't walk in there cold and start making deals. We had prepared by getting the OK from the brewery and then by making six weeks of phone calls and haggling. All Dallas did was finish things off. If you do your homework and you have the kind of backing from ownership that we had, and if you've got your budget in order and can get the other guys to sit still long enough to hear you out, then you can still wheel and deal in baseball. The trouble starts when you've got to start clearing things through lawyers and public relations men and accountants. You've got to be aggressive and be willing to throw the dice. Once you start worrying that you might be wrong, you're screwed.

By God, the Cardinals were ready. They hadn't won a damned thing since 1968, so I figured what the hell? We might as well shake things up and see what happens. Part of what happened was that I got roasted in St. Louis. The fans there are some of the best in baseball, conditioned by the Cardinal heritage that some of the old-time writers still write about every week. One result of this is that fans in St. Louis tend to become very attached to their players. It's like a small town in that way, with hometown heroes and traditions. The trouble is that baseball isn't played that way anymore.

Ted Simmons is a case in point. He'd been a Cardinal for a long time and had become very involved in the community. He was on the board of directors of the art museum and was heavily involved in charity work. And he had a pretty good off-season job as a banker. He was a fine ballplayer and had been a team leader for a lot of years. The town simply got used to him. Even so, they'd been booing the hell out of him the year before. Yet when we traded him, you'd have thought we'd traded the Gateway Arch.

The guy who took most of the abuse was Darrell Porter. Nobody in town liked the deal because all they knew about Darrell was that he'd been in drug and alcohol trouble. They accused me of going back to Kansas City and signing my fishing buddies.

◇   ◇   ◇

When we got to spring training in St. Petersburg, Florida, I thought we had a good shot at winning the division title in 1981. Porter was catching, Hernandez was on first, Herr on second, Oberkfell on third, and Templeton was the shortstop. Our outfielders were George Hendrick, Tony Scott, Dane Iorg, and Lezcano. Our starting pitching wasn't the greatest—Bob Forsch led the staff in wins with ten—but we had Sutter in the bullpen, and that covers a lot of mistakes. Our pitching got better in June when we sent Scott to Houston for Joaquin Andujar, a right-hander we liked very much. Both he and Scott were in the last years of their contracts, and I knew for sure I wasn't going to re-sign Tony Scott. I thought we'd be better off taking a shot at Andujar, who had great stuff but is temperamental as hell. I'd brought Hub Kittle, my old Mexican League manager, to the Cardinals as pitching coach, and he'd worked with Andujar before. Hub got him to forget about throwing sidearm and come back on top with his delivery. Joaquin became a dominant pitcher after that.

Getting Joaquin put the finishing touches on a very good team. Good enough, it turned out, to win more games than any other team in the division that year. But that wasn't good enough because 1981 was the year of the fifty-two-day baseball strike, the year that the commissioner, Bowie Kuhn, made one of the worst rulings in the history of the game. He split the season in half, pre-strike and post-strike, and we finished second both times. Our total number of victories was greater than that of the Phillies, who finished first in the first half, and the Expos, the second-half winners. It was a travesty. The whole idea of the long season in baseball is to reward consistency, but the commissioner couldn't figure that out. We got cheated, and so did the Cincinnati Reds in the Western Division.

Strange as some of the players in this game are, they can't touch the owners.

The worst thing about Kuhn's decision wasn't the money part of it; hell, owners have to make money. But the money tainted the whole idea of competition. For example, after the Phillies were declared the winners of the first half, they loafed through the second half, knowing they would be in the mini-playoffs anyway. The Phils, I think, were secretly rooting for the Cardinals to win the second half because they knew they could throw Steve Carlton at us in the mini-playoffs and we'd fold like a cheap tent. For years, all Steve Carlton had to do was throw his glove out on the mound and the Cardinals would surrender.

The Phillies were worried about Montreal beating us out because the Expos had a bunch of good right-handed pitchers to throw at Philly's right-handed hitters. So when the Phils came into St. Louis late in the year, they didn't pitch Carlton or any of their top pitchers. I think it was the first time since Carlton was traded by the Cardinals to Philadelphia in 1972 that he didn't face us. It was a hell of a plan, but we fooled them. We kept giving up ten runs a game, and their second-line pitchers breezed right through us. And then their worst fears were realized when Montreal beat them in the mini-playoffs. The Expos went on to lose the real playoffs to the Dodgers, who shouldn't have been there in the first place because the Reds had a better record than they did, and the Dodgers went to play the Yankees in the World Series, which is the matchup that the television networks always dream about.

◇　◇　◇

One of the great misfortunes of 1981 was what happened with Garry Templeton, our shortstop. He had his troubles all year long, dogging it on us and complaining all the time. Here he was, twenty-five years old, the first man in history to get a hundred hits from each side of the plate in a single season, and he's whining that he's too tired to play day games after night games. It came to a boil one hot August afternoon in St. Louis. We'd played the night before and we had a Ladies' Day game that afternoon. I told Tempy he'd have to play even if he didn't feel like it; we were still in a pennant race, even though it was Bowie Kuhn's version of a pennant race.

So Tempy goes out and loafs his way through the first four or five innings. Everyone in the park could see what he was up to, and the fans were booing the shit out of him. I didn't blame them; if I'd paid good money to see a professional ballplayer put out, I'd have been booing, too. So Templeton comes off the field after one inning, stops in front of the pitcher's mound, grabs his crotch, and gives the fans the finger.

When he got to the dugout, I reached out and pulled him down the steps, and if the other players hadn't come between us, I guess we'd have had a pretty good fight right then and there. I'd never been so mad at a player.

I suspended him, of course, and the club got him to go into a hospital for treatment. We put out a press release saying he'd had a "chemical imbalance." He came back after three weeks and played pretty well the rest of the year, but he asked to be traded at the end of the season. I had to do it; there was no way the fans of St. Louis were ever going to forgive him. They still boo him when he comes to town, although I think he's settled down and gotten his life together.

I hated to part with him because he is a tremendously gifted athlete. Because Tempy is a switch-hitting shortstop who could run and hit .300 from either side of the plate, he may have been the most valuable commodity in the league at the time. I knew that when I moved him, I was going to have to get good value in return.

There were only a handful of shortstops I was interested in: Alan Trammell, then a young player with Detroit; Rick Burleson, a fiery guy, with the Angels; Ivan De Jesus of the Cubs, a slick fielder and a pretty good hitter; and Ozzie Smith of the Padres, a light hitter but a genuine wizard with a baseball glove. Shortstop is a key position on any team, even in the sandlots. But on Astro-Turf, it's even more critical. The ball moves so fast on fake grass, and so many guys try to hit down on the ball and then beat out the ground ball, so you just have to have a great shortstop.

I came close to landing De Jesus that fall. Dallas Green had just come over to the Cubs from the Phillies to be the general manager, and he and I almost made a deal. It would have been perfect; Tempy could have played day games on real grass at Wrigley Field. But Dallas is a hard-line guy, and he was wary of Templeton. He turned around and robbed his old club in a deal I'm still jealous of. He gave them De Jesus for Larry Bowa, a veteran shortstop, and a kid infielder that nobody had ever heard of by the name of Ryne Sandberg. I'd seen Sandberg play in the minor leagues, and I knew Dallas had a sleeper. It didn't surprise me at all when Sandberg won the Most Valuable Player Award in 1984.

◇ ◇ ◇

I was fuming. Dallas Green had Bowa and Sandberg both, and I was still stuck with Templeton. Detroit didn't want to talk about Trammell, the Angels wouldn't part with Burleson, and my old pal Jack McKeon had told me the year before that he'd never trade Ozzie Smith. I headed off to the 1981 winter meetings in a pessimistic mood.

The first guy I ran into at the manager's breakfast was McKeon, and he asked me, "You still interested in Ozzie?"

"What the hell, Jack? You told me he was untouchable."

"We still like Ozzie," he said. "It's his agent we are angry with. Everybody in the whole organization is pissed at him."

The more I thought about Ozzie Smith, the better I liked it. I knew getting him could be the last step toward having a really good club, twenty-five guys who would have the right attitude and really bust their tails. The thing I have come to understand about Ozzie is that not only he is the greatest defensive shortstop ever to play the game, but he's also a first-rate human being, a leader in the best sense of the word.

So we made the deal, or at least we tried to. We were going to send Templeton, Sixto Lezcano, and a kid pitcher named Luis DeLeon to the Padres for Ozzie and two pitchers, Steve Mura and Al Olmsted. Then I found out Ozzie had a no-trade clause in his contract.

I said to McKeon, "What the hell, Jack? A guy on a one-year deal has a no-trade?"

"You see what I mean about his agent?" Jack said.

It turned out that Ozzie really wanted the no-trade because he didn't want to be traded. He had grown up in L.A. and had sunk his roots into the San Diego area. McKeon and I made the rest of the deal, but the Ozzie for Tempy was left hanging.

Over the Christmas holidays, I flew out to San Diego to talk to Ozzie and his agent, Ed Gottlieb. I told them I appreciated how much Ozzie liked California, but that we had some things going for us in St. Louis, too. I told him what kind of club we were trying to put together and how he could be the key to the whole thing. I suggested he go ahead and come to St. Louis, sign a one-year contract, and if it didn't work out, he could take free agency at the end of the year.

A few weeks later, Ozzie took my suggestion. And we signed him to a long-term deal after the season. In April of 1985, we re-signed Ozzie to a contract for $2 million a year and the right to buy a Budweiser distributorship. We got ripped up and down baseball for paying that much money to a glove man, but Ozzie turned around and had the best offensive year of his life in addition to playing shortstop like he invented the position. I knew when we got him that he was good, but watching him every day I've found out just how good he is. Of all the shortstops I've seen, and I've seen some good ones—guys like Marty Marion, Mark Belanger, and Luis Aparicio—Ozzie is the best. I've never seen anyone do the things on a baseball field that he can do.

We made one more deal that winter, one that kind of fell into our laps. I came into the office one morning and found Joe Mac already there, talking on the phone (the man was born with a phone in his ear). He said, "Phil Seghi called. He wants to know if you have any interest in Lonnie Smith."

Phil Seghi was running the Cleveland Indians at the time, and like everyone else in baseball, he knew I was looking for a right-handed–hitting outfielder who could run. What I didn't know was how Seghi was going to get me Lonnie Smith, who was with the Phillies at the time.

"He's moving Bo Diaz to the Phillies for Smith," Joe said. "He says he needs pitching more than he needs Lonnie Smith, and you can have him for Silvio Martinez and Lary Sorensen."

"Get him on the phone and make that deal right now," I said. "I'll tell Gussie about it later."

And that's just what we did. All Lonnie did for us in 1982 was hit .307, lead the league in runs scored, steal 68 bases, and finish second in the Most Valuable Player voting. All we gave up for him was two guys who didn't figure to pitch much for us anyway. It's deals like that which make you look like a genius.

◇   ◇   ◇

With the two Smiths in the fold, I had completed what I'd set out to do eighteen months earlier. Our starting lineup had only two players in it—George Hendrick and Keith Hernandez—who'd been there when I arrived. Bob Forsch was the only starting pitcher left. We'd cleaned house, gotten the speed, relief pitching, and catching we needed. More importantly, we had twenty-five good guys on the club, no more drag-asses, no more prima donnas. It was a club that could win a pennant, and so I figured I'd end my career as a general manager. I had the team I wanted, and if I couldn't win with it, I didn't want to have to fire myself.

I hated being general manager. I liked making the deals, but I didn't like having to live in St. Louis year-round. I despised sitting in the office, talking on the phone to agents. I wanted to spend my winters fishing, hunting, and skiing, not sitting across a desk from some clown who'd never worn a jockstrap in his life, who was trying to tell me what a great player his client was when he'd probably never even seen him play. The things agents ask for: clauses, bonuses, incentives, special treatment, and things you wouldn't believe. I threw a couple of them right out of my office, right on their asses. Then I had to call the player up and tell him, "I just threw your agent out of my office."

"Why?" the guy would ask.

"Because I don't like the son of a bitch. You come in with him next time and we'll talk."

I figure it like this: 99 percent of all the people in the world are good people and the other 1 percent are assholes, and life's too short to spend it talking to assholes. The trouble with agents is that too many of them come from the 1 percent, and I won't mess with them anymore.

So, in February of 1982, I drove Mary Lou down to St. Petersburg and then caught a plane from Tampa to Phoenix, where Gussie was spending the winter. I told him I didn't want to be general manager anymore.

"Two years of negotiating contracts have just about killed me, Chief," I said. "I don't want to be sitting around the office listening to bullshitters anymore."

"I don't blame ya," Gussie said.

So we worked it out where Joe McDonald would be general manager, and I'd work closely with him. We agreed to hold off on the announcement until the start of the season. And then Gussie did one more thing that just about floored me: he extended my contract for two years and gave me a $75,000 a year raise. He said he never wanted me to get into the final year of my contract.

"Holy cow," I told myself. "Here I am, giving up half my job, and he gives me a two-year extension and a $75,000 a year raise. And I don't have to listen to any more bullshit. Who needs an agent?"

◇   ◇   ◇

I flew back to St. Pete and looked over my team. The thing that impressed me the most was that they were the hardest-working bunch of players I'd ever seen. I don't work a club too hard in the spring, but what I tell them to do, I expect them to do full tilt. These guys did it—the fundamentals, the running, everything. They had such a feeling of confidence that I knew we were going to be good.

The key in 1982 was that everybody knew who was going to do

what. We were set everywhere, even with the pinch-hitters, the utility men, and the middle relief. I had a bunch of hard-working coaches who weren't afraid to come to the park early and work with the players. Everything was in place, and then we got a couple of nice surprises.

The first was that a couple of rookie pitchers, Dave LaPoint and John Stuper, were able to take over two spots in the rotation when two other guys, Andy Rincon and John Martin, had their problems. Stuper was a right-hander and LaPoint a left-hander, and they did the job. All they had to do was get us five innings, and then Jim Kaat or Doug Bair would come in and set the table for Sutter. The kids did it, while Forsch and Andujar each won fifteen games. We didn't get a lot of complete games from our starters that year, but if you're paying a relief pitcher as much as we were paying Sutter, you use him. We also got twelve victories out of Steve Mura that year, and he didn't win another game in the big leagues for three years. That's the kind of freak thing that has to happen if you're going to win a pennant.

The other thing that has to happen is that you must keep away from injuries. We had only one really bad injury in 1982, and even that turned out to be lucky. David Green, who'd finally made it to the big leagues, was playing center field for us until he tore a hamstring muscle in May. We brought up a kid named Willie McGee from our Louisville farm club to replace him.

I didn't know much about Willie McGee at the time—only that he was a pretty good prospect and our scouts were high on him. He'd been in the Yankees' chain the year before and had hit .322 for their Triple-A club in Nashville. The Yankees had protected him on their forty-man winter big-league roster after the 1981 season, but when they signed Dave Winfield to a big free agent's contract, they outrighted McGee to Nashville. It meant that Willie was available in the minor-league draft, and we planned to take him if he was still on the board when it got to be our turn to draft.

But since we were drafting pretty low that year, I told Joe McDonald to call Bill Bergesch, then the general manager in New York, and see if we could make a deal for McGee. Hell, they didn't think much of McGee if they thought they had forty guys better than him. They knew they were going to lose him in the draft anyway, so they asked for Bob Sykes, a left-handed relief pitcher. You always want to get a player instead of the $25,000 draft price. Bergesch and McDonald also made a little gentleman's agreement on the side that if McGee turned out OK, we'd give the Yankees the traditional "future considerations"—which means we'd make it up to them.

Willie McGee turned out to be better than OK—we brought him up and he became the biggest story in baseball that summer. He hit .296, stole 24 bases, drove in 56 runs, and played center field like the second coming of Willie Mays. Every time we'd go into New York to play the Mets, the writers there would write about how dumb the Yankees were to let McGee go for Bob Sykes. They were still writing about it in 1985, when Willie won the MVP Award.

We wound up giving the Yankees a couple of real good prospects—shortstop Bobby Meacham and outfielder Stan Javier—as future considerations.

Once Willie McGee hit town and the kid pitchers started coming through, I began to feel that 1982 might be the Cardinals' year. We kept on winning the close ones as well as the lucky ones. We won one game in the twelfth inning when our backup catcher, Glenn Brummer, who is slower than I am, stole home with two out. Still, we didn't wrap things up until we went into New York in the third week of September and took five games from the Mets in three days. We won eight in a row and coasted in, and I had my fourth division title—and another shot at the World Series, if we could get past the Atlanta Braves in the playoffs.

◇   ◇   ◇

We took the Braves in three straight—league championship series were then best-of-five—but that was the closest three-game sweep anyone has ever seen. The problem was our pitching; pitching is always the problem in a short series. The team with the hottest staff usually wins. I had it set up where Andujar would open up for us, at home. We needed to win each of the first two games at home since the final three games were to be played in Atlanta's stadium, and our pitchers usually gave up a lot of home runs in that launching pad.

The first game got under way but then was rained out, so there went my pitching rotation. Andujar's turn was wasted; he wasn't ready again until Game Three. Luckily, Forsch came through with a big shutout the next day, when Game One was finally played, and Stuper pitched well enough for us to win Game Two. We went down to Atlanta, and Joaquin did the job to get us the sweep. I hate to think what would have happened if he hadn't. LaPoint would have pitched Game Four, and he never pitched very well in that park, and neither did Forsch, who would have started Game Five. Everybody talked about how we rolled over the Braves, but they don't know how close that series really was.

But it got me to the World Series. Finally. I'd been in baseball for thirty-three years by then, and I had never been in uniform for the Series. Lord knows, I was glad to be there, but I found myself strangely underwhelmed by it all. Every year I'd set the World Series as a goal—think about it, plan for it, dream of it. When I finally got there, it just seemed like part of the job.

The Series is kind of a hassle for the managers and players anyway, what with all the press attention. The guys from the cornfield radio stations and the local television stations come out and ask their dumb questions and get in the way of the regular baseball writers. Stengel always asked those guys, "Where the hell were you in August?", and I guess that's kind of the way I feel about it. You do pregame and postgame press conferences for the television guys, and then they traipse after you to your office after the game and expect you to answer their questions all over again. They're always asking you about your team's "mental attitude," like you're supposed to be some kind of psychiatrist. When we made it to the Series again in 1985, I finally got fed up with it and threw all the television guys out of my office after the game until I was finished with the writers. The writers loved it, but the TV guys ripped me good.

But 1982 was my first time there, so I put up with most of it. Our opponents were none other than my old friends, the Milwaukee Brewers. I knew I told Harry Dalton back in Dallas that I'd help him win the pennant, but I sure as hell didn't expect we'd wind up playing each other. Harry and his manager, Harvey Kuenn, had a hell of a ball club; every guy in the lineup was capable of hitting the ball out of the park. "Harvey's Wallbangers" is what they were called, and they scared the hell out of me.

The key to the Series was the fact that Rollie Fingers had hurt his arm in September and couldn't pitch. We had our big man in the bullpen, and they had theirs in the trainer's room—that was the difference.

They pounded on us in the opener in St. Louis, but we came back to take the second game before we moved on to Milwaukee for Game Three. Joaquin beat them in that game; Sutter got the save and McGee had two homers and made two great catches at the wall. We screwed up Game Four when LaPoint dropped a ball on a play at first, and they beat us again in Game Five. So we came home down three games to two, and I had to pitch Stuper, a rookie. We scored about a dozen runs for him, and it rained like hell, but John pitched great and got the victory. Game Seven was all ours; Joaquin pitched well and Sutter finished up. It seemed appropriate, since he was the main reason we were there. Darrell Porter finally got the fans on his side, winning the MVP Award for the series.

So Gussie finally got that "one more championship" he'd been asking for. The first thing he said to me in the clubhouse, with all the champagne flying around, was, "We're pretty young, aren't we? We ought to be able to win it again next year. Maybe I can get a couple more."

I thought it was possible, even though the hardest thing in baseball is to repeat as World Champions. We were young, and all the key guys were signed for at least a couple more years. Everyone I'd gone out to get had done just what I'd gone out and gotten him for. The club had drawn more than two million fans in Busch

Stadium, so the brewery was happy. I thought we were solid; the team should have been a contender for years.

Even so, there were a lot of people around baseball—writers, mostly—who just couldn't believe the Cardinals were World Champions. They said we didn't fit the mold, whatever that was, because Hendrick was the only guy in the lineup who could hit the ball out of the park with any regularity. They weren't too impressed with our pitching, either, so they wrote us off as a fluke. They seemed to think there was something wrong with the way we played baseball, with speed and defense and line-drive hitters. They called it "Whitey-ball" and said it couldn't last.

Well, I don't know what "Whitey-ball" is, unless it's the same kind of inside baseball that John McGraw was winning with eighty years ago. Big parks with artificial surfaces are here to stay, and if you're going to win on them, you'd sure better be able to do the things we did in 1982. If I have a motto, it's "Run, boys, run." And I didn't see why we couldn't keep running for another couple of years.

What I didn't count on was how quickly things can go sour on you in this game. Over the next two years, a lot of very sour, very strange things began happening to the St. Louis Cardinals.

Rebuilding

Baseball has a lot of dumb rituals, and one of the dumbest is the annual dynasty prediction.

It always comes the day after the World Series. You pick up the newspaper or turn on the TV, and there's somebody predicting that the team that just won the Series is about to become a dynasty. Sometimes it's the team owner who's doing the predicting, and sometimes it's a player who's had too much champagne. Sometimes it's a sportswriter or a sportscaster. But it's never, ever a manager. We're too smart for that.

We know there are just too many things that can go wrong when you try to repeat. Injuries. Drugs. Free agency. A key guy or two having a horseshit year. Even if you manage to survive all that and win your division, chances are never much better than even that you'll win the playoffs and the Series.

Baseball has only had one real dynasty, the great Yankees teams in the middle part of this century. They were richer than other clubs, and if their farm system didn't provide them with the players they needed, they'd go out and buy them from some owner who needed the money.

There have been a couple of mini-dynasties since then. Charlie Finley's Oakland clubs in the early 1970s qualified, and so did

Cincinnati's "Big Red Machine" teams in the mid-1970s. Since then, everybody's been knocking each other off pretty regularly.

The reasons are obvious: free agency and the draft. The best you can hope for is to contend every year, play good baseball, and put people in the stands. If you catch a break or two and win a pennant every four or five years, that's pretty damned good. That's a modern dynasty.

As far as I can tell, there's only one tried-and-true way to build yourself a modern dynasty in sports. You find yourself one guy who knows the sport inside out, top to bottom, and you put him in charge. You let him run the show totally. No bullshit. No committees. No second-guessing. No having to answer to half a dozen different people. If he doesn't get the job done, you get yourself a guy who can.

It's worked pretty well in basketball. Red Auerbach has run the Boston Celtics for years, through four or five different ownership changes, and they're always at the top. It's worked well in hockey, too. Al Arbour did it with the New York Islanders, and Glen Sather is doing it now with the Edmonton Oilers. And look at pro football. Which teams are always in the playoffs and the Super Bowl? The Raiders, with Al Davis in charge. The Dolphins, with Don Shula. The 49ers, with Bill Walsh. Other teams will sneak in for a year or two or three, but the clubs with a strong guy in charge are always in the hunt. And that's the best you can hope for.

I'm not the guy who invented this theory, but believe me, I've had a chance to see how it works. In St. Louis, from 1982 through 1984, I saw an organization go through about as many changes as an organization could. We had all the problems: injuries, free agency, drugs. We had big changes in the front office. We went from the penthouse to the outhouse. My belief in this theory came the hard way.

◇   ◇   ◇

The Cardinals won ninety-two ballgames and the World Series in 1982. A year later, we finished four games under .500 and ahead of only two other clubs in the Eastern Division. We had two big problems. One, lousy pitching, was easy to spot. The second, drugs, wasn't so easy to figure out.

In 1982, we had two starters, Joaquin Andujar and Bob Forsch, who each won fifteen games. Almost every time you strapped them out on the mound, they'd give you seven or eight good innings. The players were confident behind them, and they knew they could avoid long losing streaks.

But in 1983, Joaquin and Forschie both collapsed. Joaquin won six games that year and lost sixteen. He kept complaining about bad luck and how God must be watching the American League instead of him. Well, it's sure bad luck when your earned run average goes from 2.47 to 4.16. Forsch won ten games, but his ERA was even higher than Andujar's. Both of them got hammered repeatedly, and we never did come up with a dependable No. 1 starter. Forsch and Andujar won thirty games between them in 1982, but won only sixteen in 1983, and the club won thirteen fewer games.

But it wasn't as simple as that. Some of the key guys on the club just weren't working as hard as they had the year before. Lonnie Smith was just terrible. Balls were scooting by him in left field, and then he'd fall down when he chased them. Any ground ball that got through the left side had a good chance of turning into a double or a triple.

Keith Hernandez was dogging it. He was playing good defense at first base, but he always does. I've never seen a ballplayer bear down as much at first base as he does. He's the best defensive first baseman I've ever seen. But on offense, he was loafing. He loafed down the line on ground balls, and he wasn't aggressive on the bases. Keith hits a lot of line drives that a hustling player, a George Brett or a Pete Rose kind of player, could turn into doubles. Keith would always pull up at first base, and he very rarely tried to steal a base anymore.

I can't say that I knew Keith had been doing drugs. What the hell? Unless you spot a guy snorting coke or smoking marijuana, or unless some reliable witness comes to you or it blows up in the press, you never know for sure.

At the same time, a manager has to be either stupid or looking the other way when a player's work habits change as much as Hernandez's did. There were things about him that made me suspicious, but I can live with suspicions. What I couldn't live with was his attitude. I've got two basic rules—be on time and hustle —and he was having trouble with both of them. A couple of the players came up to me and asked why Keith was loafing. I couldn't tell them. It seems to me that you shouldn't have to tell a man making as much money as he was making to hustle, but maybe I'm wrong.

His practice habits were atrocious. He'd come out for batting practice, then head back to the clubhouse to smoke cigarettes and do crossword puzzles. We got on him a couple of times, so he'd do better for a few days, and then he'd go back to his lazy ways. I asked a couple of my coaches to get after him, but he'd ignore them. It was getting to the point where I was fed up with him. A couple of my coaches even told me, "You'd better get rid of that guy. He's poisoning the whole ball club."

All the troubles started coming to a head in early June. We were in first place, but we were in trouble. I knew that unless we got some pitching, things were only going to get worse. I went to Mr. Busch and told him what the deal was, that we needed pitching and that I thought the best way to get it was to shop Hernandez around. Sooner or later, I said, the other players were going to decide that if Keith was loafing, they could, too.

I told Gussie that I thought we'd have trouble signing Keith the next year anyway. His contract was up for renewal, and he was on the verge of becoming a five-and-ten man in the big leagues, which would severely limit what we could do with him.

Under the rules with the Players' Association, players with ten years in the big leagues and five with one club have the right to veto any trade. You can buy out the veto, but as the Ted Simmons trade had shown me, it can cost you plenty. I told Gussie that my reading of the market indicated that Hernandez would demand about $1.5 million a year, and that I didn't want to pay him that much money and put up with his horseshit attitude.

"Trade the son of a bitch," Gussie growled.

Easier said than done. Joe McDonald shopped him around the major leagues and found only one club, the New York Mets, with any strong interest in him. Here's a guy with a lifetime batting average of .299, who'd been co-winner of the Most Valuable Player Award in 1979, the best defensive first baseman in the game, and we can't drum up any interest in him. Don't tell me there's no grapevine in baseball. The other clubs were scared of his contract, and they'd heard all the rumors about his off-the-field habits, too.

Keith later admitted, as a witness in the trial of a drug dealer in Pittsburgh in 1985, that he'd been doing cocaine. He was one of a half dozen or so ballplayers who testified under immunity in that trial, and Keith called cocaine "the devil on this earth." He said he'd kicked the habit on his own, and for all I know, he did.

All that came later, though. Early in 1983, all I knew for sure was that we had troubles. The club was informed that the FBI had two witnesses who claimed to have been at a party where two of our players were doing drugs. Hernandez, incidentally, wasn't one of the players in question. I called a meeting and laid down the law. I didn't mention any names, but I asked the players to come forth privately, on their own. Neither one of them did.

While all this was going on, and while Joe McDonald was trying to make a deal for pitching before the June 15 trading deadline, I was busy trying to keep our club together along with trying to figure out what the hell was ailing Lonnie Smith. Finally, he came to me and asked for help. He said he'd tried, but he couldn't stop taking coke. He had a bad, bad problem.

It later developed at that drug trial in Pittsburgh that Lonnie was using coke with Hernandez and Andujar. He didn't tell me that at the time. He only asked for help, and we got it for him. I admired him, and still do, for having the guts to ask for help.

On June 13, we announced that Lonnie had been put on the disabled list and sent to a rehab center in St. Louis. And then, two days later, Joe made a deal with Frank Cashen of the Mets. We sent them Hernandez for two pitchers, Neil Allen and Rick Ownbey. We called up a kid outfielder named Andy Van Slyke, who was hitting .368 in Louisville. I figured we'd move George Hendrick, who was having a hell of a year, to first base. We'd use Van Slyke in the outfield along with Willie McGee and David Green until Lonnie came back, and then we'd try Andy at other places. He could play all three outfield positions as well as first and third.

People always say it's the worst deal I've ever made, but I don't believe that. Allen, who'd been the Mets' top reliever, never worked out in St. Louis, although he won ten games for us in 1983. Ownbey is still trying to make it. Van Slyke is a decent ballplayer and may one day be a star, but he hasn't hit in the big leagues like he did in the minors. Hernandez, thanks to me, is making $1.7 million a year and is the pride of New York. The man can truly hit, and when he plays against us, he cranks it up a few notches. I think he knows that I did him a favor by trading him.

But you can't always judge a deal strictly by the talent involved. Getting rid of Hernandez was addition by subtraction. I really feel that if we had kept him, his attitude and his bullshit would have ruined our ball club. I know he never would have been as good for us as he has been with the Mets. Ballplayers are like Missouri mules—sometimes you have to hit them on the head with a two-by-four to get their attention.

Well, the shit hit the fan when the trade was announced. We were at home, playing the Phillies, and I must have told the story to every reporter in town at least three times. The fans, those loyal, die-hard, hero-loving Cardinals fans, were outraged. They'd been mad about the Simmons deal, but that was nothing compared with the reaction about the Hernandez deal. Nobody remembered that two years earlier, when I'd traded Simmons, the consensus among the fans was that we ought to trade Keith and leave Teddy alone.

Since we'd announced two days earlier that Lonnie had gone into rehab, a lot of reporters were asking whether drugs had anything to do with the Hernandez deal, too. I said no, that the deal was made simply because we needed pitching and that Van Slyke was ready, and that with Keith's contract situation, he was the best bait we had. I told them that as far as I knew, Keith Hernandez wasn't doing drugs at the time. This was true enough. I didn't know for sure.

But I didn't tell the reporters everything that was behind the trade, and I didn't tell them my suspicions. It was none of their damned business. I don't look at it like I was trying to cover up for Keith; rather, I was only giving him the benefit of the doubt. I try to do that for everybody—and not just ballplayers. For all the stuff that's been written about Keith Hernandez and me, I still think he's the greatest defensive first baseman I've ever seen, and I'm happy for the success he's had in New York.

Keith went on a tear for the Mets. Every time he'd win a game for the Mets, the outrage among our fans would start all over again. It continued like that for two years, until the first time he came into St. Louis after testifying on the stand in Pittsburgh. Then the fans booed his ass off.

I tried not to pay much attention to what the fans were saying. If I didn't want to be second-guessed, I'd have to get a new job. I had enough to worry about with the way we were playing after the trade.

◇   ◇   ◇

We just couldn't get anything going, but neither could anyone else in the division. If Andujar or Forsch had gotten on track, we might have stolen the division. Lonnie came back from rehab and finished strong, missing the batting title on the last day. We weren't much better than .500, but nobody else was either. As a result, we were still only a half game out of first place the day after Labor Day. I wouldn't mind being in that position every year. If I'm that close on Labor Day, I'll take my chances in the last five weeks of any season. That's when you have to hope the schedule-makers have been good to you. A lot of times the pennant is won or lost the year before, when they make out the schedules.

In 1983, the league handed us a five-city, thirteen-game road trip in September. It was suicide. When I saw the schedule in the spring, I knew we were screwed; and sure enough, we were. We beat the Cubs two out of three to start, but then we won only one game the rest of the trip. We lost in the damndest ways. Forsch, a very good fielding pitcher, threw a bunt away. Sutter messed up a bunt play, too. We lost another game when Chuck Hiller, our third base coach, was called for "aiding" a runner when he pushed Van Slyke toward home plate. The Phillies beat us six straight in September and fourteen of eighteen on the year, and that was the season.

A couple of good things happened that year, though. We really got our running game going, stealing 207 bases, which was a club record at the time, but which we would break time and again. The running game creates exciting baseball, which puts people in the seats, so we broke the Cardinals' all-time attendance record with more than 2.3 million people. That record wouldn't last either.

We weren't very good in 1983, but we weren't as bad as we were made out to be, either. Writers kept coming by, doing stories on "what happened to the Cardinals," and I tried to tell them we weren't that bad off. Our staff was ninth in the league in earned run average and gave up 101 more runs than they had the year before, but hell, we scored only six fewer runs. We'd had a hell of a lot of injuries: Herr had knee surgery, Dane Iorg had a broken wrist, and Lonnie was in rehab.

All in all, I didn't think we were so bad off. I figured if we could get one or two of the pitchers back on track, maybe make a minor trade or two, we'd be in good shape in 1984.

◇   ◇   ◇

Well, we weren't. The one thing I thought I could count on for sure was that we would score runs. When you play the running game, you create a lot of opportunities, and all you need is a timely hit every now and then and you've got a run or two. We couldn't get a big base hit to save our lives in 1984. It was incredible.

Very few things leave me speechless, but night after night the writers would come into my office after the game, and I had nothing new to say to them. It was one of the strangest times I've ever been through. Everything in my baseball experience, all my theories and all my beliefs, is based on the fact that if you run and you hustle, sooner or later you'll break something open. But most nights in 1984 it just didn't happen. We'd get a man on, steal a base or hit and run, be sitting pretty. And then we'd get a strikeout, pop-out, fly ball and be out of the inning.

Part of the trouble was that the middle of our lineup was just not producing. Hendrick had his worst season in ten years. Darrell Porter was just not producing. He'd gotten his life turned around after kicking his drug habit, but in the process, he'd lost his aggressiveness. Van Slyke didn't do the job. Lonnie Smith, after finishing so well in 1983, was terrible. He hit .250, which was sixty-six points below his lifetime average. Like Porter, it seemed as if he'd not only gotten over his drug habit, but he'd gotten over being aggressive at the plate, too.

The biggest disappointment of the year was David Green. Here was a guy with all the potential in the world, the guy who'd been the key to the big trade with the Brewers a few years earlier, and he just wasn't hacking it. We thought he might be troubled because his family was caught in the middle of the civil war in Nicaragua, so some of the people at the brewery got to work and got permission for his mother to come to the United States in August of 1983. She lived with David and cooked for him, and he had a pretty good year. She didn't like the cold weather in St. Louis in the winter, so we found her a place in Florida. David was going to live with her and play in the Instructional League. The club was going to pick up all the expenses.

But Mrs. Green got homesick. She went back to Nicaragua in November and died there four months later. David had a hard, hard time coping with it, as anybody would. The young man developed a real problem with alcohol. Everybody on the club knew it. He'd show up late, hung over real bad. There were times I'd get calls in the middle of the night saying David was in trouble somewhere and asking if I could come get him.

After a couple of these incidents, I sat him down and told him, "Son, one of these times you're going to get mean with somebody who's carrying a pistol, and when I come get you, I'm going to have to carry you back in a box."

He'd try to handle it, but he couldn't. His tolerance for booze was about zero. Finally, we asked him to submit to rehab, and he went in for a month of the 1984 season. He didn't play much better when he got out than he had before he went in, but he was coping with the problems a little better.

So there I was, with Green having troubles and with Van Slyke struggling. And with three veterans—Hendrick, Porter, and Lonnie Smith—struggling as well. McGee and Herr and Ozzie Smith were playing well, but there was nobody to drive them in when they got on base. The one bright spot in the season was the emergence of Terry Pendleton as our regular third baseman. We brought him up from the minors in the middle of July, after we traded Ken Oberkfell to Atlanta, and he gave us the kind of offensive firepower you have to have from a third baseman. He changed our season around. Everyone seemed to take a cue from his aggressiveness.

There's an axiom in baseball that you have to have power in the corners—that is, at first and third. I don't think it's necessarily true, but in the big ballparks, it's critical that you get run production out of your first and third basemen. They've got to hit line drives with runners on, and they've got to give you good defense.

Kenny Oberkfell is a hell of a defensive third baseman, and he'd hit .300 for me. But for some mysterious reason, he couldn't drive in a run to save his life. He'd come up with nobody on base and hit ropes. And then he'd come up with men on second and third and pop up. It was as if he was allergic to RBIs. So when the Braves came up with an injury to their third baseman, Bob Horner, Joe McDonald got on the phone and gave them Obie. In return, we got a left-handed pitcher named Ken Dayley who has done a very good job for us.

In Pendleton, we came up with a jewel from the farm system. He only played sixty-seven games for us in 1984, but he hit .430 for the first three weeks he was in the big leagues. He finished at .324 and drove in 33 runs in 67 games. Oberkfell had driven in a grand total of 38 in the whole season the year before.

But Pendleton couldn't do the job by himself. Our hitting didn't come around until August, and if it hadn't been for Andujar and Sutter, we might have finished in last place. As it was, we finished very strong and took third place. We wound up 84–78, twelve games behind the Cubs. Considering that the Cubs beat us in thirteen out of eighteen games in 1984, I felt the Cardinals contributed more than our share to their first divisional title ever.

Joaquin was just superb. He became the Cardinals' first twenty-game winner since Forsch in 1977, won the Comeback Player of the Year Award, and didn't even bitch as much as usual. He was our only real dependable starter because Forsch was on the disabled list with back problems for most of the year. We came up with some good young arms, and Dave LaPoint won a dozen games for us. But the real key to our pitching in 1984 was Sutter.

Bruce saved forty-five games for us, tying the big-league record, and his earned run average was 1.54. I spent the whole season worrying about the starters going six innings, hoping we could scratch a run or two and get to the eighth so I could bring Bruce in. He was money in the bank. And he was more than that. He was absolutely the key to our entire ball club. I had built the Cardinals based on the assumption that Sutter would be there to close the door in close games in the late innings. He had done everything we'd asked of him, winning 26 and saving 127 games in his four years as a Cardinal. We'd won 334 games in those four years, and Bruce had won or saved 46 percent of them. How valuable is that?

He was a good guy in the clubhouse, a leader in a quiet way. He was just the same on the rare occasions that he got rung up as he was most nights when he blew 'em down. Bruce had had a down year in 1983, like the rest of our pitchers. He'd saved only twenty-one games, mostly because he wasn't getting the work he needed. That's because we didn't have a lead for him to protect most of the time.

In 1984, we'd brought in Mike Roarke as pitching coach. Mike had been the pitching coach with the Cubs when Sutter was there, and he was the man who'd taught Bruce the nasty split-fingered fastball that became his bread and butter. Mike is a great pitching coach with any pitcher, but with Sutter, he was more than a coach.

He was a guru. He knew Bruce better than Bruce knew Bruce, and with Mike in the dugout, Bruce had the best year of his life.

As far as I was concerned, there was only one problem with Bruce Sutter. His contract was up.

◇　◇　◇

That worried me a lot. In fact, I found myself almost obsessed with the question of Bruce Sutter's contract. It didn't help that writers were always wandering by and asking about it. I'd always tell them, "If we don't sign Sutter, it means I'll be twenty-five games dumber next year." He just meant so much to what we were trying to do.

Players like Sutter, the late-inning closer, are one of the big differences between the game today and the game that was played when I was young. When I first started in baseball, in 1949, only a few teams had guys who specialized in short relief. There was Jim Konstanty with Philadelphia and Joe Page with the Yankees, and later Luis Arroyo with the Yankees. In those days, pitchers were tougher. They were expected to go nine innings every four days, and for the most part, the good ones did. Even as late as 1963, my last year as a player, we went with a four-man rotation on the Tigers: Paul Foytack, Jim Bunning, Frank Lary, and Don Mossi. A guy would start on Sunday, rest Monday, throw batting practice on Tuesday, rest Wednesday, and go back after 'em on Thursday.

Try telling a pitcher today that he should follow a routine like that. Some guys don't even want to warm up between starts. None of them will throw batting practice, and very few of them want to pitch with three days rest. They're all worried about rotator cuff injuries. Hell, when I was playing, nobody'd even heard of the rotator cuff.

So pitchers today baby their arms, pitch every fifth day, and most of them can't go nine anyway. Overall, pitchers today are in better shape, but I don't think they develop their arms as well while growing up. They pitch in Little League, where their number of innings is restricted, instead of playing sandlot ball fifty innings a day. The kids today are bigger and stronger, but they can't pitch as much. It's strange to me.

You'd think it would be easier for a guy to go nine these days. With the big parks and the Astro-Turf, all he would have to do is decide he was going to use the whole park, use his defense, and move the ball around. But today, for some reason I can't explain, pitchers can't exploit weaknesses the way they did when I was playing. They can't pitch up in the strike zone when they have to, can't move it in and out, can't get a curve over for a strike. Most pitchers are afraid to go away from their own strengths, even if their strength happens to be a hitter's strength.

There are exceptions to this rule, of course. Catfish Hunter was great at tying guys up in knots, and John Tudor won twenty-one games for me in 1985 by moving the ball around and using the park and our great defense. But most guys are content to go six or seven innings every fifth day and hope like hell there's a guy in the pen to bail him out.

It's a sign of how specialized the game has become. We've got all these "role players" out there, and the man with the most important role is the short reliever. Basically, these guys come in three flavors.

No. 1 is the power pitcher, a reliever who can blow people away with his fastball. Goose Gossage is the prime example, but there's also Lee Smith with the Cubs and Tom Henke with Toronto. I've got great hopes for our young guy, Todd Worrell, because he's got that kind of fastball.

No. 2 is the reliever with the freak delivery. Dan Quisenberry of Kansas City, who brings the ball in underhand, is the best of the breed, the logical successor to guys like Ted Abernathy and Dick Hyde. Quisenberry came up to the Royals toward the end of my last season there. He got hit with a line drive in one of his first appearances for me and was out for two weeks. We lost the division by three games, and I sometimes think that if I'd had Quiz for those last six weeks, I might still be manager there.

No. 3 is the reliever with one freak pitch. Sutter with his split-fingered fastball. Sparky Lyle with his great left-handed slider. Mike Marshall with the screwball. Rollie Fingers with that nasty slider. The key to these guys' success is their consistency and the fact that hitters don't see them very often. They only get one chance at them, and that's not long enough to adjust.

The common denominator in all three types of relief pitchers is what baseball people call "makeup." It's the most important thing about any pitcher, but with relief pitchers makeup is absolutely critical. They have to want the ball when the game is on the line. You want them frothing at the mouth when they get to the mound, but still in enough control to do what they have to do. And that means they don't beat themselves. They don't come in with the bases loaded and walk somebody. They make you hit their pitch. They don't hang a curveball at a crucial time.

And finally, the great relief pitcher knows that some nights he's going to get beat. They're like matadors dancing with wild bulls every night. Every once in a while, they're going to get a sharp poke in the ass. But the next night they want the cape and the sword all over again.

You get a reliever like that, such as Bruce Sutter, and you have to keep him. Nowadays it's what baseball is all about: whether my bullpen can out-do yours. If you don't have outstanding relief pitching, you might as well piss on the fire and call in the dogs. My whole team was the preliminary act to Bruce Sutter's show-stopper, and the whole world knew it.

◇   ◇   ◇

Well, maybe not the whole world. The Cardinals front office didn't seem to have caught on entirely, which brings up another problem we were having in 1984.

During the time I was general manager of the club, from August of 1980 to the spring of 1982, I probably had as much authority as any executive in baseball. I reported directly to Gussie Busch, and in fact, I had it in my contract that I didn't have to take orders from anybody else. Because I had such a great relationship with Gussie, it made it easy to do the job.

Even after I turned the general manager's job over to Joe Mc-Donald, I still kept a lot of authority. Joe and I would discuss player moves almost every day, and he wouldn't do anything without running it by me first. But after we won the Series in 1982, something happened in the higher echelons of the brewery which started to change things. They formed a three-man executive committee to run the club. Gussie was still the top man, but Lou Susman and Fred Kuhlmann were put on the committee, too. Susman was Gussie's lawyer, of course. Kuhlmann was a lawyer, too. He'd been legal counsel for Anheuser-Busch and vice chairman of the board. He'd retired recently, but was on a consulting contract and was still a heavyweight. And Fred just loved baseball.

I suppose that in most businesses it makes sense to have an executive committee to put some checks and balances on things. But in baseball, you can't really sit around discussing things and give everybody a vote, especially when most of the guys voting don't have the foggiest idea how the game is really played. Joe McDonald and I were told we could do anything we wanted as long as it didn't cost more than $50,000. Anything more than that and we needed a vote of the committee. Hell, you can't sign a rookie shortstop for $50,000.

To me, this was a slap in the face. When I came to St. Louis, the Cardinals were last in the division but second in the league for the highest payroll. Two years later we won the World Series and were seventh in the league for the payroll. I've always been as careful about spending other people's money as I am spending my own. Joe McDonald was the same way, and you could ask any agent who ever dealt with us. I think the agents were glad to see us out of the negotiations.

Once we got the committee together, we could usually make our case pretty well. But everytime we called, we'd find Susman in Washington, Kuhlmann in New York, and Gussie in Arizona. Getting them all together in the same room was a major problem.

The whole executive committee system hamstrung efforts to sign Bruce Sutter.

◇   ◇   ◇

I had started lobbying for signing Sutter before his contract was up. It's just good business sense to deal with a guy before you have to. Once the contract expired and he declared for free agency, he could play us against other clubs and might cost us a lot more money. But if we negotiated while there was still a year left on his contract, we might save some money. I got nowhere with that argument.

The front office saw that he'd only saved twenty-one games in 1983 and had had some arm problems. They were worried, and rightly so, that if they gave him a bunch of money and he went down the tubes in 1984, they'd be out on their ass. We were gambling, in a way, that he'd have another so-so year so we could sign him for less.

By the middle of June, it was clear that we were losing the bet. Sutter was better than he'd ever been, and I started pushing to get him signed before the season was over. I told management that if we weren't going to sign him, we sure as hell had better trade him before the September 1 deadline so we'd at least get some value out of him. If we lost him to free agency, we wouldn't get much of anything for him. As a matter of fact, when we did lose him to free agency, we wound up getting shortstop Argenis Salazar in the compensation draft, which was just the sort of thing I was afraid of.

But Bruce and his agents, Frank Bronner and Bob Gilhooley, weren't stupid. In fact, as agents go, I kind of like them. Both of them are from Chicago, and they didn't bullshit me as much as some agents do. They knew that every game Sutter saved made their position that much stronger, so they started waiting us out. They would exchange letters and phone calls with Joe McDonald, but Susman had decided that he was going to do the negotiating.

By August, it had become pretty clear that Joe was in hot water. He was getting the blame for a lot of things that weren't his fault, and his job was in jeopardy. I told him to stay out of the line of fire and let me handle it. It didn't help much because he got fired at the end of the year anyway.

In late September, we found ourselves in a hell of a spot. We were out of the race, our key player was about to become a free agent, and the front office was in turmoil. Mary Lou and I were invited out to Grant's Farm for dinner with Mr. and Mrs. Busch, and they asked me to submit a "game plan" for 1985. I sat down right at the end of the season and wrote one out. Basically this is what it said:

To: Gussie Busch, Joe McDonald; copies to Lou Susman, Fred Kuhlmann
From: Whitey Herzog—1985 Game Plan

Since the Chief told me last spring, "I'm eighty-five and would like it one more time," I feel the ball club is not that far away, and it possibly could be done if we do the following:

1. Sutter. If we don't sign him, we won't win. Probably will never be as good again as in '84, but don't feel there's any alternative but to sign him.

2. Biggest need: Another starting pitcher. This would give us a chance for seven-plus innings from a starter. Outside of Andujar, we are just into our bullpen too often, too early. Will have to part with an outfielder for this type of pitcher and feel we could part with either Hendrick or Lonnie Smith.

3. Other needs: Not satisfied with our catcher. But maybe we have our ace in the hole because '85 will be Porter's walk year and maybe he'll start playing better. He just doesn't compete like he used to. Feels the Lord will take care of everything. I wish the Lord knew more about hitting. A catcher with any ability will be hard to find. Probably have to go with what we've got. Don't sign Porter at this time.

4. Other place we must strengthen our club is left-handed relief pitching. Feel possibly Andy Hassler, Rick Horton, or Ken Dayley could do the job. Should shop around.

5. Good things: Strength of our club is defense, team speed and overall youth. If we retain Sutter our bullpen is as good as anyone's. Pendleton and Green have come along fine, and Van Slyke will still

be a good player, and Vince Coleman will be less than a year away.

6. Consensus: We must resolve the Sutter situation as soon as possible. If we sign Sutter, everything is in a different perspective, as we would have a chance to win for Gussie next year if we could come up with a starter. If we sign Sutter, we should get into negotiations immediately with Gottlieb on Ozzie Smith. We should negotiate with Herr's agents but hold off on Lonnie Smith. Realize we can't sign them all.

If any questions about the above, give me a call.

Well, nobody called. We messed around with Bruce and his agents until he finally filed for free agency. They wanted a five-year deal or better and a boatload of money—most of it up front in an annuity contract with a long payout—and they wanted interest-free loans and a no-trade clause. All of these things were poison to the brewery, which feels that it has better things to do with its risk capital than invest it for ballplayers. This is just common sense and one of the many reasons why Anheuser-Busch is the most successful brewery in the world.

Still, I didn't think the situation was hopeless. There weren't many other clubs who were willing to spend that kind of money. By the time we went down to Houston for the winter meetings in early December, I still thought we could sign Sutter. Gussie had told me the club would make every effort to sign him, and I felt that if I could just get into the room alone with him, I could make a deal. I wish I'd had the authority to sign him myself. I'd have taken him fishing over at Herb Fox's strip pits during the season. I'd have whipped a contract out of my tackle box and signed him before he got off that pond. Bruce and his wife liked St. Louis, and he'd told me time and again that money wasn't the biggest thing in his life. What the hell? It's easy to say that when you're talking about the difference between $1.4 million and $1.8 million.

But then Ted Turner entered the sweepstakes. He's a man with absolutely no idea about what a ballplayer is worth because he measures talent in different ways. He's got his cable television superstation, and his Atlanta Braves are the No. 1 attraction on it. He doesn't care if the ball club loses money so long as he's got the games on television and the sponsors are buying commercials. The best way to attract sponsors is to attract viewers, and the best way to attract viewers is to put a winning ball club on the field, so he backed up an armored truck at Sutter's feet.

Turner offered Bruce the moon. With the annuities and all, the offer worked out to something like $36 million over forty years. The actual cash value was something like $9.6 million. Turner offered him everything he wanted and really put the fire to our feet. In fact, until Turner's offer was on the table, we never made what could be called a firm offer to Sutter.

His agents negotiated with Susman and Kuhlmann on Wednesday during those meetings, and I think they got pretty close. In fact, I got back to my hotel room that afternoon and found the message light blinking on the phone. Sutter had called, and when I called him back, he told me the biggest hangup was on the no-trade clause. The Cardinals had offered a modified no-trade, stipulating eight clubs that he couldn't be traded to unless they paid him $200,000.

"Whitey," Bruce said, "if you can get me four more teams on the no-trade and $800,000 on the buyout, I'll be down in the morning to sign."

So I got off the phone, went to Susman and Kuhlmann, and said, "What difference does it make if you give him eight clubs or twelve? You're not going to trade him anyway. If he's going good, you won't want to trade him—and if he's horseshit, nobody will want him."

I said I thought I could get him to settle for $500,000 on the buyout, so why didn't we just make the deal? They said they'd think it over. I went downstairs to a big dinner that CBS was having, and when I got back to my room the message light was blinking. It was Bruce again.

"What the hell is going on?" he asked when I reached him. "They just called back and withdrew the offer."

That's when I knew we'd been screwed. Bruce flew down to Atlanta and signed with the Braves, with the whole thing telecast on Turner's station. He said some nice things about Joe McDonald and me and sort of blasted Susman, which didn't help me and Joe very much. In fact, Joe got the ax about a month later, and I began to wonder whether I might be next. In fact, I kind of wondered whether the decision not to sign Sutter might have been part of a larger scheme to get rid of me. Thank God it wasn't.

From then on, everybody I met would ask me about losing Sutter and what it meant to our ball club. I told them all over again that if we stood still and didn't do anything, I'd be twenty-five games dumber. If that happened, I knew I'd be out on my ass. But I didn't intend to stand still.

I never stand still. If you're standing still, you're losing ground.

Run, Boys, Run

When people ask me what's the best baseball team I've ever managed, I tell them the Kansas City team of 1977. Lord, that was a good team, and it played like it, too, which doesn't always happen. But the more I think about what happened with the Cardinals in 1985, the more I think that they may have been the best. That was sure the most fun I've had as a manager, the perfect team for the way I like to operate.

What made the year especially satisfying was that we were supposed to be terrible, but we won the pennant instead, and we should have won the World Series. I started the year as a leading candidate, according to Bill Conlin in *The Sporting News,* to be the first manager who'd be fired. I ended the year with a new contract extension that made me one of the highest-paid managers in the game, and I picked up another Manager of the Year Award.

We had two twenty-game winners, the Rookie of the Year, and the Most Valuable Player. We stole 314 bases, becoming only the fifth club in big-league history to steal 300 bases in a season. And we had a bullpen, minus Bruce Sutter, that didn't blow a ninth-inning lead until the sixth game of the World Series—and that one wasn't all their fault.

Losing Sutter to free agency forced us to make some hard decisions and to take some gambles. Nearly all of them worked out just fine. We had some incredible strokes of good luck, and even some of our injuries turned out to be blessings in disguise. But most of all, we played hard and we played consistently, and the Cardinals became the talk of baseball.

The year started strangely, and it ended strangely, too. But in between, oh, what a time we had.

◇　◇　◇

I don't blame the writers who picked us to finish fifth or sixth in our division. They all said that losing Sutter would create big problems for us, and I knew that better than anyone. They said the front office was in turmoil, and I knew that, too. Joe McDonald had been forced to resign at the end of December, which meant that nobody was taking care of business.

I'd never seen an organization that was as screwed up as ours was when 1985 began. People would ask me about it, and I'd tell them I was just the manager, and I didn't know what was going on. But I had a pretty good idea, and I knew that something had to give or else I'd be in big trouble. A manager who thinks he can ignore what goes on in the front office in the wintertime and win ball games by sitting in a dugout in the summertime is on his way to being an ex-manager.

So, in mid-January, I called Fred Kuhlmann, who was running the club for the brewery, and I told him I had some ideas I wanted to express to him and Gussie Busch. Mr. Busch was in Florida, at his winter home in St. Petersburg, but Fred arranged the meeting. He, Lou Susman, and I met in St. Louis on January 18 and flew down to St. Pete on one of the brewery's planes.

We spent the day with Gussie and Margaret, and I took my best shots. I told them there were a lot of bad feelings toward the Cardinals around baseball, mostly because of fallout from Bowie Kuhn's losing his job. Baseball people aren't any different from anybody else—they hold grudges. Rightly or wrongly, Gussie and

Susman were being blamed for getting rid of Kuhn, and as a result, we'd lost a lot of clout with the commissioner's office.

Baseball is so goddamned political it's hard to believe. You've got factions upon factions in the league offices, the commissioner's office, and among the various team owners. So-and-so doesn't like so-and-so because of such-and-such. It's like a girl's school. Trying to get those people to get together and do something for the good of the game is damned near impossible to begin with. And with Susman as our representative at the owners meetings, with all the people who were mad at him, we didn't have a chance.

So I suggested that Kuhlmann, who is a far less political person than Susman, be our spokesman. I presented my ideas about expansion and what I call "complex baseball," which is restructuring player development. I think these ideas, which I'll explain later on, would be good for the entire game of baseball, but unless we mended our fences in the commissioner's office, we weren't going to get anywhere with them.

And then I laid my big project on them—a complete restructuring of the Cardinals' front office to deal with modern baseball economics. Put one guy in charge of the business side—ticket sales, promotions, accounting, and so forth. And on the other side, have a guy like Al Davis or Red Auerbach, a managing partner or director of baseball operations, or whatever title looks best.

This person, I said, would know the organization from top to bottom. He'd know the big-league team and every prospect in the minor-league system. He'd always be thinking a couple of years down the road, keeping in mind contracts and trades, trying to keep the talent flowing upward at a reasonable budget figure. Who are the keepers? Who can we get rid of? Who's overrated and what's the best time to get rid of him, and for what?

This person would be in charge of the manager and the coaches, the traveling secretary and the player development people. He'd have the final word on contract negotiations and on all player personnel decisions. He'd be given full authority by ownership, and if things didn't work out, there'd be no doubt about whose fault it was. No more committees, no more finger-pointing. Fish or cut bait, or you're out on your ass.

Well, I said all these things, and after we had talked a while, Gussie got me over in a corner, and he growled, "Goddammit, Whitey. Why don't you just take that job?"

That really took me by surprise. I asked him for time to think about it, to talk it over with my wife. He didn't say anything to the others about it, and obviously I didn't either. After we flew back to St. Louis that evening, I got back in my car and drove 240 miles west toward home.

All the way home I thought about how much I liked managing and how much I didn't want to work over the winter. I figured they wouldn't want to pay me what I was making as a manager to do a front-office job, even that big a job.

But at the same time, I knew that unless we straightened ourselves out, we were going straight downhill anyway, and I knew who'd get fired over it. So I called Margaret Busch a couple of days later and told her that her husband had asked me if I wanted the job. I told her I'd like to talk about it some more, but we never did. I never heard any more about it, and maybe that's just as well. I don't think Kuhlmann and Susman were too crazy about the idea, and things worked out pretty well anyway.

They wound up hiring Dal Maxvill to replace Joe McDonald as general manager, and although I had my doubts about him when he was hired, he turned out to be a hell of a baseball executive. Maxie had played shortstop for the Cardinals for ten years and then had gone on to coach with the Mets and the Braves. He'd never made a trade, never negotiated a contract, and I wondered what the hell was going through their minds when they hired him.

But Maxie is smart, and he caught on fast. We got along great, and since he won a pennant in his first year, he must be a terrific general manager.

Even so, I think that one of these days some baseball team is going to try operating the front office the way I suggested. If they get the right guy on the job, give him enough time, and stay the hell out of his way, they'll win themselves a couple of pennants, and everyone will say how smart they are. I hope I'm still around to say, "I told you so."

◇   ◇   ◇

By the time spring training started, I had changed my mind about our finishing in last place. I'd been telling writers who asked that we could finish anywhere from first to last, but by the opening of camp on February 26, I was saying I still didn't know where we'd finish, but it wouldn't be last. There were two reasons for that. One was named Jack Clark and the other was named John Tudor.

Jack Clark is one of the great power hitters and RBI men in baseball today, one of those guys you stick in the cleanup spot and then build your lineup around. He'd been in the big leagues with the San Francisco Giants since 1977, and I'd always wondered what it would be like to write his name down on my lineup card.

We went after Jack Clark hammer and tong in the winter of 1984–85. By the middle of the season in 1984, when our hitting was miserable, I'd begun thinking that we really had to get ourselves a big bat in the fourth slot in the lineup. George Hendrick wasn't producing the way he'd done in the past, and neither was Darrell Porter.

Our whole game was geared to getting the jackrabbits at the top of the lineup on base and then having someone drive them in with a shot in the gap. But without an RBI threat, that game doesn't work. The guys start pressing, trying to do things they can't. And with Sutter gone, we needed a big bat in the middle of the lineup more than ever. Bruce was a gold mine in one-run games, but without Bruce, I knew we'd need to get runs in bunches if we could. So part of my preparation for life after Sutter was to get that big, aggressive hitter.

Another part of the preparation was getting a solid No. 2 starting pitcher. In our division, we were always faced with going into a three-game series with our pitching overmatched in at least one —and usually two—of the games. We'd go into Philadelphia and they'd send out Steve Carlton and John Denny. Or to Chicago against Rick Sutcliffe and Dennis Eckersley. Or to New York against Dwight Gooden and Ron Darling. Against them, I'd have Andujar and crossed fingers. The other guys on the team tend to play better, more confidently, when they think your pitcher is going to keep them in a game. Too many times in 1983 and 1984, our guys would play like one team behind Andujar and like a whole different team behind whoever else we sent out there.

I had high hopes for a young pitcher named Danny Cox in 1985, but I didn't know if he'd be good enough to be the No. 2 guy behind Joaquin. So when the Pirates came shopping around in December, we made a deal for Tudor. He'd been 12–11 for them in 1984, but I knew he was a smart pitcher. He'd spent most of his career in Boston, and left-handers who pitch in Fenway Park, with that short left field, have to be smart or they get killed. A left-hander in Boston who makes a mistake inside to a right-handed hitter can spend a lot of time watching the ball sail over the Green Monster in left field. I figured that John Tudor would be a hell of a pitcher in a big park like ours, with a shortstop and outfielders like ours behind him.

To get Tudor, we gave up George Hendrick, who, despite what people say about him, is a hell of a good guy. George was one of the first professional athletes to stop talking to reporters, and as a result, a lot of writers ripped him. I think players ought to talk to the press because it usually does a lot more good than harm. But if they don't want to, I figure it's their business—as long as they are good guys around the clubhouse and play hard on the field.

George Hendrick did that. He was one of the leaders on our club. He drove in runs and he was a smart hitter, and he was one of the best defensive right fielders in the game. When he played, he played hard. The trouble was that in the last couple of years he played for me, he wanted to play less and less. He knew the pitchers he could hit and the ones he couldn't, and he'd ask out of games against guys he didn't want to face. He didn't want to face Joe or Phil Niekro, or Dwight Gooden, or Don Gullickson, or Rick Rhoden. He didn't like to play in Candlestick Park in San Francisco or in Wrigley Field in Chicago. Now, I don't mind sitting a guy down against a pitcher who's tough on him. Why hang an 0 for 4 on him? Why not get the extra men some at-bats? But with George, I was looking at the prospect of going into the season with my No. 4 hitter missing sixty games. So it was time for George to go. We sent him to Pittsburgh for Tudor and Brian Harper, a utility player who did a good job for us in 1985.

With Hendrick gone, we stepped up the campaign for Clark, the same kind of hitter George had been, only better. We knew he was unhappy in San Francisco, playing in that disgraceful ballpark of theirs. The Giants were down on him because he was unhappy there, so we made them an offer they couldn't refuse: four for one. We sent them Dave LaPoint, a left-hander whom we could afford to part with since we had Tudor; David Green, whom we finally had to give up on; Jose Gonzales, the top shortstop in the minor leagues; and a minor-league first baseman named Gary Rajsich.

Gonzales, who changed his name to Jose Uribe for reasons I never have quite understood, was someone we hated to give up, but he was the key to the deal for the Giants. After the 1985 season, they traded La Point and Green back to the American League, and Rajsich wound up in Japan, so Gonzales/Uribe was the only one left. Trading him created another problem for us.

Ozzie Smith was in the walk year of his contract in 1985, and without Gonzales, we didn't have another shortstop in the system. So we picked up Argenis Salazar from the Expos as compensation for Sutter, and later we made deals for Ivan De Jesus of the Phillies and Jose Oquendo of the Mets. After Ozzie re-signed, we had the shortstop market cornered.

But all of this shows how much you need a careful game plan, and a man in charge who's thinking about things like this. You trade a Hendrick to get a Tudor, but that means you have to get a Clark, even if it leaves you without a shortstop for the future, so you make another deal. The whole thing goes round and round, and unless you're on top of it, it'll cost you badly.

◇   ◇   ◇

We left St. Petersburg to open the season in New York on April 9, and I felt pretty good about what we'd accomplished. I thought we had a pretty good lineup—good enough to be respectable, play .500 or better, and challenge for the pennant if we got the breaks. The big question was the bullpen, and it went sour right away.

The big guy out there was supposed to be Neil Allen, the right-hander we'd gotten in the Hernandez deal. I had hoped he'd settle down and be the stopper, but I was also counting on giving him a lot of help. I didn't think he'd save forty-five games like Sutter, but I thought that he and the other guys in the pen might combine for forty saves or so, and that might be enough.

It didn't take long for that plan to go out the window. Allen gave up an extra-inning home run to the Mets' Gary Carter to lose the season opener. In the second game, he walked in the winning run, and after that, his confidence was shot. A relief pitcher without confidence is like tits on a boar hog. Neil Allen, a fine young man with a live arm and a great curveball, kept expecting disaster to strike, and it usually did.

Having lost both games in New York, we proceeded to lose the next two in Pittsburgh and went to 0–4. Joaquin got us our first win there, and then we came home. Bob Forsch, who'd been hurt nearly all year during 1984, gave us nine innings and we won the home opener. Ozzie Smith, who'd signed a new contract that day, celebrated by hitting one of his rare home runs, and I thought we were off and running.

A word here about Ozzie's contract, because it has gotten an awful lot of attention. We gave him four years at $2 million a year, and everybody said we were destroying baseball by paying that much money to a one-dimensional ballplayer. The brewery, having lost Sutter, gave Ozzie everything he wanted because of the public relations problems that losing him would create.

Whether Ozzie Smith, or any ballplayer, is worth $2 million a year is not for me to say. All I know about Ozzie is that in addition to being a gentleman and the greatest defensive shortstop ever to play the game, he's also a bear-down ballplayer. He played the last six weeks of the 1985 season with a torn rotator cuff muscle in his throwing arm, and it hurt him like hell every time he made a throw. But he never griped, never complained, and that's the kind of player who wins pennants.

After he signed his contract, he seemed to relax a little bit, and the team started playing a little better. Then McGee, our center fielder, aggravated a hamstring muscle, and Tito Landrum, our fourth outfielder, pulled a muscle in his side. I thought, uh-oh, here we go. I really thought this would be the start of a series of injuries that would doom us.

Dal Maxvill and I talked it over and decided to bring up a kid outfielder from Louisville to fill in for a week. The kid had been with us in the spring, but the consensus was that he wasn't ready to hit big-league pitching yet—and we sent him out. Dal brought the kid up, sat him down in his office, and explained that he shouldn't get his hopes up, that he'd only be here for a week.

Vince Coleman looked at Dal and told him, very politely, that he planned to stay a lot longer than that.

◇   ◇   ◇

Vince got that right. I kept him out of the lineup the first day he showed up but put him out there the next night against the Pirates. Vince Coleman took the fans, the opposition, and the whole town by storm. He stole two bases, the first of what would turn out to be 110 on the year, and got the game-winning hit off John Candelaria, one of the toughest left-handers in baseball. He ignited our ball club and was absolutely the key to our season.

From that night on, we were the talk of baseball. Everybody wanted to see Vince Coleman, who'd stolen 145 bases in Single-A ball in 1983, 101 in Triple-A in 1984, and wasn't slowing down a bit in the big leagues. I put him in the leadoff spot, dropped McGee down to second, which is his natural slot, and put Tommy Herr in the third slot ahead of Jack Clark in the four-hole. Vince's confidence on the bases seemed to energize Willie, who may be even faster than Coleman but lacks his brazen attitude. Tommy had the discipline to take pitches and let those guys run, and he was bright enough to know that with Clark behind him, he was going to get good pitches to hit. Herr, whose best RBI production in any previous year was 49, started driving in runs in bunches and so did Clark. They were battling for the RBI lead for most of the summer. Tommy wound up with 110 RBIs and Jack had 87 despite being injured the last month of the season.

It was the damnedest transformation I've ever seen. We started playing good baseball, and in mid-May, we began playing very good baseball. We came back from six runs behind to beat San Diego on May 16, and from that day on, we were something to behold. Andujar was winning every time out; and Tudor, after losing seven of his first eight starts, put together a 20–1 record. Cox was pitching well, and that gave us a Big Three which was the equal of any team's in baseball. Kurt Kepshire, our fourth starter, pitched pretty well in the first half of the season, but the key to the staff was the bullpen.

Someone started calling it the "bullpen by committee," which is a cute way of saying everybody got a shot at it and everybody did his job. If you've got the big reliever, like Sutter, out there, it makes the job easier. All you've got to do is get to the eighth inning and turn things over to him. But if you don't have the stopper, you have to have righty-lefty balance, two capable left-handers and two strong right-handers. That way you can use a lefty in the seventh to get you an out, and the other manager knows he hasn't got you over a barrel because you've got another lefty to throw at him. In Rick Horton, I had a left-hander who could get us an early out or two, and with Ken Dayley, I had a hard-throwing left-hander who could finish a game. I had Bill Campbell, a right-handed screwball pitcher, who could get us through the sixth or seventh, and Jeff Lahti, a hard-throwing right-hander, who could close. Later on in the season, we added right-hander Todd Worrell and left-hander Pat Perry from the Louisville club, and at that point, we had what may have been the best bullpen in history.

We were cruising, playing our game, putting people in the parks all around the National League. I've never had as much fun watching a team play baseball. We stole 314 bases, scratched out runs, found ways to win. In one game in Chicago, Vince and Willie put together the first double–double steal in baseball history. First they stole third and second, and when Vince overslid the bag and got into a rundown between third and the plate, Willie kept on coming to third. But Vince beat the rundown and got credited with a steal of home.

Defensively, Terry Pendleton and Ozzie Smith gave us the best left side in baseball, and nobody has ever had a faster or better defensive outfield than Coleman, McGee, and Andy Van Slyke. We went to Chicago in mid-June, before the Cubs' pitching staff was decimated, and swept them three straight. I think that's when our guys figured out that they could go all the way.

The only blight on the horizon was the possibility of another strike by the Players' Association. At first it was thought the strike would come at the All-Star break, and then it was pushed back to August 5. Having been screwed out of a division title by the strike in 1981, I sure didn't want it to happen again.

It turned out, of course, that the 1985 strike lasted only two days, and we made up both games. And even the strike was a lucky break for us. We'd been dragging at the end of July and into early August. The guys were tired, and when we ended a long road trip with a fourteen-inning loss to Chicago on August 1 and came home to lose three of four to the Phillies right before the strike, I thought we might be in deep trouble.

But the guys bounced back after those two days of rest like they'd been at a health spa. And even though Joaquin suddenly couldn't win a game to save his life, we got back on a roll. Andujar mystified me. He won his twentieth game in early August, and then he won only one more the rest of the year. His name had been brought into the testimony at the drug trials in Pittsburgh, and that was on his mind. But even early in the season, when he was winning, I didn't think he'd been pitching as well as he had the year before. We were scoring a lot of runs for him, and he was leaving games in the sixth and seventh innings with big leads and letting the bullpen finish. His arm may have been tired because he was dropping down and throwing from the side more and more. Any little thing that went wrong would send him into a frenzy. He had me baffled, and I began to wonder how long we could afford to keep him around.

In a way, considering his troubles, it was a miracle that we managed to win the pennant. Kepshire wasn't pitching well, which left us with Tudor and Cox as the only dependable starters. If it hadn't been for Bob Forsch and Rick Horton stepping in and doing the job as spot starters, we never would have made it because the Mets were right on our tails.

And speaking of miracles. In late August, on our second trip into Atlanta, Jack Clark swung and missed at a pitch and pulled a muscle deep in his left side. That's a nasty injury for a baseball player because the simple act of swinging a bat aggravates it. The only cure is rest, and that was a costly cure heading down the stretch.

The miracle was that we headed from Atlanta to Cincinnati, and I had breakfast with Jim Kaat, who was working as the pitching coach for the Reds. Kaat told me that Cesar Cedeño might be available to us, to fill in for Clark. Cesar was on the outs with Pete Rose, the Reds' manager; he wasn't playing much, wasn't earning the big salary the Reds were paying him.

Cedeño had been one of the best players in baseball for ten years, a triple-threat guy who could run, hit, and throw. Injuries had slowed him down a little bit, and so had some attitude problems, but Kaat said he thought he could still play. He was thirty-four, in the last year of a contract, and he wanted a chance to prove he could still play.

We gave the Reds a minor-league prospect for him and assumed the last six weeks of his salary. I told the writers if he got just one hit for us, he'd be worth the gamble. Well, just like Coleman had ignited us after coming up to replace an injured player, so did Cedeño. He hit a home run his first time up as a Cardinal and went on a hitting tear. In twenty-eight games, he hit .434 for us with 6 homers and 19 RBIs, and we never would have won the division without him.

The other thing that helped us was the fact that the Cubs and the Pirates both had such miserable years. The Cubs lost all of their starting pitchers to injuries, and we just beat them like a drum all year long. The Pirates were racked with problems all year long, and we beat up on them, too. We were 14–4 against the Cubs and 15–3 against the Pirates. What's more, we were 10–2 against the Giants and 9–3 against the Braves. That's 48–12—.800 baseball—against four clubs, and you really can't expect to do that in many years.

The Mets won 98 games and still finished second. I wouldn't mind winning 98 games every year—I'd win a lot of pennants.

We needed every one of our 101 victories, as it turned out. The Mets came to St. Louis for three games on the first three days of October, trailing us by three with six to play. The strange thing was I kept reading in the paper how their players were saying that the pressure was on us. I never did figure out how a team that was three games behind could be in the driver's seat, but that's the New York press for you.

The Mets did make it interesting, though. Tudor hooked up with Ron Darling in the first game, and those two guys pitched one of the best baseball games I've ever seen, throwing zeroes at each other for nine innings. I finally had to pinch-hit for John, and Davey Johnson sent Jesse Orosco in for Darling. We lost it in the eleventh when Darryl Strawberry broke the scoreboard clock in right field with a monstrous home run off Ken Dayley.

The next night, Gooden beat Andujar, and the Mets were really chortling then. They had cut our lead to one game, with four to play, and they thought we were on the ropes. But Danny Cox gave us an outstanding effort the next night, and we got the lead back to two games with three to go. Forsch beat the Cubs the next night, and Tudor won his twenty-first on Saturday afternoon to clinch the pennant for us.

What a great season John Tudor had. I knew he'd be a good pitcher for us, but I sure as hell didn't know he'd win twenty-one games and finish second to Gooden in the Cy Young voting. Willie McGee, who hit .353 for us, won the Most Valuable Player Award, which proved to everybody else what I'd been saying for years—

he is one of the best players in baseball. And Vince Coleman, who'd turned our team around, was Rookie of the Year.

Not only had we played better baseball than any team in the league, we had played a different kind of baseball than the twenty-five other teams in the majors. We had used speed as an offensive weapon at least as devastating as a home run. We rattled pitchers, made things happen, we played good defense, and we outpitched them.

What I didn't know as we prepared to meet the Dodgers in the playoffs was that we had decided to abandon that style of baseball and play like everybody else. If I'd known that, I never would have gotten on the plane to L.A.

◇　◇　◇

The format for the playoffs was changed from best-of-five to best-of-seven in 1985, and I approve of that. Seven games is a fairer test of a pitching staff than five games. But I didn't think the change would help us any. We were still operating with only two dependable starting pitchers, and there was no way I could pitch Tudor and Cox in all seven games.

The Dodgers, on the other hand, were rich with starting pitching, as they usually are. They always give us fits. We'd lost seven of the twelve games we played against them in the regular season, and going back over the past few years, they were usually able to beat us two of three every time they tried. They had two good left-handers in Fernando Valenzuela and Jerry Reuss, and two good, hard-throwing right-handers in Orel Hershiser, whose name I can spell but not pronounce, and Bob Welsh. I figured we could do OK if we got into their bullpen, but I didn't know if we could get that far.

The Dodgers were the most improved club in the National League in 1985. They had been a miserable defensive team for years, but they'd turned that around a little bit when they found a kid named Mariano Duncan to play short. They'd helped themselves by getting Bill Madlock from the Pirates late in the season. Madlock, a great hitter, had been dogging it with the Pirates, like most of Pittsburgh's other players. But he'd come on strong in L.A. and looked like the Madlock of old.

I didn't know if we could handle them, and it sure didn't look like it when we lost the first two games in their park. We came home for Game Three, and I was really worried. Welsh started for them, and he'd been their best pitcher against us. But he got rattled by the speed on the bases, they threw a couple of balls away, and we beat them. I felt a whole lot better. We'd gotten our "Speed kills" game back in gear, and I figured if we got the pitching, we'd be all right.

But the next night, we got hit with one of the all-time weirdest injuries in baseball history. It was cloudy and cool in St. Louis, and a light rain started to fall right before batting practice. The grounds crew was ordered to roll the tarp over the infield. At Busch Stadium, the tarp is kept rolled up on a long tube that's stored underground along the first-base side of the field. When it rains, they push a button, a portion of the Astro-Turf opens up, and the tarp pops up out of the ground. There's a motorized tractor on the outfield end of the tube; someone on the grounds crew pushes a button, and the tractor starts moving at one mile an hour, unrolling the tarp as it goes. It's a fast, efficient way to get the field covered in a hurry.

While the grounds crew was knocking down the batting cage and getting the tarp out of the ground, our players were heading in and out of the dugout. Some of them were headed toward left field, where we have a batting cage under the stands. They were hopping over the tarp like they usually do. Vince Coleman came toward the dugout and stopped near the plate to toss his glove to someone before he headed out to take some swings in the cage. And the damned tarp rolled over his leg, knocked him down, and rolled right up his leg before they could get it stopped.

Vince was scared out of his mind. Who wouldn't be, being attacked by a tarp? We got the damned thing off him and carried him into the trainer's room. Gene Gieselmann, our fine trainer, and Stan London, the team doctor, examined him and X-rayed him. They thought he was just shaken up, and he'd only miss a day or two. But when the leg didn't heal, they X-rayed him again with a more sophisticated machine and found a chip fracture. Coleman was through for the year.

Talk about one of the oddities that will go down in baseball history—the fastest guy in the game being run down by a one-mile-an-hour tarp. Nobody could believe it, least of all Vince.

For a while, though, it looked like it was another of those injuries that worked out for our benefit. Tito Landrum, a right-handed hitter who'd been platooning with Van Slyke in right field, started in Coleman's spot in left. He got four hits in the game, we got nine runs in the second inning, and we won Game Four in a walkover to tie the series at 2–2. The next day the weirdness continued. Because Coleman was injured, McGee was leading off and Ozzie was hitting second instead of eighth. Ozzie came up in the ninth, with the game tied 2–2, hitting left-handed against Tom Niedenfuer, the big right-handed Dodgers' reliever. Until that moment, Ozzie had never hit a big league home run swinging left-handed. Hell, he'd only hit thirteen right-handed. But he took Niedenfuer over the right field wall and we won again.

So we headed back for the coast, up three games to two, and Tommy Lasorda made a mistake. They had us down, 5–4, in the ninth inning, with Niedenfuer trying to nail it down. McGee got a one-out single and stole second. Ozzie walked. Herr moved them to second and third with a ground ball out to the right side. That brought Jack Clark to the plate with two out and a base open— the ideal place for an intentional walk.

Van Slyke, a left-handed hitter, was on deck. If Tommy walks Clark and brings in a lefty to pitch to Andy, I would have countered with Brian Harper, the only right-handed pinch-hitter I had left. I would rather let Brian Harper try to beat me than Jack Clark, but what the hell? A manager has to go with what's in his gut, and we've all been wrong now and again. Tommy told Niedenfuer to pitch to Clark.

Jack Clark, the best clutch fastball hitter in baseball, hit Niedenfuer's first pitch high into the left-field pavilion for a three-run homer that gave us the lead, 7–5. Dayley blew 'em down in the ninth, and we were the National League Champions.

We should have stopped right there.

◇   ◇   ◇

We lost the World Series to the Kansas City Royals, as everyone knows, after being up three games to one, after winning the first two games on the road, after being three outs away from winning the damned thing in the sixth game. I got kicked out of Game Seven, my starting pitcher in that game smashed his hand into an electric fan, my other "ace" pitcher charged an umpire and became the butt of jokes around the country. What a mess.

I'd give anything if it hadn't happened like that. I regret like hell not being able to take another World Championship home to Gussie Busch and to the people of St. Louis. The only consolation for me was seeing how happy it made the people of Kansas City, my hometown. I'd played there in the minors, I'd played, coached, and managed there in the majors. Kansas City has been my home, the place where I raised my kids, and the people have been so good to me. They'd been in the big leagues for thirty years without a champion, and if we couldn't win it, I'm glad they did.

My biggest regret was that the people who watched the World Series didn't see the true St. Louis Cardinals. We just didn't play our brand of baseball. Coleman's injury took the flash out of our offense. Nobody did the things they do best, and everyone was trying to do things he wasn't capable of. Ozzie Smith, after his homer off Niedenfuer, was swinging like Babe Ruth but not hitting them nearly so far. Willie was pressing, Tommy was pressing. Cedeño's shot had worn off. We were playing baseball like everyone else. We scored thirteen runs in seven games and hit .185. That's the reason we lost the World Series.

I really had a bad feeling about it going in, even though I liked the idea of playing in Royals Stadium. It's a big park, with the same kind of Astro-Turf surface as Busch Stadium's. I felt that for the first time there'd be no home field advantage in the Series. I'd been worried about playing the Toronto Blue Jays, whom the

Royals had defeated in the playoffs. I didn't like the idea of playing all night games in the Canadian weather. I was also worried about the travel hassles in and out of Canada.

The press made a big thing out of my "coming home" to Kansas City, trying to get me into a public feud with Ewing and Muriel Kauffman. All I said was that I admire their organization, which I do, and that it would be nice sleeping in my own bed, which it was. I did get a chance to get to a couple of Kansas City Chiefs football games, which I couldn't have done in Toronto.

The oddsmakers made us a big favorite, but I didn't buy it. I knew the Royals had outstanding pitching, especially left-handed. I knew in the back of my mind that all season long we'd been vulnerable to left-handers. We weren't much better than .500 against lefties, and the Royals had three good left-handed starters, and a right-hander, Bret Saberhagen, who won the Cy Young Award. In the bullpen they had the great submariner, Dan Quisenberry. I watched their games against Toronto, another club that had trouble with southpaws, and I got a bad, bad feeling.

But John Tudor pitched an outstanding game for us in the opener in Kansas City, and we came back with a ninth-inning rally to take the second game. There we were, up two games to none and heading home for three. Everyone kept telling me how no team had ever lost the series after winning the first two on the road. I wanted to tell them to stick around. We were playing horseshit baseball, not hitting worth a damn, and I had Andujar going with an American League umpire behind the plate in the third game.

The third game was the key to the series. I don't ever want to question the integrity of the umpires, but I've looked at the tape of that game time and again, and it just confirms what I thought looking at it from the dugout: there were two different strike zones in that game. Saberhagen's was about two feet wide; he had the black edges of the plate and then some. Andujar's strike zone was about eight inches wide. Anything he threw on the corners was called a ball. We got beat 6–1, and I was really starting to sweat.

But Tudor had another outstanding outing in the fifth game and we won, 3–1, going up three games to one. It was then that the weakness of our pitching staff showed up. Cox was nursing a tender elbow, so I didn't want to pitch him on three days rest. I gave the ball to Forsch, and he didn't have a damned thing. We got beat 6–1 again, and we headed back west on Interstate 70 for the now infamous Game Six.

Cox pitched a tough, gutty game. But so did their guy, Charlie Leibrandt. It was scoreless into the seventh, but we finally got a run when Harper, hitting for Cox, came through with the biggest hit of his life. I thought Brian Harper was going to be a hero because Ken Dayley breezed through the Royals in the seventh and eighth, and I had Todd Worrell ready for the ninth.

Worrell had started the season as a starting pitcher in Louisville, but Jim Fregosi, the manager there, and Darold Knowles, our minor-league pitching coach, converted him into a short reliever. And the kid was just spectacular. He's about 6′ 5″ and throws 94 miles an hour. We brought him up to the big leagues in late August, and he showed me he has the potential to be the next great relief pitcher in the big leagues.

Todd got Jorge Orta to hit a ground ball to Clark at first. Jack was a little hesitant on the play, but he got off a good throw to Worrell covering at first. The throw beat Orta by half a step, a close play but the kind of play the umpire calls right 999 out of 1,000 times. This was the thousandth time. Don Denkinger, the umpire at first, missed the call. Millions of people around the country saw the replay on television, and they knew he missed it. Denkinger later admitted he blew it.

It wasn't funny then, but it is now. Here's Donny Denkinger, a guy I've known for years and a guy I regard as one of the top five or six umpires in the major leagues. A veteran umpire, he misses one call, and suddenly he's famous. He gets a big write-up in *Sports Illustrated* and the newspapers all for making a mistake.

And here's the Cardinals, a team that hasn't lost a game in the ninth inning all year, a team that hasn't had a bad call, pro or con, in the ninth inning all year. And in our 174th game of the year, it catches up with us. Suddenly we can't do anything right. Clark misses a foul pop off Steve Balboni's bat, giving Balboni another shot, and he singles to left. Porter lunges at a slider, misses it, and the runners advance to third and second. Hal McRae comes up, and we walk him to load the bases.

And then here comes Dane Iorg, one of my favorite people, a guy who hit .541 for the Cardinals in the 1982 series. He flares a ball to right field that scores two runs. We lose the game, and deep in my heart, I knew we'd lost the Series.

I very seldom take a ball game home with me. I usually go home, have something to eat, watch a little television, and hit the sack. I'm asleep in five minutes. But I took the sixth game home with me, sat up late talking about it with Mary Lou and the kids. I knew we had had it.

◇   ◇   ◇

The seventh game was a nightmare. I told a couple of writers before the game that I had a bad feeling about it. The players all had their heads on their chest. There was no fire in their eyes. I called a meeting before the game, tried to give them a pep talk. I hardly ever do that, and I guess my lack of practice showed. We had nothing.

John Tudor had finally run out of gas. He'd pitched magnificently for us all year, including the playoffs and the Series, but he didn't have it in the seventh game. He couldn't get his change-up over, and they sat on his fastball. When I came out and got him, he walked into the dugout and, in frustration, smashed his hand into an electric fan and cut it pretty badly.

The Royals scored early, and they scored often. By the fifth inning, they were up 9–0. The only pitcher I had left in the bullpen with any life in his arm was Joaquin Andujar.

He had told me he was ready to pitch if I needed him. Some people later said I was looking for trouble by bringing him in, using a twenty-one-game winner as a mop-up guy. But Joaquin wanted to pitch, maybe to show me I'd been wrong not to bring him back in the sixth game.

As luck would have it, Denkinger was behind the plate. It didn't make any difference. Jesus Christ could have been behind the plate and Joaquin wouldn't have been happy. Denkinger called the first pitch a ball, and Joaquin got pissed off. He walked toward the plate, motioning for Porter to come out to the mound. Denkinger thought Joaquin was hassling him, so he came out from behind the plate and said something to Joaquin. I popped out of the dugout and suggested, kindly, that he get his ass back behind the plate. By then I was fed up.

"We wouldn't even be here if you hadn't missed the fucking call last night," I said. And he gave me the old heave-ho. That was OK. I'd seen enough.

The dust had barely settled from that argument when Joaquin threw another pitch, his last one as a Cardinal, as it turned out. It was high and inside, and Denkinger called it a ball. Joaquin went into a frenzy, charged Donny, and had to be restrained by some of our guys. Denkinger threw him out of the game, too, and Commissioner Peter Ueberroth later fined him and gave him a ten-day suspension . . . something about embarrassing baseball's finest hour.

The brewery was embarrassed, too. It's been reported that Maxvill and I were ordered to trade Joaquin, and I won't deny that. I will say, though, that he might well have been traded anyway. The other players were tired of his griping and his bitching, and it had gotten to the point where he was dividing the clubhouse. We sent him to Oakland after the season for catcher Mike Heath and a young pitcher named Tim Conroy.

At any rate, we lost the final game, 11–0. I talked with Ueberroth at the winter meetings and got a few things off my mind. I told him, and everyone else I met, that the Cardinals, aside from the final score, really had nothing to be embarrassed about.

All winter long, people would come up to me and say things like, "Too bad, better luck next year." And I'd say what the hell? Remember us? We were supposed to finish last. I was going to be fired. Our ball club won 108 games. McGee was the MVP and

Coleman was the Rookie of the Year. We put 2,662,875 people in the seats at home and drew close to 1.9 million on the road. We made it to the seventh game of the World Series.

Next year, hell. I'd take that every year.

"Amazing . . ."

Those of you with long memories will recall that this book started a long time back, on an afternoon at Shea Stadium in New York. My club had just beaten the Mets in their home opener for the 1986 season. As it turned out, this was not an omen. Beating the Mets was something that we and everyone else in the league had trouble doing for the rest of the year. That day in New York turned out to be pretty much the high watermark of the Cardinals' entire year.

The Mets had an amazing season. They had four great starting pitchers, two great relief pitchers, and a lineup that was like a hitting buzzsaw. They won 108 ball games, took on the Houston Astros in the playoffs, and beat the Boston Red Sox in the World Series.

Amazing as the Mets were, the Cardinals may have been more amazing. Of the thirty-seven years I've been in professional baseball, the 1986 season with the Cardinals was the strangest. Our club went from winning 101 regular-season games in 1985 and getting to the seventh game of the World Series to a club that, for a while at least, was the worst in baseball. For a good half year, our club couldn't do anything right.

We had veteran players—some of the biggest stars in the game

—who seemed to forget how the game is supposed to be played. We couldn't hit, we couldn't field, we couldn't throw. We had injuries, we had bitterness and backbiting in the clubhouse. By the time the All-Star Game rolled around at midseason, we were two dozen games out of first place and way, way out of the pennant race. We had gone from the penthouse to the outhouse faster than any team in the history of the game. There were times I thought we'd be the first team ever to win 100 games one year and lose 100 the next.

And then we kind of turned it around, got respectable again in the second half of the season. The same team that was 36–50 before the All-Star Game was 43–32 after it. It was a crazy, crazy year —a year which proved all over again that just when you think you've seen everything the game of baseball has to offer, you ain't seen nothing yet. It was a year when I tried every trick in the manager's book, trying to find something which would work, try- ing to cover up for all the injuries, trying to get a fire started. In a way, it was kind of fun trying to come up with a lineup every night which might have a chance of winning.

I kept all kinds of notes during the year, and the only way I know to explain how strange it all was is to put it down as it happened. It's the most amazing diary you've ever seen.

May 5

I don't know what's going on here. We've got an off-day here today, and maybe I can use it to figure it all out. The ballclub is nine and thirteen, four games under .500, but we've lost ten out of the last twelve. We're twenty-two games into the season and already we've had a five-game losing streak and a six-game losing streak. We're already eight games out of first place. The Mets are hot, scoring a lot of runs, hitting the ball the way I thought they'd hit it last year. And we can't hit worth a damn.

I can't figure it out. We hit pretty well during the last week of spring training, which is when you start playing your regular lineup and letting them tune up. The bad thing about spring training is that Danny Cox, who won eighteen games for us last year, jumped off a three-foot sea wall on his way fishing one day and broke a bone in his ankle. He missed the first couple of weeks and still hasn't come into form. Jeff Lahti, who had nineteen saves for us last year, came up with arm trouble in the spring, and I'm beginning to wonder if he'll pitch at all this year. I had counted on Lahti as the right-handed set-up man in the bullpen, the guy I'd use until I could get to Todd Worrell in the eighth or ninth inning. Lahti's a good jam pitcher, the kind of guy who can come in and strike out a batter with the bases loaded and nobody out. If he doesn't come back, and if Cox doesn't come around, we could be in deep trouble. We may be in deep trouble anyway.

The thing is, we're just not hitting. The team batting average is .204. Willie McGee and Tommy Herr are really struggling, and if they don't hit close to their lifetime batting averages, there's no way we can generate much offense. They're the number two and three guys in the lineup, and if they're not on base, there won't be any runs to drive in. My new catcher, Mike Heath, has four hits in 56 at-bats and still doesn't have a hit off a right-handed pitcher.

I'm beginning to wonder if it's a carryover from the World Series last year, when we hit .185. We started the season by winning seven out of eight ball games, but we were getting good pitching and winning games with only three or four hits. We had some rainouts and off-days, so I could pitch John Tudor four times in the first ten games, but we couldn't get away with that for long.

After we won that extra-inning game against the Mets in New York, our record was 5–1. Then we had an off-day and two days of rain at Shea Stadium, so we'll have to play two doubleheaders against them in August. I was worried about that at first, but hell, the way we're playing now, we could be buried by then.

We went from New York to Montreal, won the first two there, but got shut out, 2–0, on Sunday. We went down to Chicago, got rained out on Monday, lost 3–2 on Tuesday, and Scott Sanderson shut us out again on Wednesday. Then we went home for four games with the Mets, and we lost every one of them. The real cruncher was the first game, when we blew a 4–2 lead in the ninth inning. Worrell gave up a two-run homer to Howard Johnson to tie it, and the Mets beat us in the tenth. Last year we went all the way to the sixth game of the World Series before the bullpen blew a game in the ninth inning.

Dwight Gooden handed us our third shutout in five games the next day. The way Mr. Gooden is going—and the way baseball salaries are going—he'll be the richest man in the world by the time he's thirty. Sid Fernandez beat us the next day, Bob Ojeda beat us on Sunday, and all of a sudden we'd lost seven in a row. Then we went out to the West Coast and damn near made it eight in a row. The Cardinals seem to have trouble on the West Coast even when we're going good, so it's a hell of a place to visit when we're going bad.

We blew another two-run lead in the ninth to the Giants on Monday night, but got two in the twelfth to win it. The bullpen made it interesting, though. They walked three guys to load the bases with two out in the bottom of the twelfth. I went out to change pitchers and told the umpire I was going to hang myself if we blew it again.

Lucky for me the wind was blowing. The Giants' Dan Gladden hit a fly ball to the wall in left which the wind at Candlestick kept in the park, and we finally won one.

I thought that might turn us around, but damned if Mike LaCoss, a right-hander who's one of Roger Craig's reclamation projects with the Giants, doesn't shut us out, 2–0, on three hits. I thought that was as bad as we could get, but we went down to San Diego and got shut out again, this time on a one-hitter by Mark Thurmond. At least then I knew we'd have to get beat by a no-hitter to look any worse.

We lost one more to the Padres, then went into L.A. for three games. In three straight games there our pitchers gave up three runs, but we only won one game. Fernando Valenzuela shut us out in one of them, for our sixth shutout of the year.

We finally won one yesterday, on Sunday, when Bob Forsch gave us six good innings and the bullpen held on.

We're just not playing well in any phase of the game, mentally or physically. Andy Van Slyke cost us a couple of runs with poor baserunning in the extra-inning loss to the Mets. The great Ozzie Smith threw away a double-play ball which hurt us in another game. McGee let a fly ball get over his head in center field. Heath is not only hitting .093, but he's giving up a lot of passed balls and has made some bad throws which have hurt us. Vince Coleman has decided he's got the greatest arm in baseball and is trying to throw everyone out at the plate instead of throwing the ball into second base to keep the double play in order.

We're missing signs, swinging at balls over our heads, not getting the bunt down when we need it, generally playing stupid baseball. We're the kind of team that has to do the fundamental things right because we don't have the long-ball hitters to make up for our mistakes.

And the frustration is starting to set in. Guys see the Mets winning night after night, and they're starting to press. Jack Clark and Terry Pendleton are throwing bats. Mike Heath shot the finger at a fan in St. Louis and got into a shouting match with some fans in San Diego. I took him into my office in Los Angeles and told him to calm down a little bit, concentrate on the game instead of letting all the outside stuff get on his case. But Mike is such a hyper kid, I don't know if he'll be able to do that.

I've held a couple of meetings in the clubhouse, but you really can't rant and rave at the guys. That kind of thing never does any good. I try, as calmly as I know how, to point out the little things we're doing wrong. I tell them that at a time like this, the emphasis really has to be on fundamentals. Do the little things right and execute properly. If you don't do that, things just get compounded.

The good thing is that I don't think anyone on the club has panicked yet. Looking back at last year, which might not be the wisest thing to do (but, still . . .), we didn't really get going until May. Maybe we're just going through one of those cycles. Everyone realizes this can't last forever; we've got too many good hitters and great athletes on this team to play like this for too long.

At least I hope we do. Patience, they say, is a great virtue. But patience can also get you fired.

We've now played thirty-seven games, and we're eleven-and-a-half games out of first place. We're fifteen and twenty-two, and we're just pathetic. We're still not hitting, and we're still making mental and physical errors. Guys like Willie McGee, the Most Valuable Player in the league last year, and Ozzie Smith, the best shortstop in history, are making mistakes that you wouldn't put up with in a Rookie League player. We run when we shouldn't run, don't run when we should run. It's just a total mess.

I talk and talk with them; but the more I talk, the more meetings I have, the more they just go out and screw it up worse. I really don't know what else to do. It's got me buffaloed.

The starting pitchers have been effective, but the hitting's been atrocious. The thing is that even if we were to start hitting, I don't think our middle-relief pitching is good enough for us to do anything. We'd have to win eighteen or nineteen games out of twenty to climb back into the race, and I don't see how we can do that with the way the middle relief is going. Last year they talked about our "bullpen by committee." This year it's "the Arson Squad."

We may have made a mistake by not re-signing Bill Campbell, who did a pretty good job as a right-handed middle-relief pitcher last year. With him gone and Lahti on the disabled list, we don't have the experience, the control, and the makeup we need in our right-handed relievers. We've got some young guys out there who can't throw strikes when they need to. They won't challenge the hitters. Our left-handers are still pretty capable. Rick Horton does a good job, and Ken Dayley seems to be straightening himself out, but we don't have the righty-lefty balance that I like.

Catching is another problem. Heath has been a terrible disappointment. He always hit pretty well in the American League, and he was an excellent defensive catcher. This year he hasn't hit anything, he isn't throwing well, and he can't even catch the ball. He warms up the pitcher in the bullpen and he drops the ball. I've been platooning him with Mike Lavalliere, a rookie left-handed hitter and an excellent defensive catcher. The way things are going,

I'm going to use Lavalliere every day, even though he runs slower than I do. At least he can catch and throw.

Jack Clark is struggling. He's left twenty-six out of twenty-nine guys in scoring position and driven in only ten runs in thirty-seven games. He's in the walk year of his contract, and I think he's so worried about his future that he's let it get to him. To be fair about it, though, the guys in front of him are struggling and the guy in back of him isn't hitting, so he's not getting all that many RBI chances. And when he does get them, he's pressing, and he's not getting the good pitches to hit.

Here's an amazing stat: Jack Clark, the cleanup hitter, didn't get to bat with the bases loaded this year until the thirty-first game of the season. He struck out, and no wonder. He probably wondered what all those guys in the red hats were doing out there.

Second base is a disaster area. Herr looks like he aged ten years over the winter. As good as he was offensively and defensively last year, I can't believe he's playing as bad as he is. He's got no range at second base, no snap in his bat. And he's still got the lowest batting average in the league.

At third base, Pendleton is playing great, but he's still hitting a buck-ninety. He's the one guy, though, who hasn't let his hitting affect his fielding. He may be the best defensive third baseman in baseball right now, but I don't know how long you can afford to keep him in the lineup when he's hitting .190. If the second baseman is hitting .140 and the catcher is hitting .124, you've got to have some production somewhere.

Ozzie Smith, of all people, is the leading hitter on the team. He's really worked to become a good hitter, and despite the errors he's made, he's still the best there is at shortstop. His shoulder hurt him a lot last year, but it seems to be OK this year. He's been making the throws from the hole at short, and the only place where his arm seems to bother him is the long relay throw from the outfield.

Our outfield play has been suprisingly bad. I told people all spring that I thought with Coleman in left, McGee in center, and Van Slyke in right we might have the best defensive outfield in the history of the game. I didn't know they were going to forget everything they ever learned.

Vince isn't going back on balls well and he's still trying to throw everybody out at the plate. He consistently throws to the wrong base and has set up some big innings for the other clubs. A lot of clubs try to hide their worst defensive player in left field, but with the left-handed pitching we've got, we see a lot of right-handed hitters and they hit a lot of balls to left. Lonnie Smith was a liability in left field, but Vince played very well out there last year. I can't figure out what's happened to him this year.

McGee is an even bigger mystery. Last week in Atlanta he let a ball hit by Bob Horner get over his head and gave the Braves two runs. He's drifting on balls he used to turn on and run down. He's just so tentative in every phase of his game. He's only hitting .240, and when he gets on, he won't steal a base—or he gets picked off, or he overruns a base and gets caught in a pickle. More than anyone else on the club, he's let his troubles at the plate affect the other aspects of his game. Winning the MVP Award may have been the worst thing that ever happened to him. He's just pressing so hard to live up to everyone's expectations that he's just not playing like Willie McGee.

Van Slyke is the eternal mystery. He's still playing a good right field—I think he's the best defensive outfielder in the league. But at the plate it's like he goes to sleep. One night he'll hit four ropes, the next night he'll strike out looking three times in a row. I just can't get him going for more than a week at a time. I'm still sitting him down against left-handers, but with Tito Landrum going as bad as he is, Van Slyke may become an everyday player pretty soon. I'll give him one more chance to prove he can play every day in this league.

Damn, it's strange. When we left spring training, the one area of the club I was really worried about was starting pitching. I didn't know how we were going to replace the twenty-one wins and 270 innings that Andujar gave us. But I thought everything else —the offense and defense—would be OK. Now it turns out the starting pitching is the only strength on the team. Forsch and

Tudor have been outstanding, Cox is coming around, and the other guys have been pretty fair. We've got a left-hander named Greg Mathews at Louisville who's ready to pitch up here now, so we'll bring him in and see how he does. Can't hurt anything, now that we're out of the race. But starting pitching's not the problem. It's the only one of the four main facets of this game—offense, defense, starting pitching, and relief pitching—that we're really sound in.

I just can't believe how bad we're playing. I've never seen a club with this much talent play this poorly. It was different when I managed the Texas Rangers. Then we didn't have enough good players to play well. This club, well, I just can't understand it. There's just no intensity on the club.

This may be the reason why so few clubs repeat as division winners and pennant winners. All along I've thought it had to do with parity in the league and the breaks of the game, but the more I think about this season, the more I think that the intensity evaporates after you've won it. The motivation isn't the same. We have some players who didn't do anything all winter but lie around on their asses. They say they were tired, and that may be true. Hell, they played until the last week of October.

But you just can't expect to waltz into spring training, pick up a bat, and get it going again. Something has to motivate you. It's just remarkable how the performance levels of so many guys are so far off. Herr is hitting 200 points under what he was hitting a year ago. McGee has gone from .350 to .240, with four lousy stolen bases.

Every afternoon I sit down in my office with my charts, and I try to figure out what kind of lineup to throw out there. I say, this guy hits him well or that guy hits him pretty fair, and I figure it ought to work. But not this year. We're not even hitting the ball hard in batting practice. We got thirteen singles in four games in Atlanta, all of which we lost, of course. Every other club in baseball goes into "the Launching Pad" and knocks the cover off the ball. All we ever manage are bloop hits—nobody ever drives the thing.

I wish the players would go out with the writers who cover the team and get drunk once in a while. Maybe it would loosen them up. We've got too many tense players and not enough intense players.

June 1

Two months of the season are gone. We're ten games under .500, at 17–27, and in last place in the Eastern Division, fourteen-and-a-half games behind the Mets. We've made errors in ten consecutive games and have hit fourteen home runs in two months. Pitchers around the league have caught on to us, and we're so damn dumb or stubborn we can't adjust.

What they're doing is pitching us fastballs up in the strike zone. Jerry Koosman did that to us last year, pitching twice against us in one week and giving us just one run. Then the Royals staff did it to us in the World Series, and now the word is out all over baseball—throw the Cardinals high fastballs and don't worry about it because Clark is the only one who can take you deep. Everybody else has warning-track power.

When you pitch us high, we can't chop down on the ball and beat it out for a base hit. If it's in the strike zone, we pop it up. If it's too high, we still swing at it and strike out. And if we do happen to get a man on base, the high fastball is a nice pitch for a catcher to handle, so he has a better chance to throw us out if we're stealing. Johnny Lewis, my hitting instructor, and I have been lecturing the guys about it for a month, but it goes in one ear and out the other.

As far as I'm concerned, the pennant race is over. I know what it would take for us to climb back in it, and we haven't got the relief pitching to do it, even if the hitting comes around, which it shows no sign of doing.

The good thing is that the month of May is over. May was the longest month I've ever spent in baseball. The fact that we won only nine games all month was bad enough, but there were things going on with our club that publicly I couldn't talk about and privately I didn't know what to do about. I'm not going to get into the reasons for it all, but I will say that we had some deep divisions on our club, personal animosities that had nothing to do with baseball. The way we were playing left a lot of guys frustrated, which contributed to some of the off-the-field problems, and those problems in turn made it that much harder for us to play the kind of baseball we were capable of.

I couldn't believe that some of our players were acting the way they did. We had guys who weren't talking to each other, guys who wouldn't even carry other guys' gloves and hats out to them between innings. They were almost like a bunch of little kids, pouting out there. The team was split down the middle, with factions here and factions there. Maybe I should have played one faction one day and the other faction the next day. In my twelve years as a manager, I've never seen internal problems like that on a ballclub. I didn't know what to do. I sure as hell couldn't take sides.

I tried to listen to both sides, and I finally held a meeting. I said, "You guys are going to have to get your damn heads together and get this straightened out, otherwise we're not going to be a ballclub, and I don't want to manage the club if we're going to go in that direction."

I met with the people in the front office about it, told them the problems we were having, and offered to resign if they thought it would do any good. I told them it was just no fun going out there. I couldn't talk about it, and I couldn't figure out what to do.

In the past few days, though, I've seen signs that the internal bickering, the feuding, is letting up a little bit. Now we've got to see if we start hitting and playing baseball like we can. At least if we're going to lose, I'd like us to lose because we're horseshit, and not because of all the petty bickering among each other.

June 10

I was wrong. The bickering continues, as does the horseshit baseball. We're making mental mistakes and struggling in every phase of the game. People are making a big deal out of all the injuries we've got, but injuries are only part of the problem. The real problem is that we're just a horseshit baseball team.

Maybe "team" is the wrong word. We don't have a team any more, just a bunch of individuals who don't have their heads in the game. They anticipate nothing. Mental mistakes happen every night. The bickering and feuding continues. It looks like some of them are so mad at each other they won't catch a bad throw to save the other guy an error. It's about got me to the point where I don't want to manage the damn club any more. I halfway wish Gussie would call me up and tell me he's decided to make a change, so I could get the hell out of here, get off to the mountains and go fishing. Then I wouldn't have to watch this bullshit night after night.

I can stand losing. But I sure as hell can't stand what's going on around here. My coaches are out there, working their asses off, and nobody seems to give a damn. They just go out there and screw up, night after night after night.

Monday night, for example, we took a 4–3 lead into the ninth, and a couple of mental mistakes, a couple of bloop hits, and bang, we lose, 5–4. Last night Forsch pitched a great game, but got hurt with a couple of runs in the first inning. He screwed up, failed to cover first base on a ground ball. Then the next guy hit a bad-hop ground ball past Pendleton at third. Coleman was standing around in left field, didn't break to back up Pendleton, and the ball went all the way to the wall. Two runs scored instead of one. We got within one run, and I had to bring one of the Arson Squad in from the bullpen instead of Worrell, who I would have used if the game had been tied.

It's just sickening. People keep talking about last year. Last year, my ass. We are a bad ballclub, probably one of the worst teams in baseball. We have three or four guys who flat-out cannot hit. We've got two or three more who are so uptight they can't play at all. It's amazing how bad a club we've become.

I don't know what to do about it. I'd like to see us set a goal of reaching .500, maybe finishing in second place. There's some money there, but the money doesn't seem to impress players nowadays. I could bench a couple of people, I guess, but that wouldn't work because we don't have any bench to speak of. We could make some changes on the bench, but that wouldn't do any good because we're behind all the time. I may have to change the bench anyway, just to get a base hit once in a while, because we sure as hell haven't gotten anything from the guys who are there.

We are going to have to do something to shake up this outfit. We've been trying to make a trade with San Diego, get Terry Kennedy back in here as the catcher and get Heath off the club. I don't know if the Padres will go for it, but we've got to do something. As soon as it gets into July and people see we don't have a chance to win the pennant, attendance is going to drop. We had a chance to draw three million people this year, and all of that is going right down the drain.

June 30

After seventy-two games our record is 32–40, we're eighteen games out of first place, and if we weren't finished before, we sure as hell are now. Jack Clark made a dumb baserunning play the other night against Pittsburgh, trying to take third with two out on an overthrow. I knew he was going to be out, but I sure didn't think he'd be out for the season. He slid into third and tore up the ligaments in his right hand. It looks like if he gets back at all this season, it'll just be for the last couple of weeks. This really sinks us.

Jack is really the one guy we can't replace. We can replace all the other Punch-and-Judy hitters in the lineup because we've got a lot of them in the organization. But we don't have anybody who can drive the ball like Jack can. As much as he was struggling— and he had only 23 RBIs—he still had 9 homers and a lot of walks. He could have had a lot more walks if he'd learn to take a pitch once in a while, but Jack spent most of the year trying to hit everything 400 feet and carry the club. Without him in the middle of the lineup, we're going to be pitiful. What am I saying? We were already pitiful. Now we're going to have to fight a war with pop-guns.

I feel bad for Jack, too, because he was starting to hit the ball a little bit better, and he's in the last year of his contract. He really wanted to hang some numbers up this year, so if he had to take free agency he could get a big contract. I'd really like to get him signed, anyway, because he's the guy who makes the lineup go. When it goes.

We were just starting to play pretty good baseball again, too. We won six games in a row for the first time. The starting pitching continues to be good, and the kid left-hander, Mathews, has been very impressive. The relief pitching is still a problem. I had to stick Worrell into right field the other night when I brought Dayley in to face one left-handed hitter. If Dayley hadn't gotten him out, I would have brought Todd back to the mound to finish up. It's kind of like Little League, but when you've only got one right-hander you can depend on, what the hell?

But after we won those six games, we lost three straight to the Phillies in just about the worst fashion I can imagine. When we go back and look for the low point of the season, those three games will be it. It just couldn't get any lower.

On June 27, we lost in seventeen innings, 2–1. We left two on in the tenth, wasted a leadoff double in the twelfth and a one-out double in the sixteenth, leaving fifteen baserunners altogether. The next night we lost, 7–4, in ten innings, even though we stole five bases in one inning. We lost three guys on the basepaths and went into the bottom of the ninth tied, 4–4. We loaded the bases with nobody out and Herr coming to the plate. He got ahead of Steve Bedrosian, three balls and no strikes—you can't be any closer to winning than that. But Tommy struck out, and Willie struck out, and Lavalliere popped out. The Phillies got three in their half of the tenth, and we lost again.

I thought that had to be the low point. But yesterday we took a 7–4 lead into the ninth. With two out and two on, Ozzie Smith, of all people, threw the ball away, and they loaded the bases.

Worrell hung the next pitch and Juan Samuel hit a grand-slam home run.

We're just a bad ballclub. There's no denying it. There's just so many problems on the club. It seems like every night we go into extra innings with a 1–1 tie. I never get home before midnight. We can't bunt, we can't run the bases, we can't do a damned thing. July, August, and September may be the longest three months of my life.

July 30

Wonders never cease. What a strange month this has been. It started with an eight-game losing streak, with our playing as bad as we've played all year. Then I went down to Houston, lost another All-Star Game, came home and found my players had decided to start playing baseball the way they know how. I lost my right fielder and my center fielder to injuries, put my top left-handed relief pitcher on the disabled list, got in a fight, got thrown out of a game, and with all of that, the club has won nine of its last twelve ball games. Baseball has started to be fun again.

It's a good thing, too, because early this month I didn't know what I was going to do. We got swept by the Mets at home and then went back out West for the first time since all the troubles started in April. We lost the first two games of the road trip to the Giants in Candlestick Park, losing a game on the Fourth of July to run the losing streak to eight. The immortal Mike LaCoss beat us for the third time this season, and we helped him a lot by swinging at an awful lot of bad pitches. I think I'm going to check the players' contracts to see if there's something in them about not being allowed to take a base on balls. The players were pressing so hard it was a terrible sight to see, swinging at anything, just trying to make something happen.

All the writers out there kept coming into my office, all of them asking, "What's wrong with your ballclub?" Finally, I had to tell them, "You ever stop to think we might just be this bad?"

We lost three out of four to the Giants and then went down to L.A. and lost two out of three, including being shut out by Alejandro Peña, who hadn't won a ball game in something like a year. Then we split four with the Padres and finally the All-Star break arrived. I've said before how much I hate to manage the All-Star Game, but I was really glad to see it arrive this year. We were 36–50 in the first half, twenty-four games out of first place. And without Jack Clark in the lineup, I still thought we had a chance to lose 100 games. I told the players to go home and try to forget about baseball for a few days.

Mary Lou and I went down to Houston for the All-Star Game, where I proceeded to protect my record of being the only National League manager since 1972 to lose a game. We lost, 3–2, the All-Stars playing just like the Cardinals, but what the hell. The only good thing about this season is I know for sure I'll get three days off next summer.

I got to spend some time with Dick Howser down in Houston. We'd been friends since the late fifties, and one of the things that made the 1986 World Series loss a little easier to take was that Dick managed the Royals. He's just a genuinely good person. He wasn't feeling well in Houston, said he was tired and had headaches all the time. He even forgot to bring the lineup card out to home plate before the All-Star Game, and Hal Lanier had to run back into the clubhouse to make one out for him. I didn't think much about it at the time, but three days later the Royals announced that Dick had a brain tumor. This has been a tough year for friends, and it sort of puts the lousy season the Cardinals are having in perspective.

The day after the All-Star Game we had to put Ken Dayley on the disabled list. His elbow never did seem quite right all year long, even though he'd been throwing the ball pretty well early in the month. He makes the fifth pitcher we've had on the DL this year, and with him and Lahti both out now, Todd Worrell is going to get a chance to break the Cardinals' all-time record for relief appearances. We brought up a right-hander named Ray Soff, whom the Cubs gave up on last year, from Louisville to take Dayley's spot on the roster. I've got to find somebody who can get us through the sixth and seventh innings to set up Worrell.

The Dodgers came into St. Louis right after the break, and we beat them, 12–2, in the first game. Twelve runs in one game, man, I didn't know what to do. We got back to normal the next night when Valenzeula beat us for the fourth time this year. That's all he'll get, too, since we're finished with the Dodgers for the year.

The Giants came in after we split four with the Dodgers, and that's when we got it cranked up a little bit. McGee hit two home runs and we beat Steve Carlton in the first game, on Monday night; and we won, 10–7, the next game, the night of the Tuesday Night Fights. We got out to an eight-run lead early, but when Coleman got on in the fifth, he stole second and third, which really pissed off the Giants. There's some sort of unwritten rule in baseball that you don't run when you're way ahead or way behind, but it's a rule I generally ignore. Stealing bases is the way we score; it's the only offense we've got.

Besides, after we fell so far out of the pennant race, I gave Coleman the green light to steal whenever he wanted. The fans like to see him run, and with us being out of the pennant race, it can't hurt all that much. He might get twenty or twenty-five more steals and have a shot at Lou Brock's National League stolen base record of 118.

The Giants didn't see it that way. When Vince came up again in the seventh, their pitcher, Frank Williams, threw one at his chin. Vince ducked out of the way, and the plate umpire, Bob Davidson, warned Williams that if it happened again, he'd throw him and Roger Craig, his manager, out of the game. The next pitch hit Coleman and all hell broke loose. The dugouts emptied, and there were guys rolling around all over the place. Roger and I started shoving each other. Mike Krukow tackled Vince. Jeff Leonard slammed Mike Roarke to the ground. Tommy Herr got cut on the face, and I started wrestling with Randy Kutcher. It was a dandy. I don't fight much anymore, but when I was a kid I used to go to carnivals and take on the strong man in the tent. I'd get the snot kicked out of me, but I'd last three minutes and win twenty-five bucks.

Roger said later it was "bush" for Coleman to steal with an eight-run lead, but he forgot to mention that he had the tying run at the plate in the ninth inning after they started scoring. If he'd sent me a note promising he wouldn't score any runs, then I'd have stopped Vince from running. Roger Craig hasn't had to watch these guys all year, or else he'd know that we have to score any we can. We don't have bombers on our bench like he does.

We wound up sweeping the series against the Giants—only the second three-game sweep of the year—and then we turned around and swept the Padres three in a row, too. Then we went to Philadelphia, and Cox beat them to give us seven in a row. But we lost the next night and Van Slyke screwed up his hand; it looks like he'll be out for a week. McGee's already out with a hamstring pull, and of course Clark is still out, so there's three of my eight starters joining Dayley and Lahti in the trainer's room. We've just got to hope the starting pitching holds up. We're only eight games under .500, but I don't think we're going to see .500 again.

August 22

I was wrong about that. We did make .500 again, and hell, we were even one game over .500 for a couple of hours in the middle of a doubleheader. Right now we're three games under, at 59–62, and it's amazing the surge we've managed to put together with as many guys injured as we have. The other thing that's amazing is the attendance. We'll go over two million for the year tonight, and that's just a tribute to the baseball fans in St. Louis. We've still got the carryover from winning the pennant last year, and with our running game, we're exciting to watch even when we lose, and we've been playing better the second half. But still, for two million people to come out and watch us play is just astounding. We had 42,000 paid the other night when we played Pittsburgh, and that's just incredible for a Saturday night in August with both clubs out of the race.

The club is winning on good pitching and hustle. We're still not hitting the ball very well, and we're only hitting about two home runs a week. It's entirely possible that we as a club won't hit as many home runs this year as Roger Maris did all by himself in 1961. But the guys seem to be enjoying themselves, playing good ball, and I think all those petty personality feuds are behind us now.

We finally managed to unload Mike Heath two weeks ago. Detroit needed a catcher in a hurry after Lance Parrish got hurt, and Heath never fit in over here. If he'd hit .300, the players might have accepted him. But the harder he tried, the worse things went for him. The fans got on him, the newspapers got on him, and we really had to get him out of here. In return we got a young pitcher named Gary Hill and a left-handed–hitting first baseman named Mike Laga. We also save the money it would have cost to buy out Heath's option, so it's a pretty good deal for us. We picked up Steve Lake from the Cubs' farm system to back up Mike Lavalliere at catcher. Defensively, those two give us the top catching in the league.

Now that Heath is gone, I wonder what would have happened if we hadn't traded Andujar for him. Joaquin would have gone crazy pitching for a team that scores as few runs as this one. The other half of the pair we got from Oakland for Andujar was Tim Conroy, the left-hander who's been such a mystery for us this year. He'll have one good outing and one terrible outing. Or he'll be bad three times in a row, and just when I'm getting ready to take him out of the rotation, he'll pitch great. The kid's got a great live arm, but the A's didn't bring him along right, and now he's at the point where you've got wonder whether he'll ever be able to pitch with confidence in the big leagues. If we'd been in the race this year, I never would have been able to keep him in the rotation as long as I have. But the way things have gone, I keep sending him out there, hoping he'll put it together. The one thing Timmy can do, though, is hit. He's the best-hitting pitcher I've had around here, and I may send him to the Instructional League this fall to be a designated hitter. If he can get 100 at-bats down there, and pitch OK next spring, he might make this club as a pitcher and an extra pinch-hitter. With the twenty-four-man roster now in effect, it would be nice to have another left-handed bat.

We played some of our best baseball of the year last week in New York. We had six games scheduled in four days, to make up for the rainouts we had in April. The way the Mets are hitting, we could very easily have lost all six. But we won four of them, on good pitching and timely hitting, and it really was fun to see the club play like that again. John Morris, the young outfielder we got from Kansas City in the Lonnie Smith deal last year, came up from the farm in Louisville when McGee got hurt. I put him in right field as a defensive maneuver in the eighth inning of the Mets game on Friday night, and the first thing he did was make a great catch to rob Howard Johnson of extra bases and keep the game tied. Then, in the tenth inning, he got a base hit to knock in the winning run. Suddenly, I'm a genius again.

It was really something to go into New York and beat the Mets four of six with four players on the disabled list. I wonder where they'd be if Gary Carter and Keith Hernandez had missed 100 games and if Roger McDowell and Jesse Orosco were on the DL.

So we came out of New York on a high, then had an off-day in Cincinnati and proceeded to go flat again. The Reds beat us three straight to drop us back below .500, at 59–62. We got four runs last night, but gave up four home runs, including two by Eric Davis, and lost, 9–4. Davis is going to be a superstar, an Andre Dawson kind of player. He might hit thirty home runs and steal 100 bases one year.

I can't figure this club out. We play great baseball for a week and then go right back into the doldrums. We can't maintain any consistency at all. It's the damndest thing I've ever seen. We've got forty-one games left, and if I could ask for one thing, it would be for two or three guys to play well for two or three weeks at a time. They'll go good for two or three days, and then start dragging their asses like they're tired. They're tired? What about me?

It's over. It ended in the dark yesterday afternoon in Chicago. Thank God they have never installed lights at Wrigley Field, or else we would have had to play the second game of a doubleheader on the last day of the season. We lost both of the games we played up there to finish at 79–82. Everybody can go home now and watch the Mets vs. the Astros and the Angels vs. the Red Sox in the playoffs.

I don't want to put one of those Chuck Tanner happy faces on this season. After all, we did win twenty-two fewer games than we won a year ago. But when you think of what we went through, it could have been a whole lot worse. We played pretty good baseball after the All-Star break, going 43–32, and that's without Jack Clark for the whole time and without Willie McGee for forty games.

The bad thing is we lost six of our last eight, partly because Tudor's shoulder started bothering him and I kept him out of the rotation for the last two weeks of the season, pitching Conroy instead. That concerns me a little, not knowing how well Tudor's arm will come around over the winter. Ken Dayley will have his elbow operated on, and that's another guy I don't know how much to count on. McGee may have to have surgery, too, and you never know how well a guy will come back after that.

We sure as hell had a lot of injuries, but we can't use them as an excuse. We buried ourselves before the injuries really started (except for Cox's and Lahti's). I really think the intensity level had a lot to do with it. If you make the playoffs but don't make the World Series, the guys come out the next year and they're still after the big ball of wax. But if you make the Series, win or lose, that's when it gets tough. I think we let down after the World Series and didn't get it back together until the All-Star Game. Guys who are capable of good, fundamental baseball just flat went to hell. The mental mistakes, the shabby execution. I've never seen anything like it.

This year I told them, "Boys, go home and relax. Give yourself a break. But after the football bowl games are over on New Year's Day, you'd better get your asses back in shape."

I think they'll do it. At least I hope this year taught them a lesson or two. One of those lessons is that this is a twelve-months-a-year job nowadays. Just because they're paid well enough that they don't have to get a job in the off-season doesn't mean they don't have to work. Most of them do a pretty good job of keeping in shape. But when you finish the season on October 27, as we did last year, spring training kind of sneaks up on you.

It was strange how the year developed. The big thing was they just went so horseshit that they lost confidence in themselves and each other, and they started bickering and feuding. Then the injuries started, and by then we were eighteen games out and fading. There are only so many things a manager can do in a situation like that. I'll give the people in the front office, Gussie Busch and Fred Kuhlmann, Lou Susman and Dal Maxvill, a lot of credit. They didn't panic, and they let me try to work it out as best I could.

One thing we didn't do was make any trades. Not that we didn't want to, but they just didn't work out.

I didn't rant and rave at the players or threaten them, either. The trouble with that is you've got to try to keep the team together and keep them in back of you, and you can't do that if you get them pissed off at you. You've just got to use some common sense. Night after night I talked with them, explained what was happening. And when the feuding started, I told them I knew what was going on, and that unless it stopped, we'd never be a team again. From that day on, things started getting better.

We had some good things happen. Todd Worrell had a tremendous year out of the bullpen, setting the big-league save record for a rookie. If he doesn't get the Rookie of the Year Award, it'll be the greatest robbery since the Brinks job. Lavalliere turned out to be a better catcher than we thought. Forsch made a great comeback. Herr and Van Slyke played up to their capabilities in the second half. Mathews looks like he'll be a winning pitcher for a lot of years, and the kids in the outfield played pretty well. Ozzie kept improving with the bat and hit .280.

What we have to do now is get Clark re-signed and then find a right-handed hitter to hit behind him. And I mean a good right-handed hitter, someone who can drive the ball and get a runner in from first base. I don't care if he's an outfielder or a catcher or an infielder, I'll find a place for him to play if he can hit. If we do that, we'll be good again.

If we don't do that, then we have to hope all of our Punch-and-Judy hitters hit .280 or .290 again, and pray that everybody stays healthy. We don't have much margin for error without any big bats in the lineup. Two batting slumps and a charley horse, and we're screwed. When you're a contact-hitting team like we are, and you don't have a team batting average of .265 or so, then you're in deep trouble. Unless you're getting twelve or thirteen baserunners a night, there's no way to manufacture any runs because you can't maintain anything. You can't get the hits when you need them. This crap of getting five singles a night just won't hack it.

We'll go in this winter and try to make some deals, but who knows how that will turn out? Some of these general managers who've never won a damned thing always think we're trying to screw them. I tell them, "Look at the teams I've dealt with. Milwaukee won the pennant. San Diego won a pennant. What the hell are you waiting for?"

I think if I had absolute power to move people around, I could improve every team in baseball. This team's got three first basemen, this team hasn't got any, but it's got a lot of outfielders, so we'll move one of them there and get a relief pitcher for the team with a lot of first basemen. That kind of thing. I'll bet you I could do it.

But for the time being, I'm going to forget about baseball for a while, and then crank it up again and hope we can get the Cardinals back in the race in 1987. I'd like to get Gussie another pennant.

Right now, though, I'm going fishing.

Fine-tuning

I've been thinking about baseball almost as long as I've been thinking. Baseball people are like that. The game gets hold of you early, and it doesn't let go. You put two baseball people in a room, and I don't care what the occasion is, they start talking about the game.

I love it. It's been my life. It's made me more money than I ever thought I'd see, taken me all over this country and into several foreign countries, given me opportunities that I never dreamed of back in New Athens. I've tried to be a good representative for the game, and some day I'd like to give something back to the game.

I don't know how I could do that, though. I'm too outspoken, and my bullshit tolerance is too low, to work in the commissioner's office or the league office. I'd never make it as a roving ambassador, like my friend Tommy Lasorda, giving speeches all year long. All I've got to offer is nearly forty years of experience and the opinions that go along with them. And there are plenty of people in baseball who don't care for my opinions.

Well, too bad for them. I'm going to throw out a lot of opinions here in the last chapter of this book. Our game—my game—has never been healthier. Attendance, the truest measure of the game's popularity, has been increasing almost every year. Most clubs are

making money, no matter what their books say, and most of the
ones that aren't could turn it around if they were smarter about
it.

At the same time, the game has some problems: money problems, drug problems, organization problems. I've got some ideas
on all of these. Whether people want to listen to these ideas, I don't
know. But this is my book, and if you don't want my opinions, you
can stop reading right here.

◇   ◇   ◇

Right after the 1985 World Series, I went out on my lawn one
morning and picked up the *Kansas City Times.* I turned to the
sports page, and there was my old pal Ewing Kauffman crying
poormouth. His club had just won the World Series, but there's
Kauffman saying that even if he draws two million fans a year, he
still loses $1.8 million. There's just no way that can happen.

I don't mean to pick on Kauffman. You can use any club as an
example. I thought it was instructive when Commissioner Ueberroth forced the owners to open their books during the 1985 strike
negotiations. People got an idea of just how crazy the economics
of baseball have become. They learned that George Steinbrenner
was writing off his hotel in Tampa on the books of the Yankees.
They learned that Anheuser-Busch wasn't counting parking and
concession revenue for Cardinals' games as baseball revenue. They
were putting it in a separate pot for Busch Stadium, an entirely
legal accounting practice, but one I would argue doesn't reflect the
value of the Cardinals to the brewery.

It drives me crazy when some business whiz-kid starts telling me
he knows more about the business of baseball than I do. Baseball,
as I've tried to emphasize throughout this book, is a special kind
of business. Your assets, meaning the players, have to be judged
very carefully, by standards you don't learn at Harvard or the
Wharton School of Business. At the same time, you have to apply
some common business sense to things, or it won't make any
difference how great a judge of talent you are.

Look at Kauffman's claim that he loses $1.8 million even when his Royals draw two million people. Say the Royals payroll is $10 million, which is a pretty good guess. Kauffman gets about $6.5 million a year as his share of the national television contracts with NBC and ABC. The Royals, playing in one of the smallest television markets in the big leagues, don't get as much from local television and radio rights as the New York and California clubs, but as good as the Kansas City fans are, they don't need it.

Add his national TV money to the $6 a head he gets from the gate and you come up with $18.5 million. The rule of thumb is that you'll make a dollar a head from every fan on concessions, so now the total is $20.5 million. You get about 30 cents a head from parking, so that's another $600,000 or so. So you've got $21.1 million in your pocket, plus any local broadcast rights fees, plus marketing fees from T-shirts and stuff like that.

Against that you've got a player payroll of $10 million, front office costs of not more than $1 million, about $2 million in player development costs, travel expenses of a half-million or so. There's no way—if you draw two million people—that you can lose money. Unless you're trying.

On the other hand, there are clubs like Pittsburgh, San Francisco, Seattle, Cleveland, and the like that couldn't draw two million if they opened the gates and let people in for free. I can see why they're losing money, and I can see that Ueberroth is right when he says that overall the financial picture of the game isn't all that great.

One thing that really concerns me about our game is how dependent we've become on television. The owners use it to get over the hump financially, the players have become millionaires because of it. We have the network contracts and the local contracts, and now we've got those cable television superstations to contend with, too.

One of the first things that Peter Ueberroth did when he took over as commissioner was go to the superstations and tell them, "Hey, guys. This just isn't fair. Your games are invading the territory of other clubs and hurting them at the gate. So from now on, you're going to have to pay some rights fees."

This was a hell of a move, and even though the money Ueberroth got wasn't all that great, it did set a precedent. Let's face it: it's just not right that Ted Turner can come into St. Louis and offer Bruce Sutter the moon, knowing that he's going to make the money back from televising Braves games on WTBS, sending the games into St. Louis. The Cardinals play good, exciting baseball, so our fans come out to the park anyway. But what happens when a superstation team wants to sign stars from the Pirates or the Indians? The people of Pittsburgh and Cleveland who watch the Braves or the Cubs on superstations wind up subsidizing the loss of their home team's biggest stars.

There's beginning to be some talk in baseball that maybe all the television money should be put into one giant pool, the way they do it in football, with all the teams sharing equally. Naturally, people like George Steinbrenner of the Yankees and Nelson Doubleday of the Mets are opposed to a deal like that. They get huge sums of money from local television and don't want to share it with small-market cities. But I think the game may eventually have to go to a system like that.

If I wasn't managing in the big leagues, I doubt if I'd ever go to a ball game, even though I live two miles from a big-league park. I've got a big recreation room in the basement of my house in Independence, and it opens up onto a big patio that I built. I've got a satellite dish in my back yard that I can use to pull in ball games from all around the country.

I think that if I wasn't managing, I'd much rather stay at home, cook my own steaks on the grill, and drink my own Budweiser. I wouldn't have to pay $1.65 for a beer and $1.10 for a hotdog. Mary Lou and I could have another couple over, sit on the patio, play cards and watch the ball game on TV. If I didn't like one game, I'd get up and tune in another one. I think that would be a hell of a way to spend a summer evening.

What I'm saying is that when you saturate a market, eventually it's going to take its toll. Sooner or later, people will stop buying tickets, particularly in cities where the teams aren't any good. It's almost unbelievable to me—and a credit to our game—that overall attendance is up every year. The cost of tickets keeps going up, and yet the fans keep going out to the park. A ball game is still a good buy for the entertainment dollar, but it's getting to the point where a guy who takes his wife and two kids to the game winds up spending $50. And there are a lot of people in our country who can't afford to do that.

I can see a day coming where clubs will be forced to cut ticket prices and bus people to the ballpark just so they have a crowd in the house. Costs are going up, prices are going up, and some teams are really on the ropes. So what do the owners propose doing about it? They want to cut player costs, which everybody knows is just not going to happen, and they want to expand.

◇   ◇   ◇

Expansion would be stupid. The best thing that could happen to the game would be to shrink it instead—eliminate two clubs and go to two twelve-team leagues with four six-team divisions. You'd eliminate the weak franchises and concentrate on the prime areas. What teams would you eliminate? Well, you'd let them eliminate themselves, and as far as I can see, the ones closest to self-destructing are in Cleveland and San Francisco. I think that eventually the American League will have to worry about the club in Milwaukee, too. The town is just not big enough and is too close to Chicago to have a long-term future.

If you had twenty-four teams in the major leagues, you could take the struggling teams and let them move into the boom towns that are ready for big-league ball, places like Denver and Phoenix. The Players' Association wouldn't like it because it would mean fifty fewer jobs for its members. From a purely baseball point of view, this wouldn't be a bad thing because I can name you fifty guys in the big leagues right now who don't belong there.

I'm a realist, so I know that short of a national disaster or an unprecedented epidemic of common sense, the owners aren't going to vote to shrink the major leagues. What would happen to the investments of the owners of the teams that are eliminated? There would be at least four very unhappy United States senators who'd demand investigations and threaten to eliminate baseball's antitrust exemption. No, the game won't shrink, although it should. It will expand, again, and probably with the same kind of disastrous results.

◇   ◇   ◇

Baseball's first expansion took place in 1961, when the Cowboy, Gene Autry, got the second franchise in L.A. and the Washington politicians got a new Senators team to replace the one that had moved to Minneapolis. The new Senators later moved to Dallas to become the Rangers, so it's funny to me that the politicians today now want baseball to give them a third shot at supporting a team in Washington.

The National League added the Colt .45s (now the Astros) and the Mets in 1962, two of the worst teams in history. They were stocked with players the other teams didn't want but for whom they charged outrageous prices. The Mets had to play in the old Polo Grounds until Shea Stadium was built, and the Colts played in a dump for three years before they moved into the Astrodome.

This set the pattern for later expansions in 1969, when both leagues added two teams to make two twelve-team leagues, and 1977, when the American League unbalanced everything by adding clubs in Seattle and Toronto. Each time, the new owners paid huge franchise fees and rights indemnities and were gouged for leftover ballplayers. None of the new cities had a decent ballpark ready or any organizational framework in place to start developing players. People in the new cities were hungry for baseball, so for a while they were willing to pay big-league prices to sit in minor-league parks—and watch minor-league players. But the newness wore off pretty fast.

Now baseball wants to do it again. The owners want those franchise fees, which will be enormous, and they want to satisfy the politicians. Well, if we must expand, we must. But I think we ought to give some thought to it this time, do it right, take our time and not cheat the fans in the expansion towns.

If I were in charge, I'd say, "OK, four years from now we're going to add two clubs to the National League, and six years from now, we'll add two more in each league, for a grand total of thirty-two. We'll divide them geographically into two sixteen-team leagues, with four four-team divisions in each league. We'll have us the damndest set of playoffs you ever saw."

But I would award the franchises right away. I'd let the cities start building their stadiums. They could hire a general manager and take part in the draft. They wouldn't have to take just the leftover players we didn't want, but could have a Rookie League team the first year. Then add an A-ball team the second year, Double-A in the third year and Triple-A in the fourth year. That way maybe they could develop some of their own talent, have some bargaining power in trades. It wouldn't cost that much money, and you'd get most of it back from the fans when you opened the gates.

The existing major-league clubs will still have to give up some of their players in an expansion draft, and the question is: Where are we going to get enough players to stock six new clubs? I've got an answer, or part of the answer, for that one, too.

◇   ◇   ◇

The designated hitter was introduced in the American League in 1973. I guess there's been more debate about the DH than about anything but nuclear disarmament—and to just about the same end. We talk and talk, but nothing gets done. I always get called as an expert in this case since I managed for five years in the American League with the DH, and since 1980 in the National League, where the pitchers still hit for themselves.

I can honestly say it doesn't make any difference to me. I do know that no fan ever paid his way into a game to watch a pitcher hit, but I also know that the rule penalizes a great athlete, like a Catfish Hunter, who can help himself with the bat. Damn, in 1971, Catfish won twenty-one games and hit .350, and no DH ever hit that well in Cat's spot. He's the exception, though. Most pitchers in the National League today can't even get down a bunt. Joaquin Andujar was about the worst I ever saw, unless it was Dave LaPoint.

Pitchers come to the National League, and a lot of them haven't swung at a pitch since Little League. The National League is the only league in baseball, including college and minor leagues, where the pitchers hit for themselves. I'm not saying our pitchers would hit like Catfish Hunter if they had hit in the minor leagues, but at least they wouldn't be scared shitless when they went to the plate. The DH has definitely hurt the game in that regard.

You can't put the matter to a vote because the vote would split along league lines. But what you can do is make the rules uniform along league lines. If you're an American League team and you play in my National League park, your pitchers ought to have to hit. I don't care if it's spring training, the World Series, or what. And when I go to your park, I'll play by your rules. And what's more, we ought to expand this to the minor leagues. If an American League team's minor league comes to Louisville to play our Triple-A Redbirds, then those young American League pitching prospects have to bat for themselves. We'll use a DH when our team goes to their place.

The one place the DH ought to be used every year is at the All-Star Game. You'd take the veteran stars who make it every year—the Pete Roses, Carl Yastrzemskis, or the Willie Mayses—and you let them be the DH. It would add color and interest to the All-Star Game.

I don't think a lot of National League fans really know what kind of game it is with the DH. A manager can do a lot more things offensively in the American League. He doesn't have to worry about the hit-and-run in the seventh or eighth slot in the lineup. He can fix the lineup with the good hitters at the top, the power in the middle, and the speed at the bottom. You can really do a lot of things to change the offensive strategy of baseball. I think the statistics show the DH accounting for about eight-tenths of a run a game, and fans like to see that.

But the traditionalists say that strategy is lost with the DH, and that's partly true. If your pitcher is hitting, you have a lot more decisions to make as a manager. You have to be much more careful. You don't have to make the double-switches in the late innings, putting in a different position player when you change pitchers and flip-flopping positions in the batting order. You can't always finesse the other manager out of using his big pinch-hitter or relief pitcher. But as I've said before, I don't think many fans come to the park to watch me make decisions, and I know they don't come to watch my pitchers strike out.

Besides, there are some strategic decisions you have to make in the American League that you don't in the National. You have to know your pitchers better in the American League because you don't have a convenient spot to lift him for a pinch-hitter. You and your pitching coach have to watch your pitchers for signs they're getting tired. Is he getting his ball up in the strike zone? Is his arm dropping down? When do you go get him? That's at least as hard as figuring out when he's coming to bat and who's going to hit for him, and when you can get away with using your No. 2 man in the pen and when you have to come with your stopper.

I think the rules need to be the same in both leagues, but there's no way the commissioner can do that overnight with contracts the way they are today. An American League club that's just signed a DH to a long-term contract would scream bloody murder if the DH was outlawed. What would the Royals do with Hal McRae? What would Cleveland do with Andre Thornton? Where the hell would Cliff Johnson get a job?

But there's a solution here, and it goes hand in hand with my expansion plan. The commissioner should say that six years from now, when we expand to thirty-two teams, we're going to make the rules uniform in both leagues. I don't care which way he decides, but American League teams would get a fair warning that if they sign a pure designated hitter for beyond that date, they stand a chance of losing him if the rule is abolished.

In the meantime, the National League would also go to the DH. Rosters in both leagues would be cut from twenty-five to twenty-two guys, which would be very easy to do if you had the DH. You'd only need nine pitchers because you don't need the bullpen depth, and you'd need two fewer pinch-hitters. The Players' Association would raise hell, but you'd tell them they're getting a fair exchange because when you expand there will be a lot more jobs around. And the expansion clubs will have a lot more talent to choose from.

The owners would be happy because they'd each be paying three fewer players. The Players' Association would be happy, sooner or later, because there will be at least fifty-four more big-league jobs than there are today. The new clubs and their fans would be happy because at least they'd be getting a few decent ballplayers out of the deal. Everybody could have six more years to argue about the designated hitter rule, and then we wouldn't have to listen to that stuff any more.

I think my plan is sensible and practical, which probably means it's doomed.

◇   ◇   ◇

It's hard to imagine any group of people less sensible and less practical than the people who run baseball. They got themselves into a huge mess when free agency came in the mid-1970s. A lot of that was the fault of my old buddy Charlie Finley, who opened the gates when he screwed up and let Catfish Hunter get away. Finley failed to exercise an option clause in Hunter's contract, and Cat went on to sign with the Yankees as a free agent. The next year, a couple of pitchers named Dave McNally and Andy Messerschmidt took the option clause to arbitration and won, and it's been crazy ever since.

If the owners had spent less time cussing and screaming about the unfairness of it all and had instead sat down and negotiated a common-sense agreement with the Players' Association, we'd be in a lot better shape. Instead, every three years or so, we find ourselves facing a players strike. The owners scream about the high cost of player salaries, but they never really got themselves organized. Every year someone like Autry or Steinbrenner or Turner would sign a free agent for bigger and bigger money. They'd try to buy themselves a pennant by collecting every big-name free agent they could find. The only club that ever used free agency right was the Padres, who needed a couple of guys to solidify a young team. So they went out and signed Steve Garvey and Goose Gossage and won the National League pennant in 1984.

Ueberroth, who I think is going to be a great commissioner, may have finally gotten through some of the owners' thick heads. After the 1985 season, there was far less craziness over free agents. It may be that was because there weren't a lot of stars available, but the owners seemed to be laying off each other's talent. The one big name in the free agent pool that year was Kirk Gibson, the Detroit outfielder, a triple-threat guy who is really a fine baseball player. Gibson and his agent figured they'd be able to land a five-year deal at close to $2 million a year, but instead they found a curious lack of interest among the other owners. They and the other players and agents screamed about "collusion," and the Players' Association took the matter to the Federal Labor Relations Board.

I wouldn't call it collusion; I'd call it common sense. If you don't think a player is worth $2 million a year, don't pay it.

One real problem with all the money that ballplayers are getting paid, and with the long-term contracts that they're getting, is what it does to their intensity levels. The old cliché is that players play best when they're "hungry." Well, it's hard to be hungry when the average salary is more than $300,000 a year. When I was playing, we didn't know what the other guys were getting paid, and we didn't care. We never even thought to ask. We were just glad to be playing the game, and as long as we could put bread on the table, we were happy.

The world has changed, and I'm glad players are paid as well as they are today. I just wish that money didn't mean as much to them. Some of these guys have never known what it's like to work for a living, they don't know how much money $1 million a year really is. They just know they want it.

These long-term contracts are a killer. Unless a guy is really special, there's a natural let-down the first year after he signs a big contract. And then you'll see a guy really crank it up when his contract is up for renewal, or when he thinks he's going into the free agent market.

The other problem is the arbitration rule, which is what is really jacking payrolls out of sight. The owners, those keen businessmen, agreed to the arbitration rule in 1976 because they couldn't see what it would mean. They've been kicking themselves ever since.

A player becomes eligible for arbitration after three years in the big leagues. Before the 1985 negotiations, it was after two years. That one extra year was about the only thing the owners got out of that strike. So what you had was a kid with two years of experience who could demand a certain salary from the club. And the club would make its offer to him. If they couldn't reach a common figure, each side took its case to an independent arbitrator, who usually knew nothing about baseball. The arbitrator decided which figure was closest to the player's value—either the high one or the low one, nothing in the middle.

Crazy things would happen. A kid who made $150,000 would be offered a 100 percent raise, to $300,000. But the kid and his agent would demand $750,000. You'd take it to the arbitrator, and he'd compare what other players at the kid's position were making, and he'd give him $750,000. You'd have a Wade Boggs in Boston going from $200,000 to $1 million in his first year of arbitration, and going back the next year and demanding $1.85 million, "losing" the arbitration, and still coming away with a $350,000 raise. How in the world is a club going to project payroll costs with something like that going on?

I don't blame the players. If I was in their place, I'd do the same thing. I blame the people who are running the game. They've just got to get a handle on this thing.

◇　◇　◇

Baseball people are stubborn. They want to do things the same old way, year in and year out. They say that's the charm of the game, and I suppose that's partly true. The bases have to stay 90 feet apart; the games still have to go nine innings. But some changes could be made which wouldn't disturb the basics of the game yet would still make a big difference.

For example, why should baseball continue to have two sets of umpires, one in the American League and one in the National? All it does is cause problems whenever they get together. I won a World Series in 1982 when a National League umpire called ball four on a pitch to Lonnie Smith, a pitch that might have been a strike if an American League ump had been working the plate. I lost a World Series in 1985 when an American League ump squeezed my pitcher's strike zone in Game Three.

I don't ever want to question the integrity of an umpire. I refereed enough basketball games to know what their jobs are like. It's a thankless job, a tough job that takes you on the road for eight months a year. I think any ump who has ever worked a game for me would tell you I don't give them a bad time on judgment calls. I will give them a bad time if I think they are fuzzy on the rules, which some of them are, or don't hustle and get into position.

Umpires are human beings, and they make mistakes. They're also subject to human nature, and I think it's just human nature for an ump to want to see his league do well. That's where the problem comes in during the World Series. Some people think it's because there are two different strike zones in the two leagues. That used to be the case, when the American League umps wore the big outside chest protectors. They couldn't get down to see the low pitch as well, and they called low strikes balls. But since both leagues have gone to the inside protectors, I don't see that being a problem any more.

No, it's just human nature that's the problem. And we could solve that by taking all the umpires and putting them under the commissioner's office. Umps should work for baseball, not the leagues. Another benefit to that would be that you wouldn't see the same umpiring crews all year along. Sometimes friction develops between a particular team and an umpiring crew, and no matter how hard you try, you can't get around that.

This is one of those problems that has an easy solution and wouldn't cost anything to fix. I don't think it would make anybody unhappy, which is not something I can say about my next bright idea.

◇   ◇   ◇

I'm talking about the World Series. Ever since 1969, when baseball went to the divisional format, the Series has been played later and later in the year. After 1985, now that we've gone to the seven-game playoff format, we don't wind up until the last weekend in October. We've also added teams in Toronto and Montreal, and for all I know, we may expand to Saskatoon next.

Sooner or later, what this is all going to mean is one unholy mess. We've been lucky that we haven't had a week of snow or rain. When we played the seven-game I-70 series in 1985, we got lucky with some of the best weather Missouri's ever had in late October. One of these years, we're going to be rained or snowed out for a week. The press and television people are going to go crazy, and the fans may lose interest if the Series drags on for two or three weeks, which it very well could do.

What we need to do is turn the World Series into the greatest spectacle in sports. We sign a contract with a domed stadium in a neutral site, get guarantees on hotel rates and the like, and play seven straight days all on prime-time TV. This eliminates the home-team advantage. It eliminates those early starting times on the West Coast. It becomes a fairer test of pitching staffs and eliminates the potential for disaster.

I can already hear people griping that it's not fair to take the Series away from the hometown fans. Well, that's bullshit. Ninety percent of the people who get tickets for the Series are people who haven't seen five games all year long. They're people with connections, and the average guy has almost zero chance to see a game, even if he wants to spend $30 a ticket. Your season ticket holders could be given tickets to the Series, just as the NFL gives their season ticket holders tickets to the Super Bowl.

I don't believe this is going to happen any time soon. The Series will have to turn into a weather-bound farce a couple of times before baseball will act. But I think it would be a great thing for our game.

And while we're on the subject of spectacles, let's consider the All-Star Game. The only thing bad about winning a pennant is that you have to manage the All-Star Game the next year. I'd rather go fishing for three days.

Baseball has the best All-Star Game of any sport, but most of the players hate it. It's played on a Tuesday night, and the players are required to show up for a workout on Monday so they can be interviewed. Then there's a ridiculous press conference, where the two league presidents get together and talk about how their league is so much better than the other one. I hold the distinction of being the only National League manager in twenty years who has lost an All-Star Game, but who really cares?

Then they play the game, and the players try to catch a fast flight out of wherever it's played so they can get home and catch a day of rest. They wind up traveling all day and go back into action on Thursday, and they wind up more tired than ever.

Why not play the game on Monday night, skip the workouts and the bullshit press conference, and let the All-Stars get at least one day off with their families? It seems like that's the least we owe them.

◇ ◇ ◇

The Series and the All-Star Game would be easy, cosmetic changes. A far more important thing to change is the area of player development, which is the single most critical part of any organization's success. If you scout right, teach right, and trade right, you don't have to mess with free agency. If you move your young players along at the right pace, always keep the pipeline filled, you don't come up short and have to do desperate things. Player development is to baseball what research and development is to an industrial firm—the key to the future.

For years I've been advocating what I call "complex baseball" as a means to streamline, simplify, and improve player development systems. Right now we go about it in a crazy way, spending $2 million to $2.5 million a year per team, and for all that money, we don't do it right. We take our young players, many of whom have played in excellent college programs, and we ship them into minor-league towns where the fields are bad, the lights are bad, the housing conditions are deplorable, and where they have little or no guidance away from the field.

Some of these kids, especially those from California or Florida —where college baseball is played almost year-round in beautiful little parks—get to the minor leagues and can't believe they have to play on rockpiles in delapidated ballparks. A young shortstop trying to learn to make the plays has to worry about staying alive when a ball comes off a granite infield.

Or we'll send a kid one year out of high school into a funky little minor-league town, tell him what time to report to the park, and let him run wild. He'll get a crappy little apartment with a couple of other guys, eat nothing but greasy hamburgers and fries, and try to have a good time. A lot of them will drink too much, and I have to believe that's where a lot of the drug problems get started.

Why in the world couldn't the teams get together and create a minor-league system that made sense and insured that every club had the same basic development system? We could create fifty-two minor-league clubs, two for each big league team, divided geographically into three Triple-A leagues and three Double-A leagues. The rest of the minor leagues, the A-ball teams and the Rookie League teams, would play at our training complexes in Florida and Arizona.

Nowadays every big-league club has a decent complex for spring training, most of them with four or six diamonds, bullpens, and hitting tunnels. We could spend $90,000 to $100,000 to light one field to Double-A standards and build some bleachers. We could have day games and night games with the instructors on hand or close by. We could build dorms or lease apartment houses for the kids, charge them room and board and give them a training table to eat at. God, you wouldn't believe the crap some of these kids eat. Our supervision over them would be a whole lot better, and we'd get them off on the right foot, both with their on-the-field habits and their off-the-field habits.

Then, after a year or two at the complexes, they'd graduate to Double-A and Triple-A ball, where'd they'd face the better competition and also learn the off-the-field habits they need to be big leaguers. They'd learn how to travel with a club, how to spend their meal money, how to take care of themselves.

We'd be doing the kids a favor and ourselves a favor, and I think each club would save $800,000 to $1 million a year. We'd get better ballplayers out of it, and maybe even save a few lives.

◇   ◇   ◇

And speaking of saving lives. If you've read this far, you know I've managed my share of players who've gotten themselves screwed up on drugs and alcohol. I say "and alcohol," even though it's clear to me the only difference between alcohol and other drugs is that alcohol is legal.

In the short term, it's hard to spot a player who's on drugs. He may, in fact, play a little harder and more aggressively, particularly if he's on cocaine. But the long-term effects are always bad, and even if a guy completes a rehab program and sticks to it, he's lost up to 10 percent of his strength and quickness.

I've had players, like Darrell Porter, who have been to the bottom on drugs and worked their way back. And I've had other guys who just haven't been able to kick the habit. Up until the past couple of years, baseball didn't deal very well with drug abuse. We tended to trade our problems and look the other way.

But that didn't work, and I think the Pittsburgh drug trial in 1985 really opened a lot of eyes. Some of the biggest names in baseball were dragged through the mud. I think the players have sensed that it's a serious problem, and I think they're ready to deal with it.

I firmly believe that if we're going to pay a man an average salary of $300,000 a year, we have the right to insist that he's clean. And the players are beginning to realize that taking a drug test is not too high a price to pay for the benefits that the game gives them.

There's a new realization today that drugs are not good for anyone—not the players, not the owners, not the game itself. I owe enough to baseball to want the best for it.

It's the game that must survive.